Selling Your Business For Dummies®

Cheat Sheet

Major Documents to Have On-Hand

Sooner or later in the sale process you'll need the following materials. Use this checklist to assemble everything as soon as possible to smooth the road ahead.

- ❏ Federal tax returns for the past three years (corporate or Schedule C)
- ❏ Income statements for YTD and the past three years
- ❏ Balance sheets for the past three years
- ❏ Statement of seller's discretionary earnings for most recently completed year
- ❏ Financial ratios and trends
- ❏ Accounts receivable aging list
- ❏ Accounts payable list
- ❏ Inventory list including value
- ❏ Current building lease
- ❏ Franchise agreement, if applicable
- ❏ Fixtures, furnishings, and equipment list including fair market values
- ❏ Asset depreciation schedule from most recent tax return
- ❏ Current copies of equipment and facility maintenance agreements
- ❏ Current employee, customer, vendor, and distributor contracts or agreements

- ❏ ...ns, and
- ❏ ...strations,
- ❏ Copies of ... nts
- ❏ List of existing liens
- ❏ Product or service price list
- ❏ Employee records showing staff, hire dates, salaries, pension records, and employee benefit plan outline
- ❏ Organization chart
- ❏ Business formation documents
- ❏ Current client list
- ❏ Current list of major suppliers and distributors
- ❏ Business plan
- ❏ Marketing plan
- ❏ Employment policy manual
- ❏ Business procedures manual
- ❏ Photos of business building, work areas, and equipment

Numbers to Keep at Your Fingertips

Fill out the following chart and keep it with you throughout the sale process, as these are the people who you'll be in touch with constantly.

Name	E-mail	Phone/Fax	Cell
Accountant			
Attorney			
Broker			
Buyer			
Buyer's Accountant			
Buyer's Attorney			

Selling Your Business For Dummies®

Cheat Sheet

Buyer-Seller Navigation Map

If either you or your buyer start to lose your way, use this diagram almost like a "you are here" map to help navigate the path ahead.

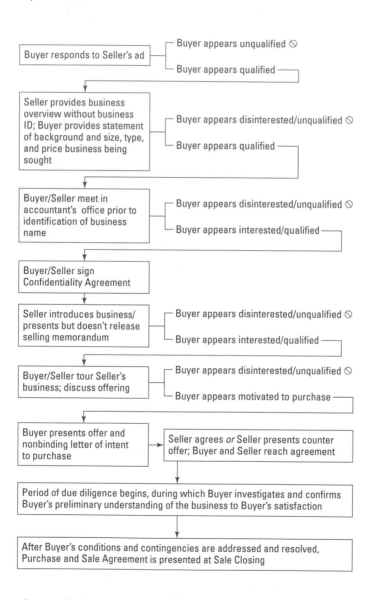

- Buyer responds to Seller's ad
  - Buyer appears unqualified ⊘
  - Buyer appears qualified

- Seller provides business overview without business ID; Buyer provides statement of background and size, type, and price business being sought
  - Buyer appears disinterested/unqualified ⊘
  - Buyer appears qualified

- Buyer/Seller meet in accountant's office prior to identification of business name
  - Buyer appears disinterested/unqualified ⊘
  - Buyer appears interested/qualified

- Buyer/Seller sign Confidentiality Agreement

- Seller introduces business/presents but doesn't release selling memorandum
  - Buyer appears disinterested/unqualified ⊘
  - Buyer appears interested/qualified

- Buyer/Seller tour Seller's business; discuss offering
  - Buyer appears disinterested/unqualified ⊘
  - Buyer appears motivated to purchase

- Buyer presents offer and nonbinding letter of intent to purchase → Seller agrees or Seller presents counter offer; Buyer and Seller reach agreement

- Period of due diligence begins, during which Buyer investigates and confirms Buyer's preliminary understanding of the business to Buyer's satisfaction

- After Buyer's conditions and contingencies are addressed and resolved, Purchase and Sale Agreement is presented at Sale Closing

For Dummies: Bestselling Book Series for Beginners

Selling Your Business

FOR

DUMMIES®

by Barbara Findlay Schenck

Foreword by John Davies
CEO, Sunbelt Business Brokers

WILEY

Wiley Publishing, Inc.

Selling Your Business For Dummies®

Published by
Wiley Publishing, Inc.
111 River St.
Hoboken, NJ 07030-5774
www.wiley.com

For general information on our other products and services, please contact our Customer Care
Department within the U.S. at 800-762-2974, outside the U.S. at 317-572-3993, or fax 317-572-4002.

For technical support, please visit www.wiley.com/techsupport.

Wiley also publishes its books in a variety of electronic formats. Some content that appears in print may
not be available in electronic books.

Library of Congress Control Number: 2008937851

ISBN: 978-0-470-38189-2

Manufactured in the United States of America

10 9 8 7 6 5 4 3 2 1

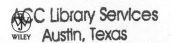

About the Author

Barbara Findlay Schenck has spent more than 20 years helping businesses — especially small businesses — start, grow, market, and brand their companies.

Her career started in Honolulu, where she was director of admissions for a private college before joining the staff of Hawaii's largest public relations firm. She and her husband, Peter, left Hawaii for an assignment with the Peace Corps in Malaysia before returning home to Oregon, where they started an advertising agency that ranked as one of the Northwest's top 15 when they sold it in 1995.

Since then, Barbara has written a number of business books, including *Small Business Marketing For Dummies*, now in its second edition; the second edition of *Business Plans Kit For Dummies*; and *Branding For Dummies*, which she coauthored in 2006 with help from branding expert Bill Chiaravalle.

Now, with *Selling Your Business For Dummies*, she guides entrepreneurs and retirement-ready small-business owners as they pursue the ultimate goal of a business sale. The book includes expert advice from John Davies, CEO of Sunbelt, the world's leading business brokerage firm, who wrote the foreword and shared his invaluable tips, advice, and real-world experience.

For more information on John Davies, visit his business Web site at www.sunbeltnetwork.com.

For more information on Barbara's background, books, and business advice, visit her Web site at www.bizstrong.com.

Author's Acknowledgments

I give thanks for making this book possible to:

Peter Schenck, who helped me realize that three quarters of a million business owners would be wanting advice on how to sell their businesses over the upcoming few years, and who heaped his wisdom, work, and a wealth of knowledge into this book's outline, research, development, and writing. The term coauthor isn't sufficient to describe his role — co-creator might come close.

Dirk Zeller, CEO of Real Estate Champions and author of *Success as a Real Estate Agent*, who didn't hesitate for a moment to name John Davies when I asked for his advice on who was the best resource for expertise on business sales.

John Davies, CEO of Sunbelt Business Brokers, who returned my out-of-the blue call and who responded to my request for business sale expertise with a depth of advice and insight that humbles me to this day, for which I and readers of this book will be forever grateful.

The team at Wiley Publishing, which never fails to impress me. First, to Acquisitions Editor Michael Lewis, who steered this book into existence and guided its format and development. To Project Editor Kristin DeMint, who worked her magic on everything from book structure to book content, backed by Copy Editor Todd Lothery. And to Howard Locker, who accepted Kristin DeMint's invitation to serve as the book's technical reviewer and who improved this book in dozens of ways.

Matthew Schenck, whose technical support and business perspective kept me current and whose humor kept me going.

Brian Bowler, who bought the ad agency that Peter and I founded, who made selling a business a pleasure and a success story that prompted the countless how-did-you-do-it questions that ultimately led to this book.

Finally and mostly, to everyone with a dream to sell a business and start a new life chapter. Thank you for trusting this book to guide you through the sale process. May fortune follow.

Publisher's Acknowledgments

We're proud of this book; please send us your comments through our Dummies online registration form located at www.dummies.com/register/.

Some of the people who helped bring this book to market include the following:

Acquisitions, Editorial, and Media Development

Project Editor: Kristin DeMint

Acquisitions Editor: Michael Lewis

Copy Editor: Todd Lothery

Assistant Editor: Erin Calligan Mooney

Technical Editor: Howard Locker

Editorial Manager: Michelle Hacker

Editorial Assistants: Joe Niesen, Jennette ElNaggar

Cartoons: Rich Tennant
  (www.the5thwave.com)

Composition Services

Project Coordinator: Katherine Key

Layout and Graphics: Joni Burns, Reuben W. Davis, Christin Swinford, Christine Williams

Proofreaders: Melissa Bronnenberg, Sossity R. Smith

Indexer: Potomac Indexing, LLC

Publishing and Editorial for Consumer Dummies

  Diane Graves Steele, Vice President and Publisher, Consumer Dummies

  Joyce Pepple, Acquisitions Director, Consumer Dummies

  Kristin Ferguson-Wagstaffe, Product Development Director, Consumer Dummies

  Ensley Eikenburg, Associate Publisher, Travel

  Kelly Regan, Editorial Director, Travel

Publishing for Technology Dummies

  Andy Cummings, Vice President and Publisher, Dummies Technology/General User

Composition Services

  Gerry Fahey, Vice President of Production Services

  Debbie Stailey, Director of Composition Services

Contents at a Glance

Table of Contents

Foreword

. . . .

Selling a business is a once-in-a-lifetime event for most people. It frequently represents the culmination of the business owner's career and his or her payoff for years of hard work. As a result, it's typically an emotional and stressful time for the owner. The best way to reduce the uncertainty and stress involved in selling your business is to develop a better understanding of the business sales process. As the old saying goes, "Knowledge is power." In writing *Selling Your Business For Dummies,* Barbara has done a terrific job of summarizing the business sale process for business owners. This book is a must-read for all small-business owners who are considering selling their business in the coming year or two.

For my Sunbelt Business Broker colleagues and me, it's a great privilege and responsibility to assist business owners in selling their businesses and transitioning management of their businesses to new owners. Working with informed buyers and sellers always makes our job easier and helps ensure a better outcome for everyone involved in the process.

John Davies, CEO

Sunbelt Business Brokers

World's largest business brokerage firm

Introduction

Crossing your fingers isn't the path to a business sale. Planning is.

Maybe you started planning for a sale the day you launched your business by naming, structuring, and running it with the payoff of a sale in mind. Or maybe you just woke up one recent morning and decided then and there to get off the business-ownership treadmill, and now you want to know what to do to achieve the sale you're hoping for. *Selling Your Business For Dummies* deals with all the variables you may be facing:

- You may be certain you want to sell, or you may be leaning toward a sale but also considering other business exit options.
- Your sale plans may involve a very, very small business or a company that's on the big-business end of the small-business scale.
- Your timeline may be immediate, or you may be willing to take up to a year or more to strengthen your business before putting it up for sale.

Every business sale involves different factors, but all sales share one common truth. Your business will sell not when *you're ready*, but when *it's* ready and when a buyer thinks it's worth the amount of money you're asking for it.

The purpose of this book is to give you an edge in the crowded marketplace you're entering by helping you get your business into sale-ready shape and walking you through every step of the sale process.

About This Book

Selling Your Business For Dummies is a guide through the world of business sales — a world to be traveled by some three-quarters of a million business owners over the next few years, according to research by well-regarded universities and business alliances. To give you an idea of the traffic on the road you'll be taking, projections are that one out of every six businesses owned by retirement-ready entrepreneurs will go up for sale by 2010, up 15-fold from the number of business sales in 2001. Those staggering numbers mean that people seeking to buy businesses will have a huge selection of opportunities from which to choose.

To guide you on your way, this book incorporates advice from an amazing group of people, including professionals in the legal, banking, and accounting fields, chief among them John Davies and the business sale specialists at Sunbelt Business Brokers, the largest business brokerage in the world.

Together, we've seen to it that this book includes everything you need to know about selling your small business.

This book also has a CD-ROM that includes planning checklists, forms, worksheets, links to useful Web sites, sample sale documents, and a template you can use in a fill-in-the-blanks manner to create the selling booklet, called a *selling memorandum*, that you'll use to explain your sale offering to serious buyer prospects.

Conventions Used in This Book

Following the famous *For Dummies* format, this book incorporates the following style conventions, designed to keep the contents quick and easy to scan and read:

- ✔ Whenever I introduce a new term you need to know, it appears in *italics*, accompanied by a short, clear description of what it means.
- ✔ Wherever possible, advice to take action is presented in bulleted or numbered lists, with the keywords shown in **bold** so they jump out at you.
- ✔ All Web site addresses appear in `monofont` to help you isolate the URL quickly and easily from surrounding text.

What You're Not to Read

You're an entrepreneur trying to sell your business while you're also likely trying to run your business, so you probably don't have time to read a word more than you absolutely have to read to get the job done. If you're time-pressed (in other words, if you're a typical small-business owner), you can skip right over the gray-shaded sidebars scattered throughout the book. Sidebars are full of interesting information and examples that will enhance — but aren't essential to — your understanding of the chapter.

Foolish Assumptions

I never introduce a *For Dummies* title without reminding readers that anyone smart enough to turn to one of these yellow-and-black books is no fool, and that's especially true with this book. If any of the following assumptions describes you and your business, then this book is especially for you.

✔ You own a small, privately held business rather than a publicly held company, or a business with a name known nationally or even globally. (Maybe that'll be your next business, but it's certainly not the one you're selling right now!)

✔ Your business fits the description of 95 percent of all U.S. businesses, with annual sales under a million dollars and fewer than 20 employees. If your business is a little larger but not a mega-million-dollar enterprise, this book is equally for you so long as your business is privately held and you plan to sell to an individual or another small business.

✔ You're not aiming to sell shares of your company to the general public through an *initial public offering*, a process that involves legalities, technicalities, investment banks, underwriters, and law firms with deep experience in securities law.

✔ You're not planning to sell your business to employees through an Employee Stock Ownership Plan (ESOP). This book isn't an ESOP how-to guide. For that, you need an attorney with specialized expertise.

✔ You want to obtain the highest possible price for your business, realizing that the faster you want the sale to take place, the more price concessions you may have to make.

How This Book Is Organized

Each of the five parts of *Selling Your Business For Dummies* deals with a different phase of the sale process, beginning with the to-sell-or-not-to-sell decision and ending with the handoff of your business keys and plans. Along the way, this book is written so you can focus on the parts you most need, whether that means getting your business ready for a sale, pulling your financial records into shape, hiring a broker, writing and placing ads, or any of the other sections covered in the book's five parts.

Part I: Getting Ready to Get Out

This part guides you into the starting gate for a business sale. Chapter 1 helps you weigh whether you're ready to leave your business, what kind of an exit you're looking for, and what's involved in the business sale process. Chapter 2 guides your assessment of how ready your business is (or isn't) for a sale, and which sale route seems the most likely path given the size and health of your business. Chapter 3 covers the steps, time, and effort you need to dedicate to getting your business ready for the inquiring eyes of buyers, righting wrongs and building strengths, and adding the kind of value that may boost your sale price. Chapter 4 prepares you to hit the Go button by helping you assemble the professionals to assist you through the sale process.

Part II: Packaging Your Business for a Sale

Selling a business and selling a house have one big thing in common: First impressions can make the difference between buyers wanting to take a closer look and buyers turning away faster than you can say, "We should have prepared a little better."

Part II leads you through the all-important preparation process. Chapter 5 — an important chapter — helps you prepare and assemble the most essential financial information for your buyer and present financial trends and growth projections for your business. Chapter 6 is the chapter no reader will skip; it's about how to price your business, including how to eliminate red flags that can cost you buyer interest and sale proceeds.

Chapter 7 is especially important for businesses whose buyers want to see summaries of business and marketing plans and operations and policies manuals. Then Chapter 8 brings the story of your business together, providing a template that lets you assemble information from all the preceding chapters to end up with a *selling memorandum*, the booklet you share — after a confidentiality agreement is signed — with serious buyer prospects.

Part III: Launching and Navigating the Sale Process

The three chapters in this part are a guide to what's involved from the moment you decide to advertise your business for sale until the day you receive a *letter of intent* confirming a purchase offer from a ready and qualified buyer. Chapter 9 helps you write and place classified print ads and all-important online postings. Chapter 10 is your guide to the process of prescreening ad inquiries, obtaining financial and background information from serious prospects, and sharing your confidential business information with likely buyers. Part III ends with Chapter 11, which takes you through the final leg of the buyer-development marathon as you receive, evaluate, and accept a buyer offer.

Part IV: So You've Got a Buyer! Now What?

Part IV is your map for the make-it-or-break-it leg of the business sale. Chapter 12 explains what's involved when the buyer does the homework, called *due diligence*, necessary to be sure your business's condition is as you've represented it to be. Chapter 13 provides the information you need as you work with the buyer to structure the financial and tax aspects of your deal and plan the payment approach. Chapter 14 helps you decipher the financing and tax aspects that come into play in most small business sales. Chapter 15 is about closing the deal and getting the paperwork signed. Finally, Chapter 16 lays out a game plan to follow as you announce the sale and pass the baton to the new owner.

Part V: The Part of Tens

This book's final part features ten-part lists of advice that you'll likely turn to over and over again. Chapter 17 presents ten deal-killers to avoid. Chapter 18 shares ten marketplace trends and truths that affect small business sales, and Chapter 19 tells you ten things you may not know about business brokers. Chapter 20 leaves you with a list of ten questions most business buyers tend to ask, for which you want to have your answers prepared, polished, rehearsed, and ready to deliver.

At the back of the book, you'll also find an appendix that introduces you to all the forms awaiting you on the CD-ROM that accompanies this book. It tells you how to use the CD as well as what's on it, so if you ever need to see a description of all the forms at a glance, the appendix is where you should turn.

Icons Used in This Book

This wouldn't be a *For Dummies* book without symbols in the outer margin alerting you to valuable information and advice. Watch for these icons:

The Tip icon marks tried-and-true approaches that save you time, money, and effort as you prepare for and navigate your business sale.

It's one thing to read advice and follow steps. It's a whole other thing to read how someone else successfully addressed the same situation. This icon flags great examples and lessons.

When there's a danger to avoid or just a bad idea to steer clear of, this icon sits in the margin like a flashing yellow light.

This icon points out essential advice and truths you don't want to forget.

ON THE CD This icon lets you know that the form or resource being mentioned is also on the CD-ROM. Whenever you see this margin marker, take note, because it signals a checklist, form, or worksheet that's available for your use, along with step-by-step instructions on how to put the material to work as you complete the selling process.

Where to Go from Here

True to the *For Dummies* format, you can start this book on any page. Every portion of the book is a self-standing component, so you don't have to read sequentially from cover to cover to make sense of the content.

You'll probably use this book by flipping back and forth, gaining input on how to figure out what your business is worth, then going back to see how to add value that buyers will pay for, then going forward to see how your decisions impact your taxes, then getting help with the processes of due diligence and deal negotiation, and round and round. If you're like most sellers, you'll be in the sale process — and within the covers of this book — for months, at least. Sooner or later, you'll probably land on every page.

If you're time-pressed, this book offers some good shortcuts:

✔ **If you're not sure whether you're really ready to leave or sell your business,** start by reading and completing every worksheet and self-test in Chapter 1. However, if you know for sure that you're ready to sell, you can just scan Chapter 1 for a good, quick overview of what's involved before heading straight to the chapters that hold the advice you're seeking.

✔ **If your business is in strong financial and marketing condition,** you don't need to spend as much time with Chapters 2 and 3 as is necessary for owners who need to get their businesses into sale-ready shape. Instead, you can head straight for Chapter 4, which guides you in building your sale team, or to the other parts of the book, which cover various stages of the sale process.

My advice: Read the book cover to cover if your schedule lets you. If you're in a hurry for specific answers, turn to the table of contents or the index to guide you straight to the information or advice you need.

Part I
Getting Ready to Get Out

The 5th Wave   By Rich Tennant

"Our goal is to maximize your upside and minimize your downside while we protect our own backside."

In this part . . .

Selling a business starts with questions. Are you sure you want out of your business? Is your business ready for a sale? Is your business likely to attract a buyer? How much might someone pay for your business? What should you expect between now and the time your business — and payment for its value — changes hands?

You and nearly a million other sellers will wrestle with these questions as they launch the business sale process over the upcoming few years.

The four chapters in this part guide you into the business sale starting lane by helping you confirm that you're personally ready to leave your business and that a sale is your best exit option, determine what it'll take to get your business to sell, get your business in sale-ready shape, and decide who to bring onto your sale team.

Chapter 1

So You Want Out of Your Business? Your Options and the Process

In This Chapter

▶ Understanding business exit options

▶ Knowing what's involved in a business sale

▶ Gauging your sale readiness

*O*wning a business is like running a marathon, and selling a business is like crossing the finish line. Getting paid to turn your business over to a new owner is the final reward for years of business creation and good management. It's also — just like finishing a marathon — hardly a decide-today-do-it-tomorrow proposition.

That you're holding this book proves you're pretty serious about harvesting sale value from your business-building efforts. That you opened to the first page instead of darting straight to a chapter on finding buyers or structuring deals indicates you're starting at square one and seeking all the information you can about the selling process in front of you, including whether a sale is your best business-exit plan or whether you should consider another way to leave the stage.

Chances are good that you're wrestling with some alligator-sized questions, such as whether you should choose to leave your business right now or ease yourself away over a longer time frame — or whether it's even possible to sell your business. You may also be wondering whether you're better off selling to business insiders — such as family members, employees, or associates — or some outsider who may actually step in to buy the enterprise you've built.

Many small business sales are driven by life-changing events such as illness, divorce, or retirement. Sometimes those circumstances force immediate sale plans, but other times, and hopefully in your situation, there's some breathing room that allows time for the steps necessary to arrive at the best sale outcome. Regardless, this chapter orients you to the range of options for exiting your business. Then it helps you assess whether a sale is your best exit route, what's involved in selling a business, and what steps lie between now and when you hand your business over to a new owner.

Much as you may want to discuss your to-sell-or-not-to-sell dilemma with friends, family, and associates, try your best to make the decision with only a few advisors, each signed to secrecy. Letting the word leak out that your business is for sale is dangerous on many fronts, especially the home front, where your sale plans may cause employee and customer concerns or defections, and the marketing front, where competing businesses may use your sale news against you as they talk with your clients or suppliers. So until you're ready to announce that a sale deal is done, plan to keep your lips sealed.

The Various Ways to Sell Your Business: Yes, You Have Options!

The number of business owners who think their businesses have no salable value — that they have no choice but to liquidate assets and close up shop — is simply staggering. Sure, if your business is located in the corner of your bedroom, you offer the same exact service or product as a list of other businesses, your sales are faltering, you keep your finances and business processes in your head, you have only a handful of customers, and hardly anyone knows your business name, selling your business will, in fact, be a very difficult task.

But if you have a business location that a buyer can take over, and if you add a valuable difference to your product or service, build solid sales, create impressive systems and marketing materials, gain name familiarity in your marketplace, and build earnings that are downright impressive, suddenly your back-bedroom operation becomes an attractive, salable asset.

To paraphrase Paul Simon, you have nearly fifty ways to leave your business, and selling comprises six of them. Your selling options range from the obvious cut-all-the-strings approach by selling your business outright to selling off a portion of your business, ridding yourself of some of your responsibilities while staying involved for some time into the future. Before you slip out the back, Jack, or make a new plan, Stan, it's worth knowing the lineup of options you can explore in your effort to get yourself free.

Selling outright and being done with it

Selling your business once and for all is probably the exit option you had in mind when you picked up this book. It's also the hope of the vast majority of entrepreneurs seeking a business exit now or in the near future, and it's the business exit option detailed in the rest of this book. After years of hard work, someone else takes over your business, it lives into the future, and you reap value that can fund either your retirement or the next chapter of your entrepreneurial life.

Who's likely to make an outright purchase of your business? Any one of the people described in the following sections.

Selling your portion to a current partner

Many business owners sell their portion of the business to a current partner, especially in professional practices where partnerships are formed around the idea that, in time, one partner will transition his or her ownership to the other partner or partners. Partnerships should always be launched with buy-sell agreements that define the terms of how one partner sells to another. If you're in a partnership, your sale game plan is set by this buy-sell agreement.

Selling to another business

If you sell your business to another business (or the owner of another business) that's engaged in the same or a similar line of business as yours (though usually in a different market), that buyer is known as a *strategic buyer*. Strategic buyers seek to expand the capabilities, breadth, profitability, and competitiveness of their existing businesses by acquiring the strengths of a business such as yours. They aren't looking to buy your business for its ability to fund a good owner salary or to build up equity for a possible future sale (that's more like a buyer with financial objectives, which is the topic of the next section). They're looking to blend or integrate your business into their own.

The way in which strategic buyers calculate what they'll pay for your business is different from the methods used by buyers with financial objectives. The businesses owned by the majority of strategic buyers fit some, if not most, of the following characteristics:

- ✔ A business that's larger and financially stronger than yours

- ✔ A business with long-range plans that would benefit from the strengths of your business — strengths the business would otherwise have to develop on its own

- ✔ A business that bases its purchase price on an estimation of how much value your business will add to the buyer's existing business over the next few years

✔ A business that will purchase your business only if it determines that the purchase price is less than the cost of creating the advantages of your business from scratch

✔ A business that's able to pay cash or obtain financing to purchase your business

Don't enter the business sale process thinking that a buyer with strategic interests will pay considerably more than a buyer with financial objectives. Most studies show that the difference between what businesses or individuals pay to purchase a business is minimal.

Selling to an individual with financial objectives

If you want to lay a bet, bet that if and when your business sells, it will sell to a buyer with financial objectives. What's more, bet that the buyer lives in or has already decided to move to your home area.

The vast majority of small business sales are to financially motivated individuals who participate in what the business sale industry calls *intramarket transactions*, which is another way of saying that all the players — the buyer, seller, and broker, if one's involved — are in the same market area. The typical small business buyer is motivated by some (if not all) of the following benefits:

✔ **A business purchase allows the buyer to be in business from Day One.** Instead of going through all the steps of starting up a business, the buyer of an established business essentially steps onto a moving train. A business that's already established has cash flow that can pay bills from the get-go. Plus, by buying a healthy enterprise, the buyer acquires an established job that can quickly fund a respectable lifestyle.

✔ **Buying a business is less risky than starting one.** Most business buyers have never owned a business before, so the fact that established businesses have a lower failure rate than business start-ups has strong appeal. Many buyers have quit or retired early from corporate careers but aren't yet ready to leave the business world. By purchasing a business they can experience ownership without the turmoil of the start-up process.

✔ **It's easier to borrow funds to buy a business than to start one.** A healthy business has established products, customers, suppliers, and employees; a proven reputation; and — most important to lenders — existing sales, profits, and cash flow. While the cost of acquiring a business, especially a healthy one, is almost always higher than the cost of starting a similar business, financing is more accessible because the risk is lower and the immediate income potential is higher. In nearly all business purchases, the buyer combines personal funds with some degree of financing — obtained either from the seller of the business, a bank, or in the form of a Small Business Administration (SBA) loan — to make the deal possible.

✔ **Buying a business delivers a three-pronged return on the investment.** When purchasing your business, the buyer is motivated by the fact that business ownership delivers more money, even after paying all expenses, than most people can make working for someone else. What's more, most buyers only consider purchases that deliver a good return on the purchase price investment. Here's what your buyer will likely want out of the deal:

- A good income ($100,000 a year seems to be the current magic number)

- A decent to downright good return on the purchase price investment

- A future payoff when the business is developed into a great success that can be sold to a new round of owners

Smart buyers (the kind you're looking for if you want your business to succeed in the future, and especially if you finance any part of the deal) only invest in businesses with strong and climbing sales, good earnings, a unique and valued product or service, a healthy marketplace, proven operations, and customers who are likely to migrate with the business under new ownership. In Chapter 2, I help you get a good feel for what buyers are looking for so you can plan your sale process accordingly. Chapter 2 also shows you how to assess how desirable your business is as a sale prospect, as well as how to improve the condition of your business in areas where it's currently weak.

Transitioning to next-generation family

One out of three small businesses transfer to next-generation family instead of being sold to outsiders. That's why you see so many businesses with names like Smith and Sons. But *sons* don't usually take over a business; instead, *one* son or daughter emerges as the controlling heir.

This book focuses on business sales rather than family transitions. If you plan to transfer your business within your family, seek legal and accounting advice on how to deal with the following issues:

✔ If you have more than one able and interested heir, determine which will assume control of your business before the transfer begins (don't leave the decision to your kids — that's a formula for a family feud). You need to develop a succession plan, groom your successor, and determine how to transfer ownership and receive compensation. Will you give or sell the business to this family member? And how will you personally reap value from the deal?

✔ Determine how the heir who takes over your business can begin to buy you out even before he or she is financially able to do so independently.

✔ Develop a means for transferring some of your business's value to your other heirs so they receive a portion of your wealth even though they don't receive business ownership or a leadership role. One way to do this is to assess your business's value at the time of its transfer to the controlling heir. That way you can allocate a portion of the value you created to other heirs (either at the time of business transfer or through estate planning) while allowing your controlling heir to benefit personally from the additional value that he or she generates after the business transfer.

Selling but staying involved

Not every owner who wants to sell also wants out of the business — at least, not right away. Many still want the sense of involvement, the security of an ongoing paycheck and benefits, and a role in the business world. In this section you find out how you can sell but stay involved in your business.

Selling part to a key employee

This approach relies on the fact that you've found an employee who has a desire to take over your business and an entrepreneurial spirit and expertise that matches or exceeds your own. What's more, the person should be one you admire, trust, and are willing to invest in, because in most cases the chosen employee won't be in a financial position to purchase all or part of your business, and you'll essentially make the person your partner until the handoff is complete.

After you identify the right person, you can begin to share ownership by selling him or her a portion of your business for cash or by transferring a share of your business in lieu of salary increases or cash bonuses with the agreement that this key employee will be your successor at some point in the future and will then fully buy you out of your business.

This approach isn't one to take lightly or without legal advice. You need to hammer out all the details, including what to do if the employee quits, dies, or is fired; what to do if you have serious disagreements; and what to do if, in the future, you want to sell your shares in the business to someone else.

One other word of warning: If you have family members with aspirations to take over your business, be upfront about your sale plans. Perhaps your desired timeline necessitates a sale to an employee rather than to a family member who may not be ready to assume the responsibility. Or perhaps an outside-the-family sale to a proven manager will result in a surer business transition and therefore greater sale proceeds to you. Whatever your reasons, know them and explain them to the affected family members, especially if the family member works in your business.

Selling part to another business

You may choose to sell a portion of your business to another business for one of these reasons:

✔ Your business would benefit from a strategic partnership with a key business partner who could lend financial, operational, distribution, production, or marketing strength to your business

✔ You're beginning a succession plan that will sell your business gradually to another business in a transition that avoids the disruption of an immediate business takeover

Taking on a co-owner or partner

Under this scenario, you value your business, determine what percentage you want to sell (and your new partner wants to buy), draw up a legally binding partnership agreement, and begin to work as one of the partners in your business rather than as the sole owner. The essential component in your partnership is a *buy-sell agreement* — a statement of the terms you'll follow if one partner buys the other out.

Do not — I repeat, do not — enter a partnership without a buy-sell agreement prepared by an attorney. When meeting with your attorney, also discuss how to protect yourself in the event of your partner's death or disability. Most partnership agreements are accompanied by life and disability insurance policies for this purpose.

Selling to employees through an Employee Stock Ownership Plan (ESOP)

An ESOP is a tax-qualified, defined-contribution employee benefit plan through which employees accumulate shares of the business. Through an ESOP, an owner can sell stock quickly or over years, and the stock sale proceeds may be tax-free. An ESOP provides tax advantages if you're planning to sell to a key employee or a group of employees.

Before considering an ESOP, decide whether:

✔ You're willing to invest the time and effort required to set up a plan

✔ You're willing to remain involved with your business over the significant transition period — usually years — between your sole ownership and assumption of ownership by one or more employees

✔ You have employees with the ability to take over your business, both from a managerial and a financial standpoint

If you decide an ESOP is a good route for your business, be aware that you're venturing way out of do-it-yourself territory.

This book is about selling your business to another individual or business. If you plan to sell your business through an ESOP, plan to work with an experienced ESOP attorney and to devote the time it'll take to plan your ESOP, value your business, obtain funding for your plan, and make your plan operational.

Other ways to leave the business life behind you

Get a few business owners together and it won't take long for the term *exit plan* to arise. Business sales top most exit plan wish lists, but other options exist. Here are a few:

✔ **Liquidating and going out of business** takes little planning. It's probably the quickest form of business exit. Basically, you inventory your merchandise, make a list of your assets, put prices on everything, and hold a sale. If your inventory is large, you probably want to seek expert assistance on pricing and conducting the sale. You also want to collect all outstanding receivables, pay off all debts, address all contractual obligations, formally release employees, and make sure all legal and financial i's are dotted and t's are crossed. If the value of the physical assets and inventory of your business exceeds the price you're likely to get from a business sale, liquidating is the way to go. It's also the way to go if you're in a tremendous hurry and your business needs time-consuming enhancements before you can sell it to a new owner. Chapter 2 helps you determine whether your business is ready for a sale, and Chapter 6 helps you with pricing formulas so you can determine whether asset liquidation or a business sale is to your financial benefit.

✔ **Mergers** are like marriages, but the players are businesses instead of people, and the baggage is emotional, financial, structural, and organizational to boot. Usually, at least one of the companies in a merger is facing some sort of struggle, and because you're the one seeking to sell, it's likely that you have issues you're hoping a merger will address. In a true merger, either both companies are dissolved and assets are folded into a new entity owned by the principals of the merged companies, or the stronger company survives and absorbs the weaker company, which essentially disappears. In many cases, mergers require owner involvement after the deal is done, so weigh this option only if you have the time and money to invest in getting the deal done and the desire to stay involved through the merger and for a transition period thereafter.

✔ *Going public* is the term used when a privately held business becomes publicly held by offering its stock for sale to investors through a process known as an *initial public offering,* or IPO. The most frequent reason, among many, that companies go public is to raise capital. The process is carefully overseen by the U.S. Securities and Exchange Commission, or SEC, which requires you to comply with a host of regulations and to fill out a mind-numbing pile of registration and reporting forms.

Warning: If you're thinking about going public, you need to seek guidance from legal, financial, and valuation professionals experienced in the public investment arena. For an overview of what's involved, read the SEC advice to small businesses considering going public, available online at http://www.sec.gov/info/smallbus/qasbsec.htm/.

A Helicopter View of the Business Sale Process

The business sale process is the same whether you sell to an individual, another business, or a strategic or financial buyer. The process is outlined in this section and detailed in the rest of this book.

What's less clear than the business sale process is the timeline involved. If you want an answer to the question of how long it takes to sell your business, you may as well ask yourself, "How long is a string?" The answer is, it depends. It depends on whether your business is ready for sale right now or whether you need time (a lot or little) to strengthen marketing, build revenues, cut costs, improve operating efficiency, firm up systems and management, update leases and contracts, and deal with all the other business-improvement issues I outline in Chapter 3.

Although you won't find a one-size-fits-all timing answer, you can arrive at a rough estimate. Plan on a year or more of preparation if your business isn't currently in prime condition, plus four to six months to market your business for sale and find a buyer. If you need to move faster, you'll probably sacrifice sale proceeds as a result. Turn to Chapter 2 for more on the time and price balance.

Step 1: Preparing your business for sale

Before offering your business, you want to get it in the best possible shape. That means you want it to be financially healthy and on a good growth track, with few weaknesses and many strengths, and with operations that are likely to continue almost seamlessly upon an ownership change.

To optimize your success in selling your business, I strongly suggest that you heed two points of advice, both of which I expand on in Chapter 2:

✔ **Know what makes a business attractive to buyers.** If you started your business from scratch, you may wonder why someone wanting to jump into the business ownership arena wouldn't want to do the same. If you understand *why* a person would want to buy an existing business, you can more effectively market right to your target audience. For instance, if you think your business will be purchased by a buyer with strategic interests, you can prepare to emphasize the capabilities your business will bring to the buyer's business. Or, if your business is likely to be purchased by someone with financial interests (as is the case in most small business sales), you can get your books in great shape for the buyer's financial review.

✔ **Assess where your business lies on the sale-readiness continuum and identify what you need to do to get it in ship-shape. Then, do it.** Most professionals advise allocating up to a year or even more to get the business into prime condition for sale. Chapter 3 helps you enhance the sale readiness of your business.

You can't keep word of your intention to sell your business close enough to your vest. Until you're certain that your business has sold and that it will continue under the careful management of a new owner, don't let word get to employees (other than the few you bring into your confidence), or especially to clients, suppliers, distributors, or lenders. Think of it this way: If you can't keep it secret, what makes you think they can? The dangers of telling employees too soon are many:

✔ Employees can become demoralized if the sale seems to drag on or stagnate and they become uncertain about the future of the business.

✔ Employees may not like the buyer at first glance and may subconsciously work against the deal as a result.

✔ Employees may leak information outside the business.

The biggest problem with letting the news out before your sale's a done deal is that it puts your business on a slippery slope that could greatly diminish its eventual value. If you tell employees and then an employee tells a friend, and the friend mentions it to someone else, and that someone else is married to one of your big clients, then your client finds out and all kinds of bad things can result; the very assets and capabilities that you're trying to sell — such as client rosters, employee team, distribution networks, and production partners — are potentially in jeopardy. For one thing, the client may feel (rightly) that you should have told clients before letting the word out in the community. For another, the client may feel (understandably) the need to protect her company by holding off on new commitments to your business until things feel more certain. Even if you request otherwise, expect your employees to share the news of the impending sale — regardless of whether they're enthusiastic or concerned — with spouses, best friends, or (your nightmare) employment recruiters or headhunters.

Step 2: Assembling your business sale team

A business sale involves a buyer and a seller, obviously. Additionally, no sale should occur without input from an accountant and an attorney. If you don't already have a business accountant and lawyer, then after you get your business ready to sell, you need to hire some pros to help you throughout the selling process.

Many business owners also involve a sale intermediary, usually a business broker. Depending on the complexity of your financial situation, you may want to bring an appraiser and a tax expert on board as well, especially if your business assets are complicated and your business value is high, resulting in a significant tax impact. Chapter 4 helps you assess your need for outside assistance and helps you figure out how to hire help where you need it most.

Step 3: Pricing your business

How to price your business depends on a long list of factors, including the size of your business and its earnings, what you intend to sell, the value of your assets, the strength of your market and industry, recent sale prices of similar businesses, and on and on.

When pricing your business, make sure you're realistic about what kind of financial outcome you can expect from the sale. Anyone who reads business articles knows about companies that were purchased at figures like 15 times earnings or other high-roller stakes, and those stories whet the sale interests and fuel the hopes of small business owners. The following fact may hit like a bucket of cold water, but it contains a healthy dose of realism: Most small businesses sell for prices that range from one to four times seller's discretionary earnings, with an average sale price of two to three times average annual earnings. Chapter 5 helps you calculate your earnings, and Chapter 6 offers all kinds of pricing advice and formulas, but for now, if you adjust your early expectations to a two- or three-times-earnings price (providing all aspects of your business make it an attractive, low-risk prospect), you probably won't face disappointment later.

Step 4: Assembling sale materials

Whether you do it yourself or rely on a business broker to help with this step, your business needs to be summarized in a document that allows prospective buyers to see what you're selling and why your business is valuable. This document should include operational, financial, and marketing information that backs up your claims with facts. Chapter 7 helps you update and summarize your business and marketing plans, and Chapter 8 shows you how to assemble your business offering into a sale memorandum for prospective buyers.

Step 5: Finding and working with buyer prospects

You have to get the word that your business is for sale out to the right people, either on your own or through a business sale broker. Either way, you need to proceed on the super-QT. Otherwise, you'll alarm and possibly scare away clients and employees, tip off competitors, and eliminate the exclusive deal you want prospective buyers to feel they're gaining access to. Chapter 9 helps you define and target your prospect, communicate your offer, and pre-screen respondents. Chapter 10 guides you through the process of receiving and evaluating offers and — if all goes well — Chapter 11 helps you move the prospect to sign a letter of intent and deposit good-faith earnest money to buy your business.

Step 6: Doing due diligence

Due diligence is the business sale term for the homework the buyer and seller need to complete to be sure that promises made on both sides of the deal hold up under examination. At this stage, the buyer will likely request information in order to learn answers to the following two major questions:

- Is your business in good financial condition and working order?

- Does your business face any problems — such as financial, legal, or marketing issues — that could threaten the future of the business?

At the same time that your buyer is determining that your business is in the condition you've represented it to be, you'll want to do some research to confirm that the buyer has the financial capability and business expertise required to purchase and run your business to a successful future. This research is especially important if you'll be providing seller financing or accepting deferred payments. Your investigation will focus on a few key areas:

- The buyer's financial condition and creditworthiness

- The buyer's business history, including the types of positions the buyer has held, the size budgets and staff the buyer has managed, and the buyer's ability to develop business, manage growth, and fulfill business commitments

Chapter 12 tells you what to expect and what steps you take during the due diligence process.

Step 7: Structuring and negotiating the deal

Business sale payment plans take many forms, from all cash (rare!) to down payments with financing ranging from seller notes to SBA loans to traditional bank loans, or even loans from lenders who specialize in helping businesses in certain industries. In addition to the buyer's cash and borrowed funds, some deals also include earn-out clauses where the seller gets paid over time based on the future performance of the business under the new owner's leadership. The structure options are myriad, and the only constant is that every arrangement comes with tax consequences that sometimes benefit the seller and sometimes benefit the buyer (but rarely both). Count on Chapter 13 to show you the structuring options and to guide you through the buyer-seller negotiation. For a one-stop financial planning resource, go to Chapter 14 for information on the implications and advantages of payment approaches, along with advice on how to proceed when you're the banker for part of the deal.

Step 8: Closing the sale

After negotiations are complete, the sale moves to the closing stage. This is the point where final price adjustments take place to account for last-minute valuation of inventory, accounts receivable, pro-rated operating costs, and other variables. It's also where the purchase and sale agreement and all loan documents are signed; business leases, contracts, and titles are transferred; and agreements ranging from covenants not to compete to such things as profit sharing plan succession agreements are executed. Chapter 15 shows you what to expect, what each closing form means, and how to participate in a closing session that gets signatures in all the right places.

The final step: Passing the baton

The sale process isn't over until the last dollar is in your pocket, which usually means that how you pass the baton matters not just to the new owner, but also to your own financial future. How you tell employees, clients, business suppliers, and others about your sale can have a big impact on how well the news is accepted and how the business prospers as a result.

Chapter 16 provides a game plan for announcing the sale and paving the way for the new owner's success. It also includes information on the legal steps you need to take to transfer the reins of your business to the new owner, along with tips for information you need to provide to the new owner before you formally exit the business scene.

Selling a franchise: A whole different ballgame

Selling a franchise (called a *franchise resale*) is only a little like selling any other business. The common features are getting your business in good financial and operating condition and gathering all the paperwork so prospective buyers can get a quick, accurate, truthful look at the condition of the business. When it's time to actually find a buyer, though, the owner of a franchised business takes a very different path from the one taken by any other business owner. If you're selling a franchise, follow these steps as you seek your buyer:

1. **First things first — review your franchise agreement, which does the following:**

   Defines whether and how you can sell your franchise. It will state whether you're required to offer your franchise first to the franchisor as part of your agreement's buy-back or first-right-of-refusal clauses. A *buy-back clause* means that the franchisor has the right to buy your franchise back before you can sell it to other buyers. A *first-right-of-refusal clause* means that you must allow the franchisor the right to match the offer from a third party before you can sell your franchise to an outsider.

   Confirms the length of time until your agreement expires. A new buyer may be able to discuss new terms with the franchisor, but the terms of your agreement will be the starting point for negotiations, and of great interest to a buyer.

   Describes whether a transfer fee will be involved if you sell and, if so, what the fee is and what services it covers.

2. **Notify your franchise organization that you want to sell.** This step is probably required by your franchise agreement. It's also to your benefit, as the franchisor will probably respond with information on how to proceed. During this step, do the following:

   Ask for information regarding how much other franchises have sold for over recent months. Especially if your franchisor has a first-right-of-refusal to buy your franchise, you can be sure that the organization watches the price of every resale transaction. It may even have a preset pricing formula, like pricing set by a percentage of sales, that you can follow as you price your business.

   Learn whether the franchisor will require upgrades to bring your franchise current with the franchisor's latest brand, marketing, and operation requirements. This is information you can't wink and walk away from. Either you or the new buyer will need to make the required changes, if any, so find out what's involved. You'll probably have to either pony up before the sale or adjust your asking price downward to account for the expenses that await the next owner.

   Clarify the franchisor's buyer qualification process. Your franchisor almost certainly has a current set of capital and credit requirements, which you need to know so you can find a buyer that will meet the franchisor's standards.

   Determine whether changes have been made to the franchise agreement that will affect a new buyer.

3. Request buyer referrals from your franchisor. Before you begin advertising that your franchise is for sale, find out whether leads are available through the franchisor. Your franchisor may want to buy back your franchise, or it may have a list of interested buyers to tell you about.

Remember: After you sell, take great care to follow the non-compete agreement you signed as part of your franchise purchase agreement. Franchisors aggressively protect their interests, so work with an attorney to know what you can and can't do after the sale to stay within the confines of your purchase agreement.

Putting Yourself through a Quick Pre-Sale Self-Assessment

A business sale starts with some pretty serious navel-gazing. It takes soul-searching to decide that you're ready to shed the title of business owner, and after that decision's behind you, a long string of deliberations awaits. After you decide what you want for your future, you have to take an unvarnished look at whether the business you've built is ready for a sale. Setting your biases aside, you have to consider whether your business is an attractive purchase prospect. Would someone (or a group of someones) want to buy your business to add strategic strength to some other business? Or, does your business earn enough profit to make it an attractive opportunity for a buyer shopping for a financial investment? After you've weighed those questions, you have to weigh your priorities to decide how to move forward.

Unfortunately, business sales aren't split-second events. I hate to break it to you, but if you need out the day after tomorrow and your business isn't in good financial and marketing condition, a business sale probably isn't in the cards — in which case you'd be better off simply selling off physical assets and closing up shop. A sale may also not be in the cards if, after some serious thought, you've decided that you'd rather close than undertake the steps (and spend the time) required to transition your business into someone else's hands. This section helps you make the starting-gate decisions that focus on *you* and what you're trying to achieve.

Figure 1-1 (shown as Form 1-1 on the CD-ROM) helps you wade through the considerations that lead to your business sale goal and objectives. Then, Chapter 2 gets you peering into the depths of your business, so you can decide whether all is where you need or want it to be before offering it for sale.

SETTING YOUR BUSINESS SALE GOAL AND OBJECTIVES

SETTING YOUR GOAL

State your desired outcome in a single sentence. *What do you want for your post-sale life? Do you want to remain involved in your business after your sale? If so, how — as the leader, as a mentor during the buyer transition period only, or as a consultant?*

_____

_____

SETTING YOUR OBJECTIVES

Timeline: *By what date do you want or need to sell?*

_____

_____

Financial: *How much money do you want to receive from selling your business? (Keep in mind that most businesses sell for 2–4 times earnings.) How do you want to receive payment — are you willing to offer a seller-financed loan? If so, what terms are you willing to offer? (Remember: You have a much higher chance of selling if you offer seller financing.)*

_____

_____

Buyer: *What are your priorities regarding the nature of your buyer? Do you feel strongly about selling to a partner, key employee, employee group, or another business? Or are you open to selling to an outsider who has the financial and business capability to successfully own and run the business?*

_____

_____

Figure 1-1:
Determining
your busi-
ness sale
goal and
objectives.

Business Continuity: *Is it important to you to ensure employment continuity for your staff, so they don't have to move or undergo personal disruption as a result of your sale decision? Do you want to ensure customer continuity, so they don't have to undergo disruption in the way they do business?*

_____

_____

Pinpointing your business-exit motivation

You may be sick of your partner, tired of feeding the kitty to keep your business in the black, fed up with fighting new competition, or exasperated from a long effort to keep your business from what feels like an ever-threatening downhill slide.

On the flip side, you may be highly successful but bored with the same old routine. Or maybe you're burned out after years spent getting your business into its amazingly healthy marketplace position. Or, if you're like the 750,000 baby boomers who are selling businesses now and for the foreseeable future, you may be just plain ready for a nonstop string of days in the sun.

Before proceeding with business sale planning, spend some time focusing on why you want to leave your business. By getting clear about your exit motivators, you'll be in a better position to consider how fast you want or need to move and how to plan the most reasonable next steps. To help focus your thoughts, consider this list of the most typical situations that motivate business exits:

- ✔ Boredom
- ✔ Burnout
- ✔ Desire or need to move to a new location
- ✔ Health challenges that make running the business difficult or impossible
- ✔ A divorce that's forcing the need to sell the business and move on
- ✔ Family obligations that require a larger income and more certain benefits than the business can deliver
- ✔ A lack of energy or resources to address the opportunities the business faces
- ✔ A desire to diversify finances so all assets aren't tied up in the business
- ✔ Conflict with partners
- ✔ Fierce competition
- ✔ Business financial troubles
- ✔ A desire to retire with money from the enterprise you've built

Before you move on to specifics, you need to determine what you ultimately want for yourself. Do you want out of the business altogether, or do you want to stay involved to some degree? What do you want to do with your time after you sell, and how much money will doing so require? Use these questions to create your goal, a statement of what you want to achieve. In one sentence, put your goal into words. Want an example? How about, "I want to sell my business, retire, and move to a golf course community in Arizona."

Weighing your priorities and setting objectives

Your objectives define how you plan to achieve your goal. Give thought to the specifics now, before you launch the sale process, and your odds of reaching a happy outcome go up dramatically. Your objectives group somewhat nicely into four main areas: money, timing, type of business owner, and business continuity. By considering these crucial decision-making aspects of selling a business, you create a clear path from which you can devise your plan of action.

Money versus time

If your business has some weak areas (as many do), selecting your sale approach is largely a matter of weighing money versus time. Is it necessary for you to launch your sale process now, or are you willing to delay while you get your business into stronger shape for a sale? In short, do you want to obtain the highest possible price for your business, or do you place higher value on getting out as quickly as possible?

Unless your business is in great financial, marketing, and operating condition, if you want out immediately, you can be sure you'll at least need to discount the price you ask, though even that may not be enough to seal a deal. Realize that many small businesses never sell, largely because they never appeal to a buyer's interests. If you can't dedicate the time it takes to get your business into the kind of financial, marketing, and operational shape that causes a buyer to see it as a good deal, you may be better off selling assets and closing up shop.

On the other hand, if you're willing to commit time to the sale process (up to a year or more), you're more apt to realize a better price when you do sell. If you're personally ready for a sale but your business isn't, the next step is to figure out what it takes to make your business salable (and how long you need). That's what Chapter 3 is all about. Realize, though, that the more revamping you need to do to get your business into attractive, salable shape, the longer the process will take.

Buyer type and business continuity

What's most important to you? If you can establish your personal priorities, setting your business sale strategy gets easier. For instance:

- **Do you feel strongly about whom you sell to?** For example, do you prefer to sell to an heir-apparent or key employee, or are you fine selling to a total stranger? If you can't stand the thought of placing your business in the hands of an outsider, or if you aren't ready to give up involvement with your business, you may want to sell to a partner or employee group and then stay on with a reduced role in your business. Or you could merge your business with another, or sell to a new owner and negotiate a consulting agreement that keeps you involved for a specified period into the future.

✔ **Do you care what happens to the business after the sale?** For instance, do you want to ensure — as much as possible — that business goes on as usual for both clients and employees by keeping your business in its current location? If so, you want to limit buyer prospects to those who are committed to running your business as it now exists, rather than to someone who wants to move to purchased assets to a new, distant location from which clients are served. (Realize, though, that all bets are off when your business transfers hands, after which time the new owner has free reign to take your business in any direction not limited by specifics in the formal sale agreement.)

Get what you want — trust me, you can

Setting your business sale goals and objectives is a personal process that results in a statement of exactly what you want to achieve through the process you're about to launch. To share an example, I'll pick the most personal one I can think of: my own.

When my husband and I decided to sell our advertising agency, we sat down and wrote out our sale goal and set of objectives following the sequence outlined in Form 1-1.

First, we decided that we definitely wanted to sell our business. That was our goal.

Then came our objectives.

✔ **Regarding ongoing involvement,** we decided we wanted to exit our business without any employment commitments. We wanted to leave the business as soon as the new owner was ready to take it over as his own. We wanted to structure the legal documents, however, to leave us each free to continue to consult in the field of marketing and advertising, and I knew I wanted to write books on the topic. (I wrote *Small Business Marketing For Dummies* as my first post-sale venture.) We both agreed to remain close to the agency for up to a year after the sale in order to help transition the agency to the new owner.

✔ **Regarding a timeline,** we agreed that we wanted to sell our business within the upcoming 12 to 18 months.

✔ **Regarding financials,** our agency was healthy and had strong tangible assets. We wanted to be paid the fair market value of our assets, and we felt a fair way to pay for the momentum of our company (its brand and goodwill value) was to structure a sale agreement that ensured us a portion of the agency's sales for each of the first three years following the sale. We were willing to self-finance part of the deal.

✔ **Regarding continuity for our employees and clients,** we decided this was an aspect of the sale that was very important to us. More than two dozen bright people worked for our business, and nearly two dozen clients nationwide counted on our agency to handle their marketing programs. We decided to rule out the idea of a merger or a sale to another agency, feeling that the other agency would likely want to serve our clients with staff working under its own roof, leaving our staff high and dry. We set as our objective to seek an individual buyer who wanted to purchase our business, move to our location, serve our stable of clients, and keep our employee team intact.

And guess what? When you're clear about what you want, you'll likely achieve your objectives. That's what happened for us, so it's a truth I can personally vouch for.

Form on the CD-ROM

Form 1-1	**Setting Your Business Sale Goal and Objectives**	A form to help clarify what you personally want out of a business sale

Chapter 2

Evaluating Your Business as a Sale Prospect

*H*ere's a statement that sounds like a Yogi Berra quote, but it's a truth that presides over the whole effort to sell your business: Your business will sell when someone thinks it's a good time to buy it. All things considered, a buyer assesses the following factors when deciding whether your business is worth its salt and has a better-than-good chance of surviving your exit and thriving under new ownership:

- ✔ The financial health of your business

- ✔ The strength of your business capabilities and processes, as well as the likelihood that your business will transfer easily into new hands

- ✔ The size and strength of your industry sector and market area

Buyers also weigh the risks that come with your business, as well as the attractiveness (or unattractiveness) of the sale terms you're offering. In many ways, the risks that accompany a business are a virtual flip of the attractive points that fall under the preceding three categories, but I run through them later in this chapter so you can see them all at a glance in order to be aware of the kind of red flags that cool many a buyer's initial interest. In regard to the sale terms, a buyer will consider whether you'll make the deal easy by offering seller financing, and whether you have enough confidence in the business to make a portion of the purchase price contingent upon its future success; the buyer will also consider whether you're willing to stick around to facilitate the ownership transition if needed.

This chapter gives you a bird's-eye view of all that a buyer looks at when considering whether the attributes and risks of a business make it a worthy purchase prospect. It helps you decide whether your business is ready or at least close to ready for a sale. After you go through the pages of this chapter, your next step will be to turn to Chapter 3, which guides you through the process of fortifying business strengths and overcoming business weaknesses to build value and allow you to raise your asking price, a topic that's covered in detail in Chapter 6. Because sale terms are a fairly complicated part of structuring a deal due to their tax implications, I cover them in Chapter 13.

Assessing the Financial Health and Growth Prospects of Your Business

Of all the factors that affect the sale readiness of your business, its financial condition tops the list. It's difficult to look attractive to a prospective buyer unless you can showcase a good financial history, with growing revenues and earnings, all documented in well-presented financial records.

Your business may keep financial records in the form of a balance sheet and an income statement that tracks sales, cost of sales, expenses, and profits. More likely, especially if yours is a business on the small end of the spectrum, you may operate from a cash flow statement, tracking your business health by watching changes in your cash position. Working from either set of records, you must be ready to show prospective buyers how over the past few years your business has grown its top line (its sales) and its bottom line (the amount that remains as earnings after expenses are covered). This recent financial history — and how neatly it's chronicled in financial statements — is what you want to evaluate before you expose the finances of your business to the masses.

The reason buyers want to see your financial history is simple. How your business has performed financially in the recent past is the best indicator they can get of how it's going to do in the near future. In other words, buyers want to study past financial statements in order to assess future potential.

As you consider the financial condition and potential of your business, be realistic and base your growth projections on sound, credible forecasts that are well justified by actual recent financial performance. (Chapter 5 includes advice for projecting future business performance.) Don't even think about stating or hinting that your business makes additional money under the table or off the books. To a prospective buyer, the reddest flag of all is a price that the owner says is justified by money generated from off-the-books revenue. If an owner makes such a statement, the underlying message is, "Trust me." By making the statement, however, the owner essentially admits to dishonesty, scaring honest buyers off as a result.

Charting your financial history

The steps throughout this section help you determine whether your business's sales and profits are likely to make it attractive to buyers. If your assessment leads you to think your financial condition isn't quite ready for show time, Chapter 3 offers advice on how to improve the situation by building sales, reducing costs, and taking other steps to improve your financial picture. On the more positive side, if your financial trends are on a good upward track, Chapter 5 helps you strengthen your financial presentation by creating the kind of financial statements buyers want to see.

To create a snapshot of your business sale and profit trends, use Form 2-1 on the CD-ROM. The form includes a spreadsheet, which shows your sales, costs, expenses, and profits for the past five years, and a chart, which illustrates how your business sales, gross profit, expenses, and profits are trending. This chart appears directly below the spreadsheet; Figure 2-1 shows the chart on its own.

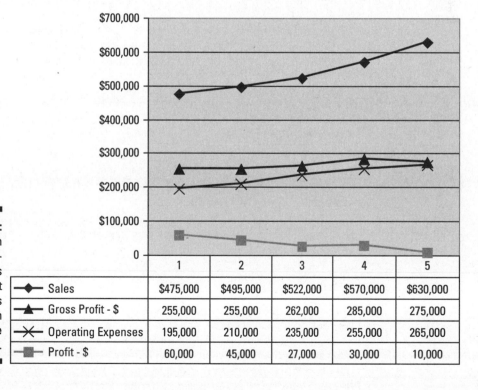

Figure 2-1: A growth chart showing sales and profit trend lines (see Form 2-1 on the CD-ROM).

	1	2	3	4	5
Sales	$475,000	$495,000	$522,000	$570,000	$630,000
Gross Profit - $	255,000	255,000	262,000	285,000	275,000
Operating Expenses	195,000	210,000	235,000	255,000	265,000
Profit - $	60,000	45,000	27,000	30,000	10,000

To use the form, simply replace the sample figures in the spreadsheet (which are shown in grey shaded boxes) with figures for your business. After you enter your numbers, the spreadsheet is set up to automatically calculate your *gross profit*, which is the portion of your sales revenue that remains after cost of sales, and your *profit*, which is the amount of money that makes it to the bottom line after all expenses are deducted. In addition to automatically calculating your gross profit and bottom line profit — both in dollars and as a percentage of sales revenue — Form 2-1 automatically creates the line chart.

Take a look at the following parts of the sample chart and then your own chart, and keep this guidance in mind:

- **The chart's top line represents sales** and provides the quickest indication to a buyer of how well your business performs in its marketplace. It shows whether sales are growing or declining, a clear reflection of whether your products are well marketed to and accepted by customers. Your top line doesn't have to be on a steep incline, but a buyer wants to see some level of steady incline, or some kind of explanation that justifies why sales were erratic or declining in certain years. In the sample chart, revenues are on a nice incline.

- **The gross margin line tracks how much the business actually earns** after it pays the costs incurred to produce its goods or services. A look at the sample chart shows that over the last five-year period, the gross margin hasn't kept pace with sales growth. Ideally, you want to see a steadily increasing gross margin that tracks on a parallel line with sales, indicating good cost management. A margin that's falling in relation to sale revenue denotes that cost of sales is eating away at revenues and, as a result, at profits.

- **Operating expenses show the cost of business operations,** including everything from rent to salaries to research and development to marketing. The trend line in Figure 2-1 shows that operating expenses are growing at about the same pace as sales, which is good.

- **The chart's bottom line represents operating income or profit.** This line gives an at-a-glance picture of how cost of sales and operating expenses affect how much of every sales dollar remains in your business. The example in Figure 2-1 shows a steadily declining bottom line. A minimal bottom line isn't necessarily a bad thing. In fact, many small-business owners include owner perks, family-member salaries, and other discretionary expenditures in their operating expenses in order to intentionally keep the taxable bottom line to a minimum. When presenting their business for sale, however, these owners work with their accountants to recast expenses, backing out all but essential operating costs to show buyers what they most want to see, which is how much money the business actually generates for the benefit of its owner. This number is called your *seller's discretionary earnings*; I describe it fully in Chapter 5.

However, in Figure 2-1, the bottom line is declining not because of operating expenses, which are actually increasing at a slower rate than sales, but because of a declining gross margin, the result of increased cost of sales that need to be reviewed and brought into line.

When monitoring your bottom line, keep a close eye on your gross profit line as well. If both your profits, indicated by your bottom line, and your gross margin are declining while your top line is increasing (as is the case in Figure 2-1), then too much of your revenues are being eaten up by your cost of sales, and you probably need to better manage the cost of producing the products or services you sell.

Assessing the financial condition of your business

After reviewing your sales and profit growth trends and other financial records, a buyer will slot your business into one of the following categories:

- **Growing revenues and earnings:** A business that's attractive from a financial standpoint will have sales and gross profit lines on a similar incline, indicating that revenue is growing and that the business is managing its cost of sales well. Further, the business will generate enough gross profit to pay operating costs and have enough left over to provide an attractive income for the owner. (For most business buyers, $100,000 seems to be the desired earnings figure.) If such is the case with your business, it's probably a good and ready sale prospect, provided that its operations, transferability, and sale terms are also attractive, as described in the rest of this chapter.

- **Growing revenues but declining earnings:** If sales are growing but your bottom line is shrinking, a buyer will look for one of two culprits. First, cost of sales may be out of control, absorbing sales revenue before it can even make it to the gross profit line. Second, the cost of running your business may be out of control. If either of these conditions leads to a weak bottom line, you have some remedial work to do, and Chapter 3 will help. On the other hand, if your bottom line is minimal for the good reason that you've expensed owner and discretionary business expenses to keep taxable income down, preparation of a seller's discretionary income statement, as described in Chapter 5, will factor non-essential costs back into your bottom line and show the strength of how much your business actually earns for its owner.

- **Moderate-to-serious growth challenges:** If your top line is declining or dipping up and down, a buyer will see a business with erratic sales, probably due to a product that's poorly accepted in its market, weak marketing programs, or other problems that lead to poor or uneven sales. To position your business as a good sale prospect, you want to improve your growth trend, as reflected by the top line in Figure 2-1, to show steadily increasing sales.

✔ **Faced with solvency issues:** Businesses that owe more than they own, and businesses that can't pay their cost of sales and essential operating expenses without eating up all their sales revenue and maybe more, face critical financial problems that scare off most prospective buyers. If your current liabilities are greater than your current assets, your business is either insolvent or close to it. Your options are to rapidly decrease debt and build assets, to try to sell at a discounted price to someone who sees value in your product or operations in spite of your financial problems, or to liquidate assets and close before incurring further financial risk.

Considering the Non-Financial Aspects of Your Business

A business that's an attractive purchase prospect has more in its favor than great financials. Most buyers want a business that not only makes money but one that makes money from a desirable location, selling a product that's in growing demand, with operations that are easy to take over, manage, and grow, and an ownership situation that's likely to transfer without disruption. To determine whether your business is a strong sale prospect, see if it lives up to most, if not all, of the attributes in the following sections.

Understanding the attributes most buyers seek

To gain a buyer's interest, your business needs to shine in the areas that buyers most value. Following is a list of the attributes that turn buyers' heads upon a cursory glance at your business. Your business doesn't need to excel in all the following areas, but to win a buyer's interest, it needs to compete in most categories and look exemplary in at least a few.

✔ **Unique and desirable products and services.** If your business sells a product that's different and decidedly better than competing options, that's a big plus. If you produce your product using a process that's difficult to copy but easy to adopt and follow, that's even better.

✔ **Desirable location.** Just like in the field of residential real estate, people pay more for businesses in growing, attractive locations where people want to live and where businesses thrive.

✔ **Modern facilities and equipment.** Businesses with modern, good-looking facilities, up-to-date equipment in top condition, and current, transferable leases that continue well into the future are more attractive than those with run-down facilities or the need for near-term relocations.

✔ **Strong staffing.** Your business is likely to be more appealing to a buyer if you, the seller, aren't the one-and-only driving force in the company. Your business will look more attractive and less risky if it has an experienced, well-trained staff with good morale, as well as strong employee relations and clear employment policies. Buyers will also look for a strong management team and employees who are likely to stay with the business after the ownership change.

✔ **Solid customer base.** A business with a large, loyal, and committed clientele and a well-maintained customer database is much more attractive than a business reliant on a few major clients.

✔ **Well-known name with good reputation, good marketing materials, and a strong online presence.** The buzzword in today's business world is *branding.* Businesses with names that are known and well-regarded have strong brands that buyers pay dearly to acquire. (Quick, shameless plug: For more information, read *Branding For Dummies,* published by Wiley, which I wrote with branding expert Bill Chiaravalle.)

To assess how good your business will look upon a buyer's first glance, rate its attractiveness using the chart in Figure 2-2 (also on the CD-ROM as Form 2-2). Answer each question as honestly as possible, and then rate your performance on a scale of 1 to 10, with 10 being exemplary. If you circle high numbers all the way down the chart, you can have confidence that your business has attributes that will be attractive to buyers. If your numbers are low or only fair, turn to Chapter 3 for advice on how to build business strengths prior to a sale offering.

Weighing the strength of your business capabilities and processes

The financial condition and attributes of your business will help you catch the eye of a buyer, but to achieve a business sale you need to convince the buyer that your business capabilities and processes are uniquely impressive and easily transferable to a new owner.

The terms *business capabilities* and *processes* aren't just MBA mumbo-jumbo; they're keys to business success. Business capabilities have to do with what kind of systems, contracts, and relationships your business has in place to successfully achieve its goals. Business processes build on business capabilities to allow your business to run smoothly and effectively.

BUSINESS ATTRIBUTES: RATING YOUR STRENGTHS	
Attribute	**Rate Your Business on a 1–10 Scale**
Products and Services: Are your products unique, decidedly better than competing options, and produced using a process that's difficult to copy but easy to adopt and follow?	1 2 3 4 5 6 7 8 9 10
Location: Is your business location desirable to buyers — both for its livability and its attractiveness as a business setting?	1 2 3 4 5 6 7 8 9 10
Facilities and Equipment: Do you have modern, good-looking facilities with up-to-date equipment in top condition, with long-term transferable leases?	1 2 3 4 5 6 7 8 9 10
Staffing: Do you have an experienced, well-trained staff with good morale, strong employee relations, and clearly defined policies?	1 2 3 4 5 6 7 8 9 10
Customers: Do you have a large, loyal, committed clientele and a well-maintained customer database?	1 2 3 4 5 6 7 8 9 10
Reputation: Is your business name well known, highly regarded, and backed by good marketing materials and a strong online presence?	1 2 3 4 5 6 7 8 9 10

Figure 2-2: Rating your business strengths.

Business capabilities fall into seven categories:

- **Operations:** The resources and systems that allow cost-efficient production of the highest-quality products or services

- **Marketing:** The process by which a business reaches, wins, and keeps customers

- **Distribution and delivery:** How you get your product into the marketplace and customers' hands

- **Customer service:** Activities that address the customer's wants and needs and enhance the customer's experience, leading to customer satisfaction and loyalty, repeat business, and positive word-of-mouth and referrals

- ✔ **Management:** How your business is led, including its vision and mission, business model (how you make money), and management team

- ✔ **Organization:** How your business is structured to make its product or deliver its service, and what systems it uses to make the most of staff and resources

- ✔ **Research and development (R&D):** Ability to research, design, and develop new products, services, techniques, or technologies

Not all the seven capabilities are equally important to every business. For example, R&D may not matter a bit to a beauty salon — unless that salon markets itself as *the* place to go for cutting-edge treatments involving the latest, greatest salon formulas and techniques. And distribution and delivery may not be anywhere on the radar screen for a restaurant — unless the restaurant has a catering division that relies on a fleet of specialized, top-of-the-line vans. What's important is that you realize which capabilities are most important to your business success and that you strengthen those capabilities as much as possible to heighten your attractiveness as a sale prospect.

Use the form in Figure 2-3, available on the CD-ROM as Form 2-3, as you take the following steps:

1. **Decide which of the seven key capabilities are most essential to the success of your business.**

   To prioritize the importance of each of the capabilities in your business, consider each capability separately, asking yourself if the capability is barely important in your business, if it's moderately important, or if it's greatly important because it provides your business with a distinct financial, production, or competitive advantage. You may decide that a single capability — for instance, marketing or distribution — gives your business its edge. Or you may decide that your success relies on several capabilities. By knowing which capabilities are most important to your business, you'll know which ones to develop even further and to showcase in your sale offering.

2. **Assess how your business ranks in each of the key capabilities you identified in Step 1.**

   After prioritizing the importance of capabilities to your business success, consider whether your performance in key areas is weak, fair, good, or great. For instance, the owner of a day spa may determine that customer service is a key capability that can make or break the spa's ability to increase customer expenditures and to win repeat business. Yet upon evaluation the spa owner may determine that the spa's customer service capability is only fair, in that it isn't a focus of employee training or rewards, nor is it an area the business promotes internally or through marketing.

As you assess the strengths of your key capabilities, reach beyond your own impressions. Think about asking a trusted manager to complete Form 2-3 independently, and then compare the findings. If the person knows about your sale plans, you can explain that the assessment is part of your sale-readiness evaluation. In most cases, though, you want to keep sale plans to yourself, in which case you can simply say you're undertaking an exercise to strengthen your business capabilities and would benefit from the manager's frank input and assessment.

Ideally, responses to Form 2-3 will lead you to the determination that your business has great strengths in the capabilities that most affect its success, but that often isn't the case. If you see areas where you've ranked a capability as highly important but you've also ranked your strength as less than great, Chapter 3 offers guidance for improving key capabilities prior to a sale.

BUSINESS CAPABILITIES: PRIORITIZING IMPORTANCE AND RATING STRENGTHS							
Capability	Importance to Your Business			Your Strength in This Capability			
	Low	Medium	High	Weak	Fair	Good	Great
Operations							
Marketing							
Distribution and Delivery							
Customer Service							
Management							
Organization							
Research & Development							

Figure 2-3: Ranking and rating your business capabilities.

Assessing the transferability of your business

Even if your business is in great financial health and operational condition, it faces a sale obstacle if a buyer doesn't believe it will migrate easily from one owner to another.

Business-transfer landmines tend to come in one of four areas:

- **Transferability of customers.** A buyer wants to be convinced that clients are more loyal to the business — and its products, services, staff, and location — than they are to you, the business owner, personally. Be ready to show the number of clients who have long-standing relationships with your business, how they're served by a number of valued employees, and how they're committed to your business through loyalty programs, formal (and transferable) contracts, credit accounts, service programs, or other indications of long-term and secure business-customer relationships. Also be prepared to explain how customer information is kept in databases that can be transferred to the new owner.

- **Transferability of business capabilities and processes.** In an easily transferred business, key capabilities are clearly defined and incorporated into formal processes that are described in manuals and understood by employees throughout the business. To assess the transferability of your key capabilities, begin by referring back to Form 2-3. Note which capabilities you ranked as most important to your business success. Then assess whether your business has developed systems around your capabilities, and whether those systems are easy to adopt thanks to business and marketing plans and production and policy manuals. If not, Chapter 7 will help you put your processes into words.

- **Transferability of business contracts.** Legally binding documents describe lasting business agreements that provide your business with continuity and marketplace advantages. A buyer wants to know that contracts for client, supplier, distributor, and other key business relationships exist and are transferable. The same goes for building and equipment leases. Especially in the case of your building lease, if your business success is reliant upon its location — as is the case with most restaurant and retail establishments — be sure your lease extends at least five years into the future. Otherwise, a wise buyer may walk from the purchase opportunity.

- **Transferability of workforce.** Key employee contracts, profit sharing programs, employee benefit plans, and other employment incentives help bind employees to a business, as do programs that inspire employee development and morale. Be prepared to explain your employment programs, plans, and policies to a buyer, preferably by sharing a copy of your employment policy manual, described in Chapter 7.

Form 2-4, shown in Figure 2-4, helps you assess the transfer-readiness of your business in each of the four preceding categories. The owner of a sale-ready business will answer the questions with Yes answers. If you answer many of the questions with the answer No, consider actions you can take to remedy the situation so your business will be ready to transfer more easily to a new owner. Chapter 3 presents information on how to ready your business for a sale, including ways to enhance its transferability.

BUSINESS TRANSFERABILITY: ASSESSING YOUR SALE-READINESS	Yes	No
Customers		
Are customers served by and loyal to key managers and staff members in addition to you personally?	☐	☐
Are customers committed to your products, services, staff, and location to the degree that they'd rather continue dealing with your business, even upon your departure, than take their business to a competitor?	☐	☐
Are customers committed to your business by participation in loyalty programs, business-customer contracts, credit accounts, service programs, or other programs?	☐	☐
Does your business maintain a complete customer database showing customer names, contact information, purchase history, and other useful facts?	☐	☐
Key Capabilities and Processes		
Have the key capabilities of your business been clearly defined and incorporated into formal processes — for product production, sales, customer service, billing, financial management, and other processes that are important to your business success?	☐	☐
Are your processes described in manuals?	☐	☐
Does your business have a current business plan?	☐	☐
Does your business have a current marketing plan?	☐	☐
Contracts		
Does your business have a building lease and if so does it extend at least five years into the future and is it transferable?	☐	☐
Does your business have contracts with suppliers, distributors, or strategic business partners and are they transferable?	☐	☐
Does your business have equipment or equipment service contracts and are they transferable?	☐	☐
Workforce		
Have your key employees signed employment contracts and are they transferable?	☐	☐
Are your employee benefit plans and incentive programs outlined in an employment policy manual?	☐	☐
Do you have a formal program for training employees and is it detailed in writing?	☐	☐

Figure 2-4:
Assessing the transfer-ability of your business.

Analyzing the Health of Your Industry Sector and Overall Market

In the same way that your business will be most attractive to buyers when your financials are on an upswing, it will also be more attractive when your industry sector is strong and growing and when the size of the market for your offering is also rising.

The truth is, though, that some industries go out of market favor, and some market areas recede in population. When that happens, the attractiveness of a business serving the industry and market also diminishes. Face it, buyers prefer to buy businesses that ride the promise of a strong industry and a growing market area.

As you assess the condition of your industry sector and market area, see if any of the following conditions apply:

- **Your industry faces regulatory, legal, or growth challenges.** If this is the case, you want to reduce the reliance of your business on the high-risk aspects of your industry and find undamaged niches that you can grow.

- **Your industry has undergone changes and your business hasn't adapted.** If this is the case, consider updating your business plan and investing time and funds to bring your business current so it's competitive in the marketplace and attractive as a sale prospect.

- **Consumers have declining interest in the products or services of your business.** If this is the case, update your business plan to bring your product or service into line with current market tastes.

- **Your market area has a declining number of prospective customers for your business**. If this is the case, you can either alter your product line to appeal to those in your market area, or you can develop new market areas to build sales to compensate for the dwindling prospective customer group in your established market area.

This section helps you get a feel for how your business's industry and market sector as a whole are faring so you can decide whether the market conditions that surround your business are favorable for a sale.

Gathering the facts and stats

Research helps you determine the marketplace situation your business faces by keeping you abreast of shifts in consumer interests, government regulations, economic conditions that affect your industry or market, and changes in the population that alter your prospective customer pool.

You can compile information on your industry and market growth trends in a number of ways, which I outline in this section.

Consulting your industry association

If you're not already a member of your industry association, or you're not sure whether your industry has an association, do an online search by entering a word that describes the focus of your business, plus the word "association." For example, enter "advertising" plus "association" in a search engine, and the first result is the American Association of Advertising Agencies. Enter "remodeling association" and the first result is the National Association of the Remodeling Industry. Try a similar search for your field.

After you find an association source, visit the association's Web site for information on industry growth and health, or call the association to request information on industry growth prospects.

Searching online for research groups

Enter a term that describes your industry into a search engine and check out some of the top results. For instance, when I enter "golf industry statistics" in my favorite search engine, one of the top results is the Golf Research Group, which describes itself as the world's leading consultant and publisher of business information to the golfing industry. As another example, when I enter "cellular phone industry statistics" into the search engine, one of the top results is for the Cellular Telecommunications & Internet Association, the self-described international association for the wireless telecommunication industry. Similar industry groups probably serve your business arena and can provide industry growth trends that are useful during your sale process. You'll probably be amazed by the amount of information that's available for free on industry online sites. Other information is available for a price, and often industry magazines invest to obtain the information. It's worth it to ask for the media kits from leading industry publications, which likely excerpt key points from industry studies they've purchased.

Looking up other business and government Web sites

Start with www.census.gov for information on population and resident characteristics in practically any U.S. community. From the home page, click Quick Facts to browse population statistics for any U.S. county and for incorporated cities. Then move on to the Web sites of the business development departments that serve your market areas, ranging from your state's economic development department to the business resource center at your chamber of commerce to the small business department center (SBDC) at your community college. These groups will likely be able to provide you with detailed local market information, including market area growth trends and growth trends by various age groups. This information helps you present the strength of the market your business serves, if in fact the prospective customers you serve are growing in number. If they aren't, the information helps you make decisions about how to target alternate market segments, if necessary to maintain sales momentum.

Studying publications in your industry and market area

Most publications post online versions of their media kits, which provide trends and forecasts that supply you with useful information on how your industry and market are growing and changing.

If the information isn't available online, call the publication and talk to a sales representative. Explain that you're compiling industry statistics for a presentation and are seeking information on issues facing the industry, industry growth statistics, growth information by market niche or segment, and any other information that affects the health of businesses in the industry sector.

Forecasting trends based on the info you gather

The whole point of compiling industry and market area information is to become clear about whether your business exists in a strong and growing environment or whether it faces problems that will likely affect the attractiveness of your business as a sale prospect.

After you have an idea of how the industry and market area are likely to trend in the near future, proceed as follows:

- ✔ **If trends point toward growth and strength in your industry and market area,** and if your business is ready financially and organizationally for a sale, then you can proceed with confidence, knowing that your industry sector and market area will contribute to the strength of the business you're offering for sale.

- ✔ **If you see a receding industry or shrinking market,** you may be wise to take some time to redirect your business toward new opportunities (see Chapter 3 for information on building strengths), or at least be aware that you may need to discount the price of your business to account for the risky times it may be entering, based on troubled industry and declining market conditions.

Watching Out for Risk Factors (Or Being Prepared to Account for Them)

A buyer can and will overlook one or even several risks if the attributes of your business are enticing enough to outweigh the weaknesses, if you present a good plan for how necessary changes can be addressed, or if you ask a price that's lower than it might otherwise be to compensate for the risks that come with your business purchase.

Some buyers actually seek out businesses in trouble, hoping they can make the purchase at a sacrifice price and then apply their own abilities to turn the business around. Others are willing to overlook certain risky aspects of a business in order to acquire strong attributes — patents, proprietary production processes, a strong brand name, or other features, for example. The reasons that buyers acquire troubled businesses are many, but in almost all situations buyers pay less for businesses with any of the following red flags:

- **Low earnings.** Remember, most business buyers want to buy businesses that provide annual income of at least $100,000. If your business earnings are too low to meet this threshold, the buyer will see your financials as a deterrent to a purchase.

- **High competition with low competitive advantage.** Your business is a risky deal if it has strong and growing competition that significantly outranks you in name awareness, sales, and product or service appeal.

- **No key staff.** Buyers see risk in a business that rests entirely on the owner's shoulders, with no second-in-command employee or employee team to help in a business transition — especially if the business has no distinct products or unique processes that clients will follow after the owner leaves.

- **Weak operations.** An unprofessional workplace and low-quality business records — especially financial reports — turn buyers away or lower price expectations.

- **Low name recognition.** Your business has lower value, due to lower brand value, if customers don't know your business name or have strong positive reactions when they hear it.

- **Dependency on a few clients.** A buyer sees risk if you serve only a few clients, especially if those clients aren't committed to your business by loyalty to your product or service (rather than to you personally) and by transferable contracts.

- **Non-transferable business capabilities and processes.** The transferability of your business is at risk if you lack managers or employees who can help a new owner keep the operation going after the old owner leaves — especially if you don't plan to stick around during a transition period. Likewise, a buyer will see a risky seller-to-buyer transfer if systems and processes aren't set up to allow a buyer to easily step in and keep the business running. Other transferability risks include a lack of client contracts, customer loyalty programs, and a good client database or detailed customer information.

✔ **A declining industry or market area.** Businesses in undesirable locations, declining neighborhoods, or ailing industries carry high risks and therefore sell for lower prices.

✔ **Expiring or problematic lease.** An iffy lease is a sky-high risk if your business success is reliant on its location, as is the case with a restaurant or a business with heavy foot traffic. In fact, many brokers won't even try to sell a restaurant with less than five years left on the lease unless the lease includes a good renewal clause.

Don't wait until the last minute to deal with this potential deal-killer. Have a confidential talk with your building owner or landlord to learn about extending and assigning your lease, including what's necessary to qualify a new tenant.

✔ **Undisclosed challenges.** Business owners who try to hide business weaknesses or challenges create a risk rather than avoid one. A buyer *will* discover business challenges during the due diligence fact-finding process. If he or she finds one that you didn't share openly, the trust established during sale negotiations can be jeopardized, and the deal may fall apart as a result.

✔ **Unwillingness by the seller to provide financing or accept any contingent payments.** If it looks like you want to wash your hands of your business the minute the sale documents are signed, buyers sense risk. By offering to provide seller financing, and by tying a portion of the payment price to future business performance, you're vouching for the future potential of your business by putting your money where your mouth is.

Deciding How to Proceed

If you've waded through the contents of this chapter, you know the kinds of attributes buyers seek, the kinds of risks they avoid, and the factors they consider when assessing whether a business seems to be a good purchase prospect. By applying the information to your own business situation, this chapter provides you the information to determine how your business rates as a sale prospect. Based on this knowledge, you can decide which of the following four actions to take:

✔ **Launch the sale process with confidence,** because your business is on an upward trend (and therefore attractive to buyers) and your operations and clients are ready to transfer efficiently into the new owner's hands.

✔ **Delay your sale launch while you right wrongs** by improving the financial, marketing, and operating challenges of your business. Realize that the project of getting your business into a more marketable condition before offering it for sale will likely take months, or even a year or more, so plan your timeline accordingly.

✔ **Launch the sale process knowing you need to plan around your business, industry, or marketplace deficiencies** by setting a lower sale price than a more attractive business would likely win, and then by making a strong case for the opportunity that awaits a buyer able to invest expertise and financial resources that you weren't able to apply to the situation.

✔ **Get out quick** by liquidating and selling physical assets to offset liabilities and avoid further financial risk.

How you decide to proceed is dependent on the personal situation that's motivating your business exit, the condition and sale-readiness of your business, and the timeline you want to follow.

Whether you decide to sell as quickly as possible or following a preparation period during which you get your business into prime selling condition has a lot to do with how much you can command in sale price. It's the old fire-sale rationale: Damaged or out-of-season goods sell at discounted prices, if at all.

As you plan your next steps, consider the following questions:

✔ Based on everything you've read in this chapter, is your business ready for a sale right now?

✔ Do you need to sell right now?

✔ If your business isn't ready, can you make time to get it into sale-ready shape (that's what Chapter 3 is about)?

✔ If your business isn't ready and you can't make time to get it into sale-ready shape, are you prepared to discount your asking price as a way to compensate for financial or operating deficiencies (see Chapter 6 for more on pricing your business)?

Your business will sell for what a buyer thinks its worth. As a result, how much you get for your business goes hand-in-hand with how much time and effort you can devote to the process of getting it into sale-ready shape. That's what the next chapter is all about.

Will the marketplace be ready when you are?

If you're like most business owners who are ready to enter the business-for-sale marketplace, you may be concerned about how current economic conditions will affect the odds for a successful sale outcome. You may wonder whether a retrenching economy will hamper the business sale environment. Here are two facts to remember: One, while a recessionary economy chills the residential real estate market, it can actually heat up the business sale market. As middle- to upper-level executives leave or are edged out of the corporate world, many decide to have a go at business ownership instead, contributing to a growing buyer pool. And two, while housing sales are reliant on mortgages through financial institutions, small-business sales usually rely on seller financing, which is largely unaffected by changes in the financial world.

You won't find anyone who'll tell you that selling a business is a cinch in any economic environment. That's why you're holding a whole book on the topic. But if you have a business that's attractive based on all the points outlined in this chapter, the marketplace likely holds plenty of buyers.

Forms on the CD-ROM

Form 2-1	**Sales and Profit Growth Trends**	Use this form to create a spreadsheet showing your sales, cost of sales, operating expenses, and profit for the past five years, along with a line chart illustrating your growth trends
Form 2-2	**Business Attributes: Rating Your Strengths**	Use this form to rate how well your business performs in the areas buyers evaluate when forming initial impressions about a business-for-sale offering
Form 2-3	**Business Capabilities: Prioritizing Importance and Rating Strengths**	A form for ranking and rating your business capabilities
Form 2-4	**Business Transferability: Assessing Your Sale-Readiness**	Questions to ask and answer as you assess the transferability of your business

Chapter 3

Sprucing Up Your Business

In This Chapter

▶ Cleaning up legal issues before you sell your business

▶ Getting your finances in order

▶ Boosting your bottom line with price hikes and cost cuts

▶ Making improvements to the most important parts of your business

To sell your business, you need to convince a buyer — quickly and clearly — that your business is a good bet because it has a long list of plusses and very, very few minuses. The most obvious attribute you want to present has to do with the financial condition of your business, because almost all buyers will want to see growing sales and positive cash flow that can fund operating and financing costs right from the day of purchase. If the buyer doesn't see a financially attractive picture, one of two things will happen: Either the buyer walks away or a bargaining process begins. If bargaining starts, a lower price almost certainly follows. To help avoid that route, this chapter shows you how to get your business into shape — financially, for sure, but also legally and operationally — before offering it for sale.

Most business owners are so busy putting out fires they don't take time to think about, plan for, or implement business improvements. Or when they do take time, they don't know where to start or how to proceed. That's where the information in this chapter comes to your rescue.

Most often, business owners take the time to analyze the strengths, weaknesses, opportunities, and threats their businesses face only when they're starting up, at a major crossroads, or facing big challenges or big opportunities. Can you think of a bigger opportunity than the once-in-your-business-lifetime chance to sell your business?

To get you started, this chapter identifies major areas for review, along with steps you can take to strengthen your business before showing it to buyers. It also has information about eliminating weaknesses and buyer red flags, cleaning up legal problems, structuring your business and its finances with a sale objective in mind, and polishing your company's image prior to a sale offering. Some of the steps are critical; others are important-but-not-crucial. Go through the whole chapter, and then you can decide how much time to devote to building strengths and fixing what may be broken — or close to it — in your business so you're ready when the first buyer prospect comes calling. *Remember:* The stronger your business is before you put it up for sale, the quicker it will sell, and the higher the price it will command.

Weighing Your Options

If your business is in prime shape for a sale — and Chapter 2 helps you make that assessment — then you can skip this chapter and head straight to Chapter 4, which helps you assemble your sale team and launch the sale process. If, however, your business is in less than ideal shape for a sale, you have three choices:

- **Pump up strengths and overcome weaknesses so your business is in shape to command the best possible purchase price** (that's what this chapter's about). If your financial picture is less than rosy, I highly recommend that you take this option, giving yourself time to improve your numbers and the strength of your operation before offering your business for sale.

- **Plan around deficiencies by offering your business at a lower price** than it would command if its growth and finances were strong (see Chapter 6 for help pricing your business). Plan to sell based on strong and attractive capabilities in other aspects of your business, compensating for less-attractive or higher-risk aspects of your business through price concessions.

- **Liquidate assets and close up shop.** If your business faces problems that business strengths can't outweigh, and you don't have the time, energy, money, or inclination to make the changes necessary to alter your business condition, you may decide that your best route is to sell physical assets, close up shop, and avoid putting yourself at further financial risk.

Only you can determine how much you can or are willing to do, and how much time and energy you're able to invest, to prepare your business for sale.

Keep in mind, though, that highly attractive businesses win higher prices than all others. If you have the time, the best thing you can do for your business is to go through this chapter, working to build strengths and overcome weaknesses in the areas that most contribute to the ability of your business to compete and succeed in its marketplace, and therefore in the business-for-sale arena.

Untangling Legal Issues

One of the quickest ways to scare off a buyer is to try to sell a business that's riddled with issues signaling legal troubles ahead. If your business is threatened by a lawsuit or a contract dispute, or if it has pending legal actions you haven't dealt with, you're sitting on a stack of buyer red flags. From product warrantee disputes to employee lawsuits to regulation or zoning infractions, when a buyer learns of unaddressed legal issues, yellow cautions flash because the buyer starts to see risk. At that point, interest is likely to ebb, price negotiations are likely to intensify, and due diligence is likely to become even more intensive.

Your best course of action is to list any possible legal issues before offering your business, and then to take whatever steps necessary to clear them, or at least to get the process of clearing them underway. Do this to smooth the sale process, for sure, but also do it for yourself, because in most small business sales, legal liabilities remain with the seller — not the buyer — even after the sale. That's because, technically, most small business sales include the sale of business assets, not the sale of the entire business entity, which would includes business liabilities. Chapter 6 explains the confusing topic of asset versus entity sales. For now, it's enough to know that most likely upon the sale of your business, its liabilities will remain seated firmly in your lap. As such, you should start cleaning up any lingering legal issues, both for the sake of an easier sale offering and for your own good.

Seek legal help to address any of the following issues:

- ✔ Are you including any patents or licenses as part of your business sale? If so, make sure they're held by the business and not by you personally, and that they're current and not nearing expiration dates.

- ✔ If you have a building lease, is it current, assignable, and renewable? This is a big deal that will stop many buyers cold if your answer isn't an unequivocal "Yes." If your location is essential to the ongoing success of your business (as it is, for instance, for a retail establishment or a restaurant), see that your lease extends at least five years into the future. Also, work to assure that lease increases are protected by rate escalation clauses.

- ✔ Is your business in violation of any zoning regulations, or do you have any unapproved regulation variances? Are there pending zoning changes that will impact your business in the near future? Will a sale trigger forced compliance with any previously grandfathered zoning regulations? You may not be able to change the facts, but get legal advice on how to address any problematic situations, if possible. Otherwise, be ready to disclose the issue so it doesn't come as a surprise later in the sale process.

✔ Are there any legal claims, encumbrances, or liens against your business? Don't think you can sweep them under a carpet. A good buyer will discover them as part of the due diligence process, so clear them up before offering your business for sale.

✔ Is there pending litigation or an unresolved lawsuit against your business? Again, you may not be able to accelerate and conclude the legal process before a sale, but if your business is involved in litigation, disclose that fact early on in the selling process.

✔ Does your business face any labor union or other employee-related problems? In addition to disclosing such problems, also outline the steps you've taken to minimize the possibility of similar issues arising in the future.

✔ Has your business had any regulation or law violations, or any environmental or safety compliance issues, that will result in major expenses to address? The expenses almost surely will remain yours to handle, but the risk is one the buyer will have to address, unless you can convince the buyer that you've already put controls in place to avoid similar violations in the future.

✔ Are business licenses up to date? If not, make the calls and write the checks to address what's probably a fairly easy-to-remedy oversight.

✔ Will the sale and transfer of your business require any third-party consents? If so, before offering your business for sale, be sure the consents can be easily obtained.

Consult with an attorney and plan to right wrongs before putting your business up for sale if you can. If you can't, address the issues frankly and factually in your selling memorandum (which is the topic of Chapter 8) and during the sale process. Ideally, you'll be able to present a plan for how the problem can be overcome in due time and without weighty ramifications.

One other legal issue to address with both your accountant and your attorney is whether the legal structure of your business should be changed prior to your sale offering. Your accountant can give you the lowdown on how the legal structure of your business affects how your sale will be structured and how your sale proceeds will be taxed. Based on that discussion, you may choose to change your business structure if a different legal form would help you structure your sale and its payout.

Getting Your Finances in Order

In addition to seeing that your business is in good legal shape, you also need to see that your finances are in good order. If your finances are a mess, it's difficult to make anything else about your business look really good.

I can't think of a single business that shouldn't rate financial health as an essential key to success. Without financial health, you can't grow your business to its potential, nor can you sell it for what would otherwise be its best price. The only kind of business that wins a top-dollar price from buyers is one in strong financial condition with positive growth trends. All other businesses sell at discounted prices, if at all.

Getting your finances in order takes four steps:

✔ Getting clear about the financial condition of your business

✔ Cleaning up financial problems

✔ Improving your bottom line

✔ Getting your financial records ready for presentation

This section helps you with the first three steps. The last step — getting your financial records ready for presentation — merits a chapter of its own. For that, turn to Chapter 5.

Getting clear about your financial condition

Form 3-1, shown in Figure 3-1 and available on the CD-ROM, helps you clarify your business's financial condition. To use the form, take these steps:

1. **Begin by deciding which of the statements in the left column best describes your business.**

2. **Then note the pre-sale condition, shown in italics in the right column, that matches your business situation.**

3. **Third, plan your next steps by reviewing the improvement recommendations that apply to businesses facing similar financial conditions, and by choosing between overcoming your financial challenges and then selling, selling now by reducing the price you ask in order to compensate for financial deficiencies, or — if you can't or don't want to turn your financial condition around — liquidating assets and closing up shop in order to avoid further financial loss.**

As you assess whether your business faces serious growth issues or solvency problems, apply these quick tests:

✔ **Determine the extent of growth challenges:** Chart the average rate at which revenues and profits or earnings have grown over the past three years (see Form 5-5). If average growth rate over the past three years is negative, that negative trend will continue until significant business changes are made.

✔ **Determine the extent of solvency challenges:** Divide the current assets of your business (cash, accounts receivable, inventory) by current liabilities (accounts payable, short-term debt, and interest on long-term debt due within one year). A current assets-to-current liabilities ratio of less than 1:1 indicates near-term solvency issues and a reason to take immediate action, as indicated in Form 3-1.

ADDRESSING YOUR FINANCIAL SITUATION	
✓ **SITUATION THAT DESCRIBES YOUR BUSINESS**	✓ **PRE-SALE CONDITION AND STEPS TO CONSIDER**
☐ Growing revenues/ growing bottom line	*Financially, business is ready for sale.* ☐ Prepare financial statements for presentation to buyers (see Chapter 5)
☐ Growing revenues/ declining bottom line	*Costs and expenses need to be reduced to strengthen bottom line prior to a sale* ☐ Reduce and manage cost of sales ☐ Reduce and manage operating expenses ☐ Delay sale offering until bottom line is stronger or ☐ Offer business now at discounted price
☐ Declining revenues/serious growth challenges	*Business needs to increase sales, which may require product and marketing improvements, prior to a sale* ☐ Invest resources to implement business turnaround ☐ Assess and improve product and marketing ☐ Consider increasing prices ☐ Delay sale offering until bottom line is stronger or ☐ Offer business now at discounted price or ☐ Seek legal and accounting advice to assist in liquidating assets and closing the business to reduce further financial loss
☐ Business faces solvency issues because it owes more than it owns	*Business needs to pay down debt and increase assets prior to a sale* ☐ Pay down debt ☐ Reduce expenditures that don't directly contribute to sales or that don't deliver a return on investment in order to decrease further depletion of current assets ☐ Delay sale offering until business is more solvent or ☐ Seek legal and accounting advice to assist in liquidating assets and closing the business to reduce further financial loss

Figure 3-1: Determining your pre-sale financial condition and improvement plans.

Cleaning up financial problems

Go through your records and work with your accountant to check on the following:

- ✔ **Asset ownership:** Be sure you have clear title, with no liens or encumbrances, to your equipment and any other major assets you sell. If you do have any liens, either pay them off or advise the buyer that they'll be paid off through escrow at the time of sale closing. Also, if you sell assets as part of a business entity sale, be sure they're held in the name of your business and not in your name personally. Additionally, determine whether your assets are undervalued or overvalued and whether your inventory is turning at a good pace. You can find more on those topics in Chapters 5 and 6.

- ✔ **Taxes:** Bring all federal, state, and local tax payments up to date, including payroll taxes.

- ✔ **Debts you owe:** Deal with bank or supplier credit problems to get them cleared before a buyer starts to look into how you do business.

- ✔ **Debts owed to you:** Collect overdue debts and accounts receivable. Buyers will look at how long credit sales remain unpaid, using their findings to form opinions both about your clientele and about how efficiently you manage your business. In most businesses, receivables that remain unpaid after 45 days represent a problem to be cleared prior to a sale.

Increasing your bottom line

A small business buyer wants to see that your business generates enough money, after all expenses, to fund a good living for its owner. As you prepare your business for sale, be sure its bottom line is as great as possible.

Most small business owners work with two bottom lines:

- ✔ One is the bottom line called *profit*, which is the taxable earnings the business shows after subtracting all cost of sales and operating expenses from the business, including such expenses as the owner's salary and perks, salary and perks for family members involved in the business, and other expenses that are important to the business success but not entirely necessary and therefore considered *discretionary*.

- ✔ The other is the bottom line called *seller's discretionary earnings*, which is the amount of money the business generates for the benefit of its owner, after adding owner's salary and perks, family member salary and perks, and other discretionary expenditures to the profit line. Chapter 5 includes information on calculating the seller's discretionary earnings for your business.

Whether you're looking at profits or discretionary earnings, you want your business to have the greatest bottom line possible. To increase your bottom line, you essentially have two options: increase prices or cut expenses. Either move delivers an instantaneous, often dollar-for-dollar impact on your bottom line. So if bottom line looks weak and you have time to turn things around between now and when you put your business up for sale, increase prices or cut costs, or both.

Increasing prices

One of the quickest ways to increase profitability is to increase prices, so long as the increases don't scare off existing customers.

A well-run business (which is what a buyer wants to acquire) raises prices on a regular but not-too-frequent basis in order to accommodate for increasing cost of sales and increasing operating expenses. Usually, the resulting price increases mirror increases in the overall economy, and as such customers tend to see the changes as understandably unavoidable. If you haven't brought your prices into line (and you'll see this at a glance if your revenues are growing but your bottom line is shrinking, due to increased cost of sales and operating expenses), bite the bullet and deal with the fact that your prices need revising. Make the fix for two reasons:

- ✔ A buyer wants to see a strong bottom line, which you can only achieve if you're charging enough for your product or service to cover all costs and expenses with money left to provide business profit.

- ✔ A buyer would prefer that you raise prices prior to the sale instead of putting a new owner in the position of having to make the increases immediately after the ownership change, possibly alienating customers who may miss you (and your lax pricing).

Take these steps:

- ✔ **Increase prices on your usual business schedule.** Most businesses raise rates on a regular basis. If it's time for a price boost between now and when you put your business up for sale, don't delay. Do it for three reasons:

  - The increase will add to your profitability, and therefore to your attractiveness as a purchase prospect.

  - The increase is on your normal business schedule, so the buyer won't perceive the price hike as a way to manipulate profits.

  - The increase is on a standard schedule that customers will understand and absorb.

✔ **Increase prices to reflect changing economic conditions.** If the cost of gas, shipping, materials, or any other business expense is eating into your profits, raise your prices accordingly. Businesses often get into financial trouble by allowing the cost of sales to balloon, taking a bigger and bigger bite out of sales revenue and gobbling up the bottom line as a result. Watch what it costs to produce the product or service you sell. If you can't trim your cost of sales, increase your prices to accommodate the extra costs involved, either by adjusting your overall price or by adding itemized charges for particular expenses, as hotels have done with utility charges and as airlines have done with checked-baggage charges.

Notice that this section is focused on increasing prices rather than on increasing sales. The problem with trying to increase sales over a short-term period is that most small businesses do so by slashing prices, staging big promotions, undercutting competitors, or whatever else it takes to bring in more sales volume. But unless your increased sales are accompanied by prices that allow you to grow your bottom line, they don't do a thing to boost profitability.

Cutting costs

Cutting costs involves reducing overhead and trimming discretionary expenditures. You certainly don't want to eliminate expenses that are necessary to the strength of the business you're trying to sell, and you don't want to set off alarms that create sale rumors or that drag morale down into the dumps. But you can make strategic cuts that help boost your bottom line without affecting your products or services or smashing your employees' morale into the ground.

The act of reducing overhead is sometimes called the Scrooge Strategy, but that doesn't mean you have to become miserly about how you fund your business.

✔ Look for expenses that aren't contributing to your business's strength and eliminate them. As a few examples, do you still need a large ad in the phone directory, or do most customers now find you through online searches? Or do you really benefit from membership in a local networking group, or would the dollars you spend on dues and attendance be better on your bottom line? Every business situation is different, but all businesses benefit from an occasional and careful review of which expenditures are being made more out of habit than as a result of careful and current decision making.

✔ Hold off on replenishing supplies and replacing staff unless absolutely necessary. For instance, if you're nearly out of stationery, compare the cost between a six-month supply and the annual supply you usually order. Or, if one of your staff members resigns, consider whether you may be able to reallocate the workload to avoid the costs involved with employee search, hiring, and training.

✔ Look for items you can purchase at lower costs and start shopping for and negotiating with competitive suppliers. While working with established vendors is often most expedient, when you're trying to build your bottom line it's often not the most cost-effective route. You probably don't want to look for a less expensive accountant or attorney, especially not now! But you may be able to find a window-washing service that's more affordable than the one you currently use, or a delivery service that charges lower rates.

✔ Begin to cull low-profit or no-pay customers you serve at a loss to your business. If you have customers that fit this description, consider whether there's a way to cut ties without creating unhappy former customers who generate negative word-of-mouth. Also, consider whether eliminating these customers will cut revenues and trim your client list to the point that your business will look less rather than more attractive to a buyer. You can start by increasing your prices so the customer is forced to pay a profitable price for future purchases. Or you can overcome slow payments by instituting an advance-payment policy for future purchases by customers with recent delinquent balances. One way or another, make it your objective to increase your business profitability and accounts receivable picture before it gets scrutinized by a prospective buyer.

Other ways to increase your bottom line profit include cutting the perks you pay to yourself and cutting or eliminating the salary and perks you pay to family members employed by your business. However, such cuts aren't necessary (unless your business is facing serious profitability challenges), because before selling your business, your accountant will help you reforecast your bottom line by adding such discretionary expenses back to your profits. (Chapter 5 has information on this process.)

Improving Your Curb Appeal

After a prospective buyer finds out your business name (a revelation that should follow the careful process of pre-screening and the signing of a confidentiality agreement, as described in Chapter 8), the buyer will start a sleuthing process. Any buyer with an ounce of sense or curiosity will go straight to a computer to start an online search for information about your company. The buyer will also drive by your business, collect your marketing materials, and take any other steps possible in an effort to form an impression of your business long before you give your polished sales pitch.

In other words, your business better be able to look good all on its own. In this section, I help you focus on the first impressions buyers take away from your business.

Polishing your external impression points

About the only way you can control the impression your business makes is to recognize all the ways your business presents itself and decide whether each presentation is as good as you'd like it to be.

Ideally, you want all your impressions to lead to a single strong image of your business. You want everything from stationery to ads, signs, brochures, T-shirts, staff uniforms, shopping bags, Web pages, and even specialty items like coffee cups and pens to convey the same logo, colors, and overall look and message. If you had years to prepare your business for sale, you'd want to polish the impression your business makes by taking the following steps:

- ✔ Be sure your business name and logo look the same on all business materials and ads

- ✔ Consistently use the same colors and type style on all your marketing materials

- ✔ Present a consistent image in terms of look, quality, and message on all business communications

But you likely don't have years to bring the image of your business into ideal condition. If that's the case, then between now and when you offer your business for sale, at least take the time to be sure that your business isn't making any impressions that harm its image. For instance:

- ✔ Signs, building fronts, or displays that are messy, unprofessional, in poor repair, or in need of cleaning deserve immediate attention and upgrade.

- ✔ Advertising and sales materials that look outdated or that present logos or taglines from years past need to be pulled from circulation.

- ✔ A Web site that fails to load quickly, or that has links that go nowhere or that lead to information that's outdated needs an immediate overhaul.

- ✔ An office or business location that's cluttered — or worse, dirty — needs immediate cleanup, possibly by a professional crew.

Especially if your business generates consumer foot traffic at your bricks-and-mortar location, then just like in selling a home, the curb appeal and first impressions of your location are very important to your sale outcome. Be sure the outside of your building is clean and freshly landscaped with good signage. When a prospect walks in, be sure the first impression is that you have modern furnishings and equipment and clean walls and flooring. A little bit of money spent to spruce up first impressions can go a long way toward helping you sell your business.

The form in Figure 3-2 (Form 3-2 on the CD-ROM) lists the ways most prospective buyers gain early impressions of a business. To use the form:

- ✔ Go down the left-hand column and check each item that represents a way your business makes impressions.

- ✔ For each impression point that you check in the left-hand column, use the center column to rate the quality of the impression being made. If the communication presents a current version of your business name and logo, with a positive message and a look that's clean and professional, rate the impression quality as Good. If the communication is outdated, sloppy, or unprofessional, give it a lower rating.

- ✔ Use the right-hand column to enter notes on how you'll deal with faulty impression points. In some cases you may decide to simply eliminate the communication point (canceling a billboard contract, for instance). In other cases you may want to replace the faulty communication with an updated and more professional version. Other points you can deal with by simple repairs — for instance, cleaning dirty windows, replacing broken glass, or enforcing employee dress codes or office maintenance policies so your place of business makes a good impression.

Boosting your online presence

What will prospective buyers find when looking for information about you and your business online? The answer is important, because an online search is one of the first steps a buyer takes upon learning your business name and purchase opportunity. It's doubly important if Internet marketing is essential to your business.

What you want, of course, is that when a buyer enters your business name into a search engine, the results lead straight to your Web site or, if you don't have a Web site, to positive mentions of your business on other sites, such as industry sites, regional business listings, or pages that include publicity or reviews featuring your business.

Imagine yourself at a buyer's keyboard and take the following steps, carefully studying the first few screens of results (that's about as far as most users go). If you don't see mentions of your business among the results, then you have work to do if you want to make a good online impression.

1. **Type your business name into a search engine and study the results.**
   If your business name is a common one, narrow down the responses by typing in your business name, the + symbol, and the name of your city and state.

MONITORING YOUR BUSINESS'S IMPRESSION POINTS				
Ways Your Business Makes First Impressions	**Quality of Impression**			**Notes on How You'll Improve Faulty Impression Points**
	Good	Fair	Poor	
A D V E R T I S I N G ☐ Print ads ☐ Radio ads ☐ Television ads ☐ Phone directory ads ☐ Billboards/outdoor ads ☐ Direct mailers ☐ Brochures/literature ☐ Newsletters Other _____	☐ ☐ ☐ ☐ ☐ ☐ ☐ ☐	☐ ☐ ☐ ☐ ☐ ☐ ☐ ☐	☐ ☐ ☐ ☐ ☐ ☐ ☐ ☐	
O N L I N E ☐ Web site look/speed/use ☐ Online ads ☐ E-mail look/response rate ☐ Online search results for you and your business Other _____	☐ ☐ ☐ ☐	☐ ☐ ☐ ☐	☐ ☐ ☐ ☐	
L O C A T I O N ☐ Building/entry signage ☐ Appearance from exterior (including doorway/windows) ☐ Appearance of reception area and promptness of greeting ☐ Appearance of workplace including décor and cleanliness ☐ Appearance of staff ☐ Nature and promptness of phone greeting ☐ Appearance of product/product displays/product presentations (such as menus, price lists, packaging, and so on) Other _____	☐ ☐ ☐ ☐ ☐ ☐ ☐	☐ ☐ ☐ ☐ ☐ ☐ ☐	☐ ☐ ☐ ☐ ☐ ☐ ☐	
L O C A L ☐ Publicity ☐ Customer word-of-mouth ☐ Business leader comments ☐ Community participation ☐ Business networks Other _____	☐ ☐ ☐ ☐ ☐	☐ ☐ ☐ ☐ ☐	☐ ☐ ☐ ☐ ☐	

Figure 3-2: Determining, rating, and improving your business impression points.

2. **Enter your own name, putting quotation marks around your first and last names to improve the results.** If your name is a common one, enter both your name and your business's name to narrow results.

3. **For comparison, repeat the above two steps but enter a few top competitors' names.** This will give you a sense of how companies that are a little stronger than yours are managing their online presence and will give you ideas for how you can boost your online profile.

If your search doesn't turn up any pages on your business, then follow these steps to strengthen your online presence:

1. **Work with a Web site developer to improve your site so it appears when your business name or your own name is entered into a search engine.** This is called *search engine optimization,* and almost any good search engine consultant should be able to help with the task.

2. **Look for organizations, media outlets, or groups who've given positive online reviews to your competitors.** If they haven't yet given a positive review, ask how your business may be included in the future.

3. **Add posts to forums where businesses like yours are being discussed.** Also work to add your business to sites listing businesses in your community or industry sector as a way to further increase your online visibility.

Fact-checking and fine-tuning your reputation

If you search for your business online and find sites containing less-than-flattering reviews or comments, do your best to rectify them. Consider these suggestions:

✔ If you find negative comments about your business that are accurate, fix the wrong and add news of your improvements to both your Web site and the Web site where the negative story is posted.

✔ If you find negative comments about your business that aren't true, politely ask that the blog, forum, or site owner remove the erroneous content. Offer to provide correct information if appropriate. If the site won't remove inaccurate, damaging information, contact a lawyer, especially if the site is visible enough to make a difference in your ability to attract a buyer.

✔ Improve your own site by adding an area where you spotlight positive reviews, publicity, customer comments, or other favorable testimonials.

✔ Overcome negative comments that you can't avoid by asking customers if they'd be willing to put their own good remarks into words to offset the damaging comments.

Overcoming Business Weaknesses and Building Business Strengths

Getting your business ready for sale is a delicate balance between getting rid of glaring problems and polishing strengths. The question you're probably weighing is where to direct your energy. Are you better off embellishing positives, fixing negatives, or finding some middle ground where you do a little of both?

If time, energy, and resources aren't an issue, the answer is to build positives *and* erase negatives. But usually, time, energy, and resources *are* an issue, and so the solution is usually to find a middle ground that tips in favor of building strengths. Put differently, where your business is strong, make it stronger. Certainly, you also have to get rid of big problems, which is a topic I deal with throughout this chapter. Keep in mind, though, that if your strengths are strong enough, they just may compel a buyer to look beyond deficiencies in your business. That's especially true if your strengths give your business a decided edge — one that a competitor can't easily replicate and a start-up can't easily create.

The following sections guide your diagnosis and prescriptions for strengthening each of the major capabilities of most businesses.

Improving your business one capability at a time

Chapter 2 describes the capabilities that fuel the success of most businesses, including operations, marketing, distribution and delivery, customer service, management, organization, and research and development. It also includes a form, Form 2-3, that helps you focus on which capabilities are most important in your business. As you work to improve your business for a sale, concentrate on the capabilities you check in Form 2-3 as being most important to the success of your business. If you believe your performance in an essential capability is poor or only fair, then that capability represents an area where you need to overcome weaknesses prior to a sale. On the other hand, if your business is good or great in an essential area, be ready to build your strength even further and to spotlight the key capability when you present your business to prospective buyers.

The upcoming section describes major business capabilities and gives advice on how to overcome weaknesses and build strengths in every area key to your business success.

Operations

As you assess the importance and strength of your operational capability, consider four key areas:

- ✔ **Location:** Your location is where you do business. Ask yourself, does your location — both your physical location and your online presence — give your business an edge over competitors? If it does, then it's an attribute to highlight in your sale offering.

- ✔ **Equipment:** This area includes computers, software, fixtures, furnishings, and equipment you use to produce your product and run your operation. Ask: Does your equipment set your business apart and give it an advantage?

- ✔ **Human resources:** This area includes the people who help you get the job done. Buyers want to know if your business has a management team that's capable of easing the seller-to-buyer transition. They also want to know about your employee team and your subcontractor network, which is especially important if yours is a very small business that relies on vendors and freelancers.

- ✔ **Processes you use to get the job done:** How you produce your product or service may give your business a real advantage. If you have a special production process — perhaps even a proprietary production system — you want to promote that fact in your sale offering. Similarly, if inventory management and control and quality control systems distinguish your business, then these are key areas to strengthen and spotlight.

In addition to thinking about how well your business rates in terms of location, equipment, human resources, and processes, think about whether your strengths are easily transferable to a new owner. For instance, if you rate human resources as a great strength but you have no employee contracts or compelling benefits that keep employees with your business, then a new owner may face a transferability issue. The same concern applies if your processes give you a competitive edge but they aren't systemized or detailed in manuals.

Use the form in Figure 3-3, available on the CD-ROM as Form 3-3, to rate your business operations and consider how to improve them. Follow these steps as you fill out the form:

1. **Check the operational aspects that are most important to your business's success.**

Look through the list in the left-hand column and put a checkmark in front of each entry that describes an advantage of your business. The boxes you check will describe operational aspects that you believe distinguish your business, give it an advantage, or enhance its ability to compete.

2. **Check steps you believe you should take in order to strengthen the operational advantages of your business.**

To take this step, begin by reviewing the operational aspects you checked as most important to your business in the left-hand column. Then look through the list of suggested improvements or actions that accompany the important aspects you checked. Consider whether your business would grow stronger if you took the action listed in the right-hand column. If so, put a checkmark in the box. The list of action items that you check will form the action plan to follow as you overcome weaknesses or build strengths in key operational areas.

Marketing

A big part of the reason people buy businesses rather than start them from scratch is that an established business comes with established customers and name recognition, resulting from strong marketing. A business buyer wants assurance that your enterprise is a moving wheel with all spokes intact and with full capability of maintaining and attracting customers without pause after the change of ownership.

Want to know how a buyer will judge your marketing capability? Look at your sales figures (the top line in the chart you create when using Form 2-1). If sales are going up, a buyer knows that your business is doing something right when it comes to creating a product or service people want, getting the word out, and converting consumer interest to business sales.

If your marketing isn't going so well, your sales are probably flat or declining, in which case you have to ask yourself: With time and money, how can we boost sales? The answer will lead to decisions about how to improve your marketing by improving your strategies in four marketing areas:

- ✔ **Your product strategy:** Does your product need to be altered to address current market tastes or trends? Do you need to revise your packaging or labeling to inspire market interest? What about the ways that you offer your products for sale — would the market respond better if you bundled several products together into one offering, or if you added warranties or service programs to address market interests and build sales?

- ✔ **Your distribution strategy:** Distribution is how you get your product in front of customers. It's both a key business capability and an important marketing strategy. Distribution is the topic of the next section.

STRENGTHENING BUSINESS OPERATIONS		
	Aspects of Importance to Your Business Success	Areas for Pre-Sale Improvement or Action
L O C A T I O N	☐ Physical location	☐ Improve physical location exterior, signage, and interior (use Form 3-2 to assess your physical location impression points) ☐ Check length and transferability of building lease if you rent your location and renegotiate if necessary
	☐ Online presence and domain name	☐ Improve Web site design ☐ Increase and document Web site usage and traffic counts
E Q U I P M E N T	☐ Equipment	☐ Replace or repair equipment if necessary ☐ If equipment is part of a business entity sale, confirm that it's owned by the business (not by you personally). Also see that titles are free of liens or encumbrances ☐ Review the nature, length, and transferability of equipment leases and service contracts; work with attorney to revise as necessary
	☐ Fixtures and Furnishings	☐ Upgrade fixtures and furnishings if necessary
W O R K F O R C E	☐ Management team	☐ Create organization chart ☐ Create job descriptions and profiles of key managers ☐ Review key employment contracts with attorney, including non-disclosure, non-compete, and transferability clauses ☐ Add key managers only if necessary for near-term operations or to heighten transferability of business ☐ Define recruitment and retention programs; improve retention programs if you have time and if improvements will inspire key employees to remain after ownership transition
	☐ Employee team	☐ Define employee training program ☐ Update or create employee policy manual ☐ Define profit sharing and deferred compensation programs, including how they inspire retention and their transferability to a new owner
	☐ Subcontractor network	☐ Create database of subcontractors, freelancers, and key independent contractors ☐ Define policies for independent contractors, temporary and leased employees; review with attorney
P R O C E S S E S	☐ Product/service production process	☐ Define your product/service production process ☐ Update or create production/service process manual
	☐ Inventory management and control	☐ Define how you acquire, manage, and control inventory
	☐ Quality control process	☐ Define your quality control processes ☐ Systemize and enhance transferability of quality control process if it represents a distinct business advantage

Figure 3-3:
Prioritizing
pre-sale
operation
improve-
ments.

✔ **Your pricing strategy:** Most businesses follow a pricing philosophy that aims to make their products the high-end, mid-range, or low-end price choice in the marketplace. As you review your pricing, consider your philosophy and then compare your prices with like-minded competitors. If you believe your business offers higher value than competitors, be sure your pricing is an accurate reflection of your product or service offering, and adjust it if it isn't. Also adjust your price if your costs have increased but haven't been reflected by price increases. At the same time, consider whether you might increase sales if you offered bulk purchase options, contract purchase offers, and financing or other payment options. Price adjustments are a direct route to a heightened top line, so long as the prices are justifiable in the customer's mind and don't lead to customer defections. Most buyers appreciate a business that has a defined pricing philosophy and a system for reviewing and adjusting prices on a regular basis.

✔ **Your promotion strategy:** Your promotion strategy defines how you communicate your marketing message and sales offer to prospective customers. Some businesses rely on advertising; others rely on one-to-one marketing, sales promotions, publicity, and other communication approaches. If you're not clear about how you promote your offerings, or if you think your promotion strategy — the approach you use to get word of your product or service to customers — needs improving, consider picking up a copy of my book *Small Business Marketing For Dummies* (Wiley) or one of the many other marketing books available at the bookstore.

As you incorporate these four marketing strategies into an improved marketing program for your business, turn to Chapter 7 for help. It includes a section on how to update your marketing plan and turn it into a document you can follow to improve your business sales and to present to your buyer as a marketing blueprint to follow.

Distribution and delivery

Some businesses distribute their products directly to the consumer through their own retail outlets or via direct sales driven by mail, phone, or online marketing. Others rely on distributor networks to sell products via intermediaries such as wholesalers, distributors, agents, or other retailers.

Businesses that sell directly to consumers don't have to give a lot of thought to distribution. For example, an accountant or doctor, the local shoe repair shop, and the restaurant around the corner (unless it has a catering division) hardly need more than an open door and a phone to get products and services to customers. Other businesses can't survive without strong distribution systems, whether that means contracts with shipping partners, retail channel agreements, or agreements with sales intermediaries such as travel agents or online booking sites. If distribution is a key to your business success, take some pre-sale planning precautions to ensure that the distribution systems and networks that give your company a competitive edge are formalized with contracts or agreements that can transfer without interruption to a new owner.

If you plan to offer your business for sale over the next couple months, you don't have time to make changes to the distribution capability of your business, so focus on detailing the distribution strengths you already have in place:

✔ Outline the steps you take to get your product or service to your clients or customers, basically providing the prospective buyer with a diagram of how your product goes to market.

✔ Describe the geographic area you serve, including market expansions over recent years and plans for new markets or distribution channels you believe should be opened in the near future.

✔ List relationships and agreements you've established with distribution or delivery partners and how those relationships will transfer to a new owner.

If your timeline is a little more generous, the form in Figure 3-4, available on the CD-ROM as Form 3-4, helps you define your distribution system and consider ways to expand upon it. Follow these steps as you fill out the form:

✔ Answer each question in order to put your distribution approach into words.

✔ Under each question, list the top one or two actions you can take, if any, to make your products more accessible to customers.

DEVELOPING YOUR DISTRIBUTION STRATEGY

How do you sell your product or service to customers? Do you sell directly through your business, either in person, by phone, by mail, or online? Do you use one or several intermediaries to sell you product, including sales representatives, wholesalers, or other retailers?

In addition to your current distribution channels, can you think of one or two ways you might enhance the availability of your product to customers, such as by making your offering available through other retailers, by direct mail, or for sale on your Web site, as a few examples?

If you use sales representatives, could you build sales by providing additional training or new incentive programs?

How do you deliver your product to customers? Do they carry it away on their own, or do you provide delivery services?

Can you think of one or two ways you might increase sales by adding new delivery options, such as same-day or overnight delivery, subscription delivery, free delivery to volume customers, or other delivery options?

Figure 3-4: Describing and enhancing your distribution and delivery systems.

Customer service

Customer service is the key to customer loyalty, and loyal customers are the key to many business buyers' purchase decisions. It's crucial that you keep your customer service at an all-time high throughout the pre-sale and sale process, even though your attention will be pulled in a million other directions. There's truth in the old saying that squeaky wheels get the oil — because loyal customers don't squeak very loud, they can get overlooked at the very time you need them most. If their loyalty ebbs and they leave your business, your attractiveness to a buyer can fall fast.

To assess and present the strength of your customer service capability, take the following steps (which aren't for naught, because you'll need to include this information in your selling memorandum, which I cover in Chapter 8):

✔ Create a profile of your typical customer, including customer geographic location and demographic or lifestyle facts (such as gender, age, income level, and so on). Chapter 8 includes a form you can use to create this profile.

✔ Track and summarize increases in the number of customers your business serves and the length of time customers have been with your business.

✔ Calculate and summarize rates of spending and profitability per customer.

✔ Track and present the number of customers who demonstrate loyalty to your business through contracts, loyalty programs, or other ways that demonstrate commitment to your company.

Use the form in Figure 3-5 (adapted from *Small Business Marketing For Dummies* [Wiley, 2005] and available on the CD-ROM as Form 3-5) as you follow these steps to benchmark and set customer service improvement standards:

1. **Rate your current performance in each area that contributes to customer satisfaction.** Be as objective as possible as you evaluate your business, giving yourself a 10 if your performance is superb and a 1 if it's riddled with problems. If you have a trusted key manager who can provide another opinion, ask that person to complete the form as well.

2. **Prioritize which areas with low performance ratings most need immediate attention and improvement.** Go down the list and note each area that you rated with a performance indicator of 6 or less and pick out a number of areas where you think your business can undergo near-term improvements. You can't fix everything at once, but even some improvement in areas you think are most important to your customers will make a difference, especially if customer satisfaction and loyalty are essential to your business success.

3. **Create a plan to reverse poor-service indicators in priority areas.** Meet with key managers or hold a staff meeting to brainstorm customer service ideas, focusing on the priority areas you've targeted. Create service standards and systems, and define ways to improve and monitor customer service. Then implement employee training and announce customer service incentive programs and rewards for customer compliments.

Beyond improving customer service, also work to see that customers are committed to your business by contracts, loyalty programs, or attachments to the unique benefits provided only by your company in your marketplace. If you believe that customers are more loyal to you personally than to your business's offerings, take time between today and when you offer your business for sale to increase customer loyalty to other staff members, to the unique attributes of your product or service, and to the loyalty programs of your business to increase the odds that they'll remain with your business after the sale.

Management and organization

A prospective buyer wants to know that your business doesn't tick only to your personal heartbeat but runs smoothly as a well-managed enterprise that can be carried forward without any great lurches by other managers or by a new owner.

To assess the management capability of your business, answer these questions:

- ✔ Does your business have a mission or vision statement that describes the principles of your business and what you're working to achieve?

- ✔ Can you explain the business model, or how your business makes money?

- ✔ Do you have key employees who can provide leadership and direction upon your departure from the business?

- ✔ Have you prepared manuals or documents that describe how your business runs, how your products or services are produced, and your employment policies and procedures?

The best way to improve your management capability prior to a sale is to get some of the weight off your own back. That means assembling a team of key managers or employees who customers trust and admire and who can help run the business in your absence. It also means creating processes and systems that can be easily transferred and adopted. And most of all, it means building a product or service so exemplary that customers will migrate with your business simply for what it offers — and not for the fact that you, personally, deliver the goods.

CUSTOMER SERVICE ANALYSIS & IMPROVEMENT			
Customer Satisfaction Factor	**Current Performance (1-10)**	**Improvement Priority (1-10)**	**Describe Plan for Improving Low Ratings**
COMMUNICATION			
Clear, friendly, informed, courteous staff			
Error-free correspondence, estimates, invoices			
Open to ideas, concerns, complaints			
Attention by owners/managers			
RESPONSIVENESS			
Customized solutions			
Flexible to special requests			
Prompt response to customer ideas/problems			
Prompt response to phones, mail, e-mail			
Prompt greeting upon customer's arrival			
No unnecessary management layers			
COMPETENCE			
Expertise in customer's field of interest			
Experience with customer's problems			
Delivers high value			
CONVENIENCE			
Convenient hours, phone system, Web site			
Good location, parking, access, services			
Convenient payment/delivery options			
Enjoyable, attractive atmosphere			
RELIABILITY			
Meets deadlines/exceeds promises			
Delivers accurate, quality products			
Stays within estimated costs			
Good reputation/highly recommended			

Figure 3-5: Rating customer service and planning improvements.

If you're more or less the one-and-only driving force in your business and you don't have a team to back you up, you may consider creating a board of advisors that could offer continuity after your exit.

And even if you're on a short timeline, it shouldn't take too long to enhance the transferability of management by putting a summary of what your business is and how it runs into words. Chapter 7 includes step-by-step guidance to follow as you formalize a business plan, marketing plan, employment policy manual, and operations manual for your business.

Research and development (R&D)

Though R&D capability is the backbone of many large companies, it's not a key capability in most small businesses. If cutting-edge technology and new product development are important to your business's success, however, then formalize your R&D approaches prior to a sale, if you haven't already done so, by documenting your R&D procedures. That way you can present not just a capability but also a process that a new owner can easily adopt.

Also, be prepared to show how key R&D managers are committed to your business by contracts and benefit programs, because the departure of a brilliant research mind could be devastating to a buyer.

Also be prepared to present a list of your research success stories, including patents, product introductions, publicity, and other indicators of success.

Improving the transferability of your business

Even if the capabilities of your business are in top condition, your business is only attractive to a buyer if he or she believes those capabilities will transfer seamlessly from seller to new owner.

Figure 3-6 (available as Form 3-6 on the CD-ROM) presents issues that affect the transferability of a business, along with steps to take to build your business into one that will transition efficiently into new hands.

To use the form, follow these steps:

- ✔ Review conditions that affect business transferability, listed in the left-hand column, and check any situations that apply to your business.

- ✔ Note the pre-sale advice that accompanies each of the situations you feel apply to your business.

- ✔ Choose the sale approach you'll follow, given your situation and the actions necessary to address the situation.

ASSESSING THE TRANSFERABILITY OF YOUR BUSINESS		
✓ **SITUATIONS THAT APPLY TO YOUR BUSINESS**	**PRE-SALE ADVICE**	**SALE APPROACH OPTIONS** (✓ **Approach You Plan to Take**)
☐ Clients are loyal to you personally more than to the products and services of your business	Launch a leadership and client contact transition plan; emphasize your product/systems over your individual presence or advice	☐ Implement a client-contact transition plan and to enhance client belief in and loyalty to your business product, service, and systems before offering your business for sale ☐ Offer your business now with an agreement that you'll remain during a seller-to-owner transition period
☐ Your products and procedures aren't unique and are easy to duplicate	Update marketing plan to establish a point of difference and unique market position	☐ Create distinct product value and unique advantages that lead to customer preference and loyalty before offering your business for sale ☐ Offer business now at discounted price using marketing plan to demonstrate product potential
☐ Your products and procedures are unique but not transferable as processes are "in your head"	Systemize processes; establish proprietary approaches; create operation and process manuals	☐ Invest time and funds to create systems and process manuals ☐ Offer business now with agreement to remain during transition period to transfer system and production knowledge
☐ Leases and contracts (building, equipment, supplier, distributor, key employees) don't exist, are about to expire, or aren't current or transferable	Review all legally binding documents; update where necessary	☐ Review/update contracts prior to sale offering ☐ If contracts can't be obtained or aren't transferable, determine if business is saleable without contract advantages or whether the business has aspects that can be carved away and sold separately

Figure 3-6:
Taking steps to make the transfer of your business to a new owner a smooth transition.

Accounting for Market Area and Industry Weaknesses

If your industry or market area has seen much better days, you need to decide whether you're willing to invest the time and resources necessary to complete the recommended pre-sale steps to address your current industry and market realities. If not, be prepared to price your business around its unaddressed marketplace challenges. Chapter 2 helps you figure out whether the industry and market are favorable for a sale. Here, you decide what you're going to do if you're facing weaknesses on those fronts.

Use the form in Figure 3-7 (available as Form 3-7 on the CD-ROM) to determine which conditions apply to your business. Then consider the advice that accompanies each condition.

To use the form, follow these steps:

✔ Review conditions that affect the marketplace condition of your business, listed in the left-hand column, and check any situations that apply to your business.

✔ Note the pre-sale advice that accompanies each of the situations you feel apply to your business.

✔ Choose the sale approach you'll follow, given your situation and the actions necessary to address the situation.

ACCOUNTING FOR THE CONDITION OF YOUR INDUSTRY SECTOR AND MARKET AREA		
✓ **SITUATIONS THAT APPLY TO YOUR BUSINESS**	**PRE-SALE ADVICE**	**APPROACH OPTIONS** (✓ **Approach You Plan to Take**)
☐ Your industry faces regulatory, legal, or growth challenges	☐ Look for undamaged aspects of your industry and grow your business around healthy niches in your industry ☐ Rewrite your marketing plan to focus on new product/service lines ☐ Rewrite your business plan to develop new capabilities to address the changing industry situation	☐ Reduce business reliance on industry high-risk aspects and to build business in undamaged areas of your industry before offering your business for sale ☐ Isolate healthy portions of your business for a partial-business sale ☐ Offer your entire business now at discounted price
☐ Your industry has undergone changes and your business hasn't adapted	☐ Create an updated business plan to bring your business current with industry trends and market preferences	☐ Update your business plans and bring your business up to date in your industry before offering it for sale ☐ Offer your business now at a discounted price using your updated business plan to demonstrate its potential
☐ Consumers have declining interest in your business offering	☐ Update your business plan to bring your product/service into line with market preferences ☐ Update your marketing plan to incorporate product values and a marketing message and brand image that appeals to current market tastes and trends	☐ Update your product line and business and marketing plans; implement business and marketing changes before offering your business for sale ☐ Offer your business now at discounted price using your business and marketing plans to demonstrate product line potential

continued

Figure 3-7: Dealing with the pre-sale condition of your indus- try and market.	☐ Your market area has a declining number of prospective customers for your business	Conduct market research; adapt product/service and promotions; identify new market segments and geographic areas	☐ If you have several years of planning time before offering your business for sale, invest resources to develop new customer groups or market areas to offset declining prospects in your established market. ☐ Offer business at now discounted price using business and marketing plans to demonstrate market expansion potential

Forms on the CD-ROM

Form 3-1	**Addressing Your Financial Situation**	A form to use when determining your pre-sale financial condition and improvement plans
Form 3-2	**Monitoring Your Business Impression Points**	A form to help determine how your business makes first impressions and how to improve those impressions where necessary
Form 3-3	**Worksheet: Strengthening Business Operations**	A form for prioritizing pre-sale operation improvements
Form 3-4	**Worksheet: Developing Your Distribution Strategy**	A form for describing and enhancing your distribution and delivery systems
Form 3-5	**Customer Service Analysis & Improvement**	Rate your customer satisfaction levels and then enter your plan to improve low-ranking areas
Form 3-6	**Assessing the Transferability of Your Business**	A form to use when taking steps to make the transfer of your business to a new owner a smooth transition
Form 3-7	**Accounting for the Condition of Your Industry Sector and Market Area**	A form that helps you deal with changes in your industry and market that affect the strength — and therefore the salability — of your business

Chapter 4

Assembling Your Business Sale Team

. . . .

In This Chapter

▶ Finding out who can help and how

▶ Deciding what to do yourself and what to hire others to do

▶ Evaluating whether you need a broker

▶ Choosing the key members of your team

. . . .

*B*efore you put the business sale process into motion, first tap into the expertise you need to help you craft, negotiate, and steer your sale to a positive end.

The following pages discuss who to invite onto your sale team, steps to follow when contracting for professional services, and when to bring the various experts on board.

At some point during the sale preparation process you may choose to bring one or two business confidants into the loop as well, but do so only if absolutely necessary. As much as possible, keep news of your sale to yourself and out of the business grapevine. Work with your accountant, attorney, and broker — all under the protection of confidentiality agreements — instead of relying on people within your business for help. If you must inform your key people of the impending sale, do so and enlist their support only after your decision to sell is final and you're sure you won't change your mind. Otherwise, you risk causing alarm among your staff, making them feel vulnerable about their jobs and possibly scaring right out the door those whose support you most count on.

Knowing Who's Who on the Business Sale Team

Making the decision about who to bring onto your sale team isn't clear-cut. One thing is certain, though: Selling your business isn't a time for flying solo. You need to bring some professionals — from accountants to attorneys to business sale brokers to appraisers — aboard to assist you. The following list shows which professional resources are available, and Figure 4-1 provides a flow chart for your quick reference:

- **Accountant.** This is probably the first business sale team member you'll recruit. The financial condition of your business, and the way your financial story is presented, is fundamental to sale success. Your accountant will have all the information at hand to help you prepare the numbers you need to plan your sale offering and present your business to buyers. If you've worked with an accountant over the years, be sure that person has experience in business sale transactions and the resulting tax implications. Your accountant will likely participate on your sale team at his or her regular hourly rate.

- **Attorney.** If you already work with an attorney to advise you on issues regarding your business structure, employees, contracts, and other legal matters, you probably want to involve that person on your sale team, maybe from the onset but certainly as you reach the negotiation stage and closing point. Your attorney can help you with preparation of legal documents such as confidentiality agreements, seller disclosure statements, and, of course, the purchase and sale agreement that will finalize the sale. It's especially important to bring an attorney with business sale-transaction experience on board if you're trying to handle the sale on your own without a broker. You'll pay either hourly rates or a flat fee.

- **Business broker.** Some business owners handle their sales with only the help of an accountant and an attorney. Others use a sale intermediary, most often a business broker, but sometimes a merger and acquisition (M&A) specialist if the business is large and the deal is complex. The decision of whether to hire a broker weighs heavy on most sellers' minds, and no one answer prevails. Some sellers will tell you their sales went through just fine without a broker, and others will say the broker was essential to their sale success. For that reason, the rest of this chapter helps you weigh the benefits of using a broker against the costs involved. In a nutshell, a broker can help maintain confidentiality about your sale, find and deal with prospective buyers, and free you from the demands of selling your business while also trying to run it. A broker can also provide advice on how to value your business. In return, you'll pay a fee, which is usually about 10 percent of your sale price.

✔ **Appraiser or valuation expert.** If you need a formal appraisal — because of the size or complexity of your business, because you need to prove the validity of business value to the buyer or to the IRS, or because you doubt the accuracy of the value established by your broker or by your sale advisors — you can hire a professional appraiser. Appraiser fees can range from several hundred dollars to tens of thousands of dollars, depending on the complexity of your business and whether you want an oral appraisal or a formal, written document. Numbers between $2,500 and $5,000 seem to be most common for small business written appraisals, but most appraisers charge by the hour, and the final fee depends on how much time goes into the effort. Before obtaining an appraisal, talk with your broker if you're using one. Also talk with your accountant. It may well be that between these two resources and the information in this chapter, you can arrive at a good figure from which to start seller negotiations. If you decide to hire an appraiser, flip to the final section of this chapter for advice on where to look and what to look for when making your selection.

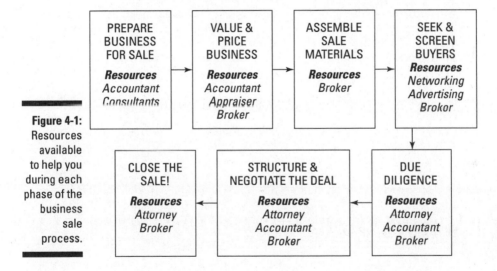

Figure 4-1: Resources available to help you during each phase of the business sale process.

PREPARE BUSINESS FOR SALE	VALUE & PRICE BUSINESS	ASSEMBLE SALE MATERIALS	SEEK & SCREEN BUYERS
Resources Accountant Consultants	**Resources** Accountant Appraiser Broker	**Resources** Broker	**Resources** Networking Advertising Broker

CLOSE THE SALE!	STRUCTURE & NEGOTIATE THE DEAL	DUE DILIGENCE
Resources Attorney Broker	**Resources** Attorney Accountant Broker	**Resources** Attorney Accountant Broker

No one, no matter how small the deal, should sell a business without obtaining financial and tax advice. At the very least, you want an accountant to help you assemble and present your business financial records and to help structure your sale with the intent of managing taxes and facilitating buyer decisions. You may also want to involve an attorney, particularly if your business has established a relationship with a lawyer whom you trust to deliver good business and legal advice, or if you plan to sell your business on your own without a broker's help.

Deciding Where You Need Help

When it comes to getting professional help, you need to consider a number of variables. Almost all sellers involve an accountant for financial and tax advice. The decisions about which other professional resources to call upon will depend on your answers to the questions posed in the following sections, on the nature and size of your business, on your personal abilities and interests, and on the amount of spare time in your calendar.

Do you know what your business is worth?

If yours is a small service business with few assets, all of which are pretty easy to value (cars, office equipment, even real estate), you can probably work with your accountant or broker, if you use one, to arrive at an estimation of what your business is worth.

If your business value involves harder-to-assess assets — such as major equipment, inventory, brand value or reputation, proprietary processes, goodwill, and intellectual property (including patents, trademarks, and copyrighted material) — you may benefit from an appraiser's professional valuation assistance.

Most small businesses can be valued without input from valuation specialists. Frequently, when appraisers are called into help with small business sales, they're there less to value the business than to confirm that an accountant's or broker's estimate is in fact a fair representation of business value.

If you're transferring your business to family or business insiders and think that a business valuation isn't necessary, you may be wrong. The IRS may challenge the value you place on your business, and a formal, written valuation by a licensed broker or appraiser can help you avoid problems or can serve as an important component in your defense.

The section "Signing Your Sale Team MVPs," later in this chapter, presents some guidance on hiring appraisers, and Chapter 6 has more valuation information to consider.

Do you know who and where your likely buyers are?

Some deals start with a ready, willing, and able buyer, but for most sellers, finding a buyer is a looming issue. In deciding whether you can find a buyer on your own, ask yourself:

✔ **Do you have a clear picture of the kind of person who will buy your business?** For instance, if you sell your accounting practice, you know the buyer will almost certainly be an accountant. If you sell a retail store, however, the picture of your prospect isn't so clear, so you have to cast a wider net to reach the far-flung group of people that may include your buyer.

The more specifically you can target your prospective buyers, the less help you'll probably need to reach them, although you may still benefit considerably from a broker's assistance to keep your contacts confidential and effective.

✔ **Will your prospective buyer be shopping for a business like yours, or shopping for a business, period?** A dental practice will probably sell to a dentist looking to buy a dental practice. A pizza parlor, on the other hand, may sell to, well, almost anyone. What's more, the pizza parlor buyer may not be looking to buy a pizza parlor specifically but to buy a business of any kind. The pizza parlor may emerge as an interesting prospect to pursue, along with a long list of other businesses that seem worth looking at.

The harder it is to define prospective buyers for your business, the harder, more expensive, and more time-consuming it'll be to reach them. It's a lot easier to market your business if your buyers are likely to come from a specific group of professionals that you can target through professional organizations, sites, and journals. If that's not your case, you may benefit by getting marketing help from a broker. The broker relationship lets you tap into a source of prospective buyers who are already shopping for businesses.

Do you have time to both run your business and prepare it for sale?

The last thing you want is for your business to suffer from neglect while you direct your energy to the effort of selling it. Letting your business slide into bad health because you're turning your time away from customers, accounts receivable, operations, and employees is *not* the formula for a happy business sale ending.

If selling your business distracts you from running your business, and if you don't have a dependable employee to take up the slack while you turn your attention to the business sale process, then get help from a broker, pronto.

As you ponder whether to seek assistance, see how you answer the following questions:

✔ Over the past six months, has running your business and serving your customers consumed all the hours in your working days, and then some? If so, you probably need sale assistance.

✔ In a typical week, does your schedule allow a good amount of time for business planning, associating with friends and colleagues, and maybe even playing a weekly game of golf or some other type of recreation or fitness? If so, you probably have time to find, screen, and negotiate with buyers on your own — so long as you have the patience and talent and you're willing to give up some free time activities (versus giving up business management activities) during the sale period.

✔ Do you have a strong and able employee team that can take over some of your client and business management responsibilities while you redirect your energies to the sale process — without tipping them off to the fact that your business is for sale? If so, you may not need to hire sale assistance.

✔ Can you redirect your efforts to marketing your business while keeping your sale plans confidential? If word that your business is for sale leaks out, is your business likely to suffer defections from important employees, customers, suppliers, or distributors? If so, using an intermediary may give you a valuable layer of protection and confidentiality.

Are you good at marketing, presenting, and negotiating?

For the same reason that you'd hire bookkeeping assistance if you were weak on the numbers front, you want to hire a business sale intermediary if you're not the best person to design and implement your business-for-sale marketing plan. This advice is even more appropriate if buyers for your business are hard to locate and screen, or if the size and complexity of your business leads to a complicated sale requiring top talent and expertise at every turn.

If your business is small and uncomplicated — a straightforward service business or a single-location retail or food service outlet, for example — you can probably handle the sale with just the help of an accountant and an attorney if (there's always a catch) you can reach the right prospects on your own, your personal talents make you the best person to market your business, and you have time to do so.

Otherwise, you should add marketing and business sale expertise to your team, probably in the form of a business broker.

Weighing the Benefits and Costs of Hiring a Broker

Almost all brokers can help you value your business and assess its sale readiness before listing it for sale and marketing it. They also help you through the process of finding buyers and navigating buyer negotiations. Like residential real estate brokers, business brokers charge a percentage, typically 10 percent, of the sale price as their fee. To spotlight the obvious, that fee alone is cause for considerable deliberation regarding whether to go it alone or to partner with a sale pro.

As you make your broker-or-no-broker decision, consider the following advantages of hiring a broker and decide whether the benefits outweigh the costs. A good broker has

- Experience in the business sale arena and process
- Time to do the tasks you'd have to jam into an already full calendar
- Knowledge of the market value of businesses comparable to yours
- Plans on how to market your business, with no additional cost for featuring your business on heavily trafficked Web sites
- Access to an extensive database of qualified people seeking to buy a business
- Customized and confidential contact with individually targeted prospective buyers
- Experienced assistance with business-preparation, valuation, and preparation-of-sale presentation materials, though sometimes for an additional fee
- Guidance and expertise to help you with due diligence, buyer-seller negotiations, financing, closing documents, and business transition from seller to buyer

To give you a general idea of the cost-to-benefit ratio, here are some guidelines:

- **If your business will probably sell for under $200,000,** it may not be a good fit for a business broker, and you may be better off proceeding with the help of this book, your attorney, your accountant, and perhaps a local realtor who also matches business sellers with business buyers. If you do list with a broker, be prepared for the broker to request a higher-than-standard percentage fee, or to charge a flat fee or additional charges, in order to make your sale worth the broker's while.

✔ **If you're selling a business for a couple hundred thousand dollars or more,** your business will be an attractive client for a business broker, who can help you in all the ways outlined in this chapter, usually in return for 10 percent of the sale price.

✔ **If your business is worth many millions of dollars,** a broker's rate will probably be less than the 10 percent fee charged to most businesses. Larger businesses seeking sophisticated valuation assistance may be best served by a mergers and acquisitions (M&A) specialist who can act as a consultant in all aspects of valuing and selling the business or merging it with another.

Use the form in Figure 4-2 (Form 4-1 on the CD-ROM) to detail the steps required to sell your business, along with the efforts you think you have the time and talent to handle on your own. This will help you make the decision about whether to retain a broker.

To use the form, take these steps:

1. **Go through the steps listed under each phase of the sale process to get clear about all the activities that need to be conducted as part of the sale process.**

2. **Then put a check in the box in front of the party you'll count on to get the activity accomplished.**

   For many of the activities, you'll check several boxes. For example, to get your financial records together, you'll probably check Self, because you'll almost certainly have to devote your time to the effort, and you'll probably check Bookkeeper or Accountant as well.

3. **After you complete the form, go through to see how many places you checked Self, and then ask yourself whether you're sure you have time to do all the things you've assigned to yourself.**

   If not, you may reconsider how you've assigned responsibilities, taking some of the responsibilities off your shoulders and moving them to a broker instead.

DETAILING AND ASSIGNING SALE PROCESS RESPONSIBILITIES

*Check to indicate how you will assign responsibilities. Confirm that you have the
time for the tasks you assign to yourself. If not, reconsider your need for assistance.*

PREPARE BUSINESS FOR SALE

Financial records and projections ☐ Self ☐ Bookkeeper ☐ Accountant
Business structure review ☐ Self ☐ Attorney
Legal condition review and improvement ☐ Self ☐ Attorney
Business analysis and improvement ☐ Self ☐ Managers ☐ Consultants ☐ Bro
Assess and improve business facilities and equipment ☐ Self ☐ Contract services
Implement necessary improvements ☐ Self ☐ Managers ☐ Consultants
Other_____

VALUE AND PRICE BUSINESS

Estimate value to arrive at price ☐ Self ☐ Accountant ☐ Broker
Obtain professional appraisal ☐ Accountant ☐ Valuation ☐ Professional

---

ASSEMBLE SALE MATERIALS

Financial and back-up records ☐ Self ☐ Bookkeeper ☐ Accountant
Organization chart and operation manuals ☐ Self ☐ Managers ☐ Consultants
Payroll records ☐ Self ☐ Bookkeeper ☐ Accountant
Leases and contracts ☐ Self ☐ Bookkeeper ☐ Accountant
Sale memorandum ☐ Self ☐ Consultants ☐ Broker
Other_____
_____

SEEK AND SCREEN BUYERS

Define and target prospective buyers ☐ Self ☐ Broker
Develop business sale marketing plan ☐ Self ☐ Broker
Network within industry and business community ☐ Self ☐ Broker
Prepare and place ads ☐ Self ☐ Broker
Prescreen buyer prospects ☐ Self ☐ Broker
Obtain confidentiality agreements; work with prospects ☐ Self ☐ Broker
Evaluate and qualify offers ☐ Self ☐ Broker ☐ Attorney ☐ Accountant
Obtain letter of intent/earnest money ☐ Self ☐ Attorney ☐ Broker

---

DUE DILIGENCE

Investigate buyer for financial and managerial ability ☐ Self ☐ Attorney ☐ Accountant
Grant buyer access to your business records ☐ Self ☐ Accountant ☐ Broker
Work with buyer ☐ Self ☐ Accountant ☐ Broker

continued

STRUCTURE AND NEGOTIATE DEAL

Structure deal □ Self □ Accountant □ Attorney □ Broker
Structure payment □ Self □ Accountant □ Attorney □ Broker
Arrange financing □ Self □ Accountant □ Attorney □ Broker □ Banker □ SBA
Negotiations □ Self □ Accountant □ Attorney □ Broker
Structure protections against default, etc. □ Self □ Attorney □ Broker

CLOSING

Closing arrangements □ Self □ Attorney □ Broker
Closing documents □ Attorney □ Financing partners □ Broker
Announcing the sale □ Self □ Buyer

Figure 4-2:
Assigning business sale tasks and allocating responsibilities.

Signing Your Sale Team MVPs

The first step in building your sale team is to enlist your accountant and, if you plan to handle the sale without a broker, a lawyer to oversee the legalities of the deal. The order in which you sign these professionals isn't as important as your belief that they can work well together. After you hire one professional and as you prepare to hire the second professional, share the name of the first person you've already put on your team. Ask, "Have you ever worked together?" and listen carefully to the response. If you sense hesitation or lack of regard, think twice about putting the two pros on the same team. If they can't work together well, you'll pay the price for the extra professional hours expended to reach accord.

Selecting an accountant and attorney

Almost all small businesses work with accounting professionals, at least for the preparation of annual tax returns. You probably want your established accounting advisor to serve on your sale team because he or she knows you and your business and may have created many of the documents that will become part of your sale presentation. If you have a business relationship with an attorney, you probably want that person's help as well.

What to look for in a candidate

Before confirming participation, determine whether

✔ Your accountant and your attorney, if you involve one, have experience in business sale transactions of about the same size as yours

✔ They have experience valuing businesses of your size and type

If your current professional contacts don't have the necessary experience, ask them to provide referrals to colleagues with deeper expertise in sale transactions for a business of your size and type. Often, the referral leads to a professional in the same firm as your accountant or attorney. Sometimes, however, the referral leads to a new professional firm. Regardless, so long as you find a professional with current experience in sale transactions similar to the one you're planning, and with a personality and professional approach that feels comfortable to you, you'll be in good hands.

What the signing will entail

If you use your current accountant as your sale team professional, you probably won't need any new paperwork. The accountant will likely participate at the regular hourly rates you're used to paying. If you hire a different accountant, you want to find out his or her hourly rates.

Your attorney will likely ask you to sign a retainer agreement that covers the following:

- ✔ Services to be provided and fee arrangement. If your attorney charges a flat fee, the agreement details what services are provided under the fee.

- ✔ Additional costs that may be charged, including whether the attorney's costs (for travel, research, long distance phone charges, delivery charges, and so forth) are billed in addition to the flat fee, and whether interest is charged on unpaid statement balances, and at what rate.

- ✔ Whose interests the attorney represents under the terms of the agreement. For instance, if you have business shareholders or partners who are also affected by the sale, or if your business is a corporation and you want the agreement to cover your interests and the corporation's interests, the attorney may agree to represent multiple parties so long as the appropriate waivers are signed. The attorney almost certainly won't agree to represent you and your buyer, however, as that would create a conflict of interest.

A retainer is usually activated by your signature and by prepaying a portion of the fee.

Bringing on a broker

Before you can hire a broker, first you have to find one. Here are a few ideas to help you locate business brokerage firms:

- ✔ Search the Internet. Open your browser and type "business brokers," along with your city and state, into the search box.

- Ask business leaders in your market area or industry for recommendations. When using this approach, proceed carefully so you don't divulge your sale plans. Instead of saying that you're thinking of selling, say you've been asked for the names of leading brokers and are compiling a list to share. Or, if you're talking to someone who recently sold a business, you can learn broker names simply by casually asking what brokerage was used.

- Check local phone and business directories under the category of *business brokers*.

- Ask your economic development or chamber of commerce directors for advice, again couching your request as part of a general fact-gathering effort rather than as part of your own sale planning.

- Contact the International Business Brokers Association (IBBA) at www.ibba.org/. On the site, click on "find a broker" and enter your state or province to find member brokers in your geographic area.

What to look for in a broker

If a broker is the right choice for your sale team, make your selection by interviewing a number of brokers and determining which one best matches your needs. To weigh your decision, use the list of questions presented on the form in Figure 4-3 (Form 4-2 on the CD-ROM). Follow these steps:

- Interview each broker you're considering by asking the questions in the left-hand column. Keep a sheet of answers for each broker you interview so you can make comparisons.

- Compare broker answers with the advice contained in each of the Form 4-2 boxes and make your broker selection accordingly.

To prepare for your broker interviews, you may want to spend a few minutes looking at Chapter 19. It goes into more depth about what you should know about choosing and working with brokers.

HIRING A BUSINESS BROKER: QUESTIONS TO ASK

Do you handle businesses of our size?
☐ Yes ☐ No

What percentage of your listings — and your sales — are for businesses with revenues roughly equal to ours?

What percentage of your listings and sales are for businesses in our sector? (The four basic business sectors include manufacturing, wholesale distribution, service, and retail.)

Advice: Rule out brokers that don't handle businesses of your size or in your sector.

When it comes to marketing a business for sale, which functions does the brokerage handle, and which functions do you prefer for the seller to handle directly?

Advice: Choose a broker who is prepared to handle all the tasks you want to assign.

How will you present our business for sale? How much do you allocate monthly for advertising expenses? Where do you advertise and which Internet sites do you use?

Advice: Choose a broker with a high-traffic Web site who also advertises on other sites and publications.

Do you cooperate with other brokers to reach business buyers? ☐ Yes ☐ No

Advice: Choose a broker with affiliations so you reach more buyer prospects.

How do you screen and research buyers?

Advice: Choose a broker with a thorough screening process that culls out unqualified inquiries before they waste your time.

How long does the listing agreement last, and is it exclusive (does it stipulate that the broker has exclusive right to sell your business)?

Advice: Expect at least a 6-month exclusive agreement but be wary of longer terms.

How will you communicate with me during the term of the listing agreement?

Advice: See that the level and nature of broker communication matches your preferences.

continued

Are you compensated entirely by sale commission, or are other fees involved? What is the commission rate, and what other fees, if any, should we expect?

When is the fee due to the brokerage? If our business doesn't sell, will we be obligated for any fees to your brokerage?

Advice: Learn the broker fees during initial interviews so you can make fair broker-to-broker comparisons.

Are you covered by professional liability insurance? ☐ Yes ☐ No

Advice: Be wary of any broker who answers "no."

Are you a member of the International Brokers Association? ☐ Yes ☐ No
Are you a Certified Business Intermediary (CBI)? ☐ Yes ☐ No

Advice: Give extra points to any broker who answers "yes."

Figure 4-3:
Sum-
marizing
business
broker
interviews.

What to look for in a broker agreement

After you select a broker, the broker will provide you with an agreement form that outlines the nature of the broker-seller relationship. The agreement should confirm all the points you discussed during your broker interview. Because the agreement is legally binding, heed the following information to be sure that the fine print corresponds to what you heard during your interview:

- **Broker fees and commitments:** This part stipulates what the broker commits to do and how much he or she charges.

- **What kinds of fees to expect:** Take care to note:

  - The percentage of the sale price the broker charges as the broker's fee

  - Whether any portion of the fee is due as a flat fee or upfront deposit, and whether such funds are refunded if a sale doesn't occur

  - What fees are due if you cancel the listing before its term is up

  - What fees are due if you sell your business to someone referred by the broker, even after the listing agreement is over

  - Whether any additional fees or charges will be billed to the seller

  - When fees are due and payable to the broker

The standard fee charged by most brokers is 10 percent on the first million dollars of sale price, with a $15,000 minimum fee. The time to do your homework, ask your questions, and negotiate fees and services is before the agreement is signed, not after. It's not pushy to ask questions or to compare answers from various brokerage firms before making your selection.

✔ **Listing time period:** The standard broker agreement term lasts six months. Just as with a residential realtor listing, if you and the broker agree, you can renew the listing when it expires.

✔ **Buyer exclusions:** Find out whether you can add (or whether the listing includes) a clause that excludes a buyer you find on your own from the standard fee arrangement.

✔ **Timing of broker payment:** Brokers are paid in full at closing. Read the payment-terms portion of the agreement carefully to understand your obligations.

Be sure your attorney reviews any broker agreements before you sign on the dotted line.

Form 4-3 on the CD-ROM presents a copy of the broker agreement used by Sunbelt Business Brokers. View it as a sample of the kind of commitment that's made between a broker and seller when listing a business for sale.

Enlisting an appraiser

For an idea of the services valuation firms offer and how they work, visit the Web site of Gulf Coast Valuation at www.gvalue.com. Or do an online search for small business valuation firms in your state or region to study the offerings of appraisers in your geographic area.

If you hire a valuation consultant or business appraiser, follow this advice:

✔ Hire an experienced professional who's certified or accredited by a reputable trade association. Professionals with these designations follow a professional code of ethics that ensures they create independent, credible valuation opinions. Look for these initials on the appraiser's marketing materials:

• ASA (Accredited Senior Appraiser, designated by the American Society of Appraisers)

• CBA (Certified Business Appraiser, designated by the Institute of Business Appraisers)

• CBV (Certified Business Valuator, designated by the Canadian Institute of Chartered Business Valuators)

- CPA/ABV (Certified Public Accountant Accredited in Business Valuation, designated by the American Institute of Certified Public Accountants)

- CVA (Certified Valuation Analyst, designated by the National Association of Certified Valuation Analysts)

✔ Order only the level of appraisal that you need to proceed with your sale. An oral appraisal may cost hundreds of dollars, while a written appraisal can run into five figures.

Forms on the CD-ROM

Form 4-1	**Detailing and Assigning Sale Process Responsibilities**	A form that details sale tasks and helps you assign responsibilities to members of your sale team
Form 4-2	**Hiring a Business Broker: Questions to Ask**	A form for recording answers obtained during broker interviews
Form 4-3	**Sample Broker Agreement**	A copy of the listing agreement used by Sunbelt when it contracts with business sellers

Part II

Packaging Your Business for a Sale

The 5th Wave   By Rich Tennant

"Cooked books? Let me just say you could serve this profit and loss statement with a fruity Zinfandel and not be out of place."

In this part . . .

No doubt you've heard stories about businesses that sell out of the blue, with no preparation beyond planning for the post-sale party. But with an avalanche of baby boomers looking for the business exit door, business buyers will soon have a selection like never seen before.

The chapters in this part get you ready to compete in a very crowded business sale environment.

Chapter 5 helps you compile all the financial documents you need to move forward in the sale process, and Chapter 6 addresses the all-important topic of how to value your business and — the master key to a successful sale — how to arrive at the price that's right. Chapter 7 helps you get your business plan in order, and Chapter 8 puts it all together in the sale memorandum you share with prospective buyers.

If it sounds like a lot of work, look at it this way: Either retirement or a nice, long break awaits!

Chapter 5

Compiling Your Financial Records

In This Chapter

▶ Getting your financial paperwork in order

▶ Choosing the accounting method that's best for your type of business

▶ Creating reports to show your important sale and earnings data

▶ Presenting your business trends and ratios

▶ Pulling together backup information

Your word alone isn't good enough when it comes to business finances. You can't get beyond the first glimmer of buyer interest without showing financial records — and the more formally prepared and documented they are, the better your chances of nabbing a sale. In fact, how you present your finances can affect the sale price of your business. Chapter 6 is full of sale pricing information, all based on the truth that attractive, low-risk businesses sell for higher multiples-of-earnings than their less-attractive, more-risky counterparts. You don't need advice from a $24.99 book to know that a business run with shoddy or incomplete financial records looks risky to a prospective buyer.

If your business doesn't already have clean, presentable financial statements, you have two choices in front of you. Create financial statements using the forms in this chapter or the ones included in any business accounting software package, or hire a professional to do the job for you. If you decide to prepare your own statements, treat your work as a first draft for a professional's review. This is a time in the life of your business where you should plan to make good use of your accountant's expertise.

The short cut, of course, is to head straight to an accountant for help. If that's the path you choose, I certainly don't recommend heading to his or her office with no clue of what to expect. By taking time with this chapter first, you'll arrive armed with your financial facts, putting you in position to save professional time and fees and to better understand the accounting advice you receive and the financial performance you'll be discussing with prospective buyers. When you finish creating your statements, either on your own or with the help of an accountant, you'll have the information you need to take the next steps in the sale process.

Getting Your Bearings

The business you're selling may simply comprise you, a desk, and a phone; or it may consist of you and a couple dozen employees in a sprawling office or shop; or you may have hundreds of employees and maybe even multiple locations. Among those points along the business spectrum is a long list of management differences, topped by the biggest difference of all — the difference in how financial records are kept.

Knowing what you need: A quick outline

A prospective buyer typically wants to see:

- ✔ **Financial statements that go back three years.** Offering to let a buyer go through a shoebox full of records won't do. You need to present financial statements that are accurate and understandable, including year-to-date and past-three-year income statements, balance sheets, cash flow statements, and a statement of the seller's discretionary earnings your business generates. You'll see samples and explanations for each of these forms in this chapter.

  Depending on the nature and size of your business, *cash basis* financial statements may be acceptable to your buyer. For most businesses, though, *accrual basis* financial statements prepared in accordance with generally accepted accounting principles (GAAP) are considered the gold standard. (The next section of this chapter describes cash- and accrual-based accounting approaches.)

- ✔ **Business financial trends.** Financial statements bare the financial soul of your business, but they require interpretation before the information they contain can actually help you sell your business. That's why it's important to present at-a-glance trend charts and financial ratios that show what the numbers in your statements mean and the kind of opportunity they represent.

  Truth is, with your financial statements in hand, a prospective buyer has all the information necessary to plot the direction your sales and earnings are heading, calculate what percentage of sales dollars make it to the bottom line, and determine how efficiently your business turns inventory or collects receivables. You're better off doing the work yourself, however (this chapter tells how), so you can present the information with your own explanations about what the calculations mean and how they support the idea that your business is a good purchase opportunity.

✔ **Backup records.** To back your financial claims you need to be ready to present supporting financial documents including bank statements, tax returns, and other forms that prove that the numbers in your financial records are accurate. You won't need these in your early dealings with buyers, but you'll definitely need them when your prospective buyer starts the homework process called *due diligence*, so be ready.

Figuring out where to begin

Every business seller will benefit from every section of this chapter, and all business owners should spend some time with the sections on ratios and projections for one of two reasons. If your ratios and projections are weak, you need to go into fix-it mode (which means heading to Chapter 3) immediately. If your ratios and projections are strong, you need to highlight your performance as a selling point in your selling memorandum (Chapter 8). First things first, however — you need to get your financial statements ready for presentation, if you haven't already done so.

Small-business owners are do-it-yourselfers, so your inclination may be to use whatever numbers you can come up with, prepare your own financial statements, and proceed full steam ahead. For very small businesses with revenues in the several-hundred-thousand dollar range and with sales coming from easy-to-track sources, self-generated statements are more likely to be considered adequate. Even then, if you decide to go it alone, rely on good accounting software such as Quickbooks or Peachtree, which can help you prepare the financial reports you need. Be aware that accountant-reviewed or accountant-prepared statements underscore that your business is professionally managed, which adds value in the minds of buyers seeking businesses that have sophisticated management systems.

Here's some advice: If you're ever going to invest in professional financial assistance, do it now. Selling your business is one time when doing everything on your own can cost more than it saves. I recommend these steps:

✔ Start by referring to the "Preparing Financial Statements" section later in this chapter to bring yourself up to speed about the content and function of each of the financial statements.

✔ Use the forms in this chapter or in your accounting software to prepare working financial statements to the best of your ability. If statement preparation is over your head, then use the forms as a guide to see what kind of financial information you need to provide to an accounting professional.

✔ Then meet with an accountant to get the following assistance:

• Have your statements prepared or, if you've prepared working versions, have them reviewed and finalized.

- Get advice about *restating your balance sheet* prior to the sale by removing assets that aren't essential to business operations.

  Your business may own fixed assets that you don't want to include in the sale, such as a business-owned car. Or your business may have money market or investment accounts that you'll remove from the sale offering (most buyers don't want to spend cash to buy cash). If your business owns the building it's located in, you may want to move that asset out of your business as well, transferring it to become a personal asset and offering favorable lease terms to the buyer.

  When it comes to restating balance sheets, every business owner's decisions are different. This is an area where you definitely need to seek counsel, from your broker if you're using one and definitely from your accountant. If you've used your sale-team accountant to prepare your tax returns in the past, he or she will probably have all the information on file to help you with this step.

- Get advice about removing loans that won't be of benefit to the buyer. Most buyers don't want to assume short-term loans that you've taken to address the operating needs of the company, so you're wise to pay such obligations off before offering your business for sale. About the only loans that buyers view favorably are long-term notes directly tied to income-producing major equipment assets. However, if the buyer is getting a bank loan, the bank won't loan money against assets that already have a lien, in which case you need to pay off loans before you put your business up for sale, or pay them off during escrow.

✔ After financial statements for your business are prepared, you can put the numbers they contain to work as you calculate the financial trends and ratios — at-a-glance indicators of your business strength — that your prospective buyers want to see. I show you how to accomplish that task later in this chapter.

Be aware that before your sale deal closes, the legal documents will include a clause saying that you *warrant* or represent that the financial information you've provided is accurate, so if you have any doubts, request a professional review by an accounting pro.

Use the following sections to find out what kinds of raw information you need to provide and what kinds of reports you're aiming to obtain.

Deciding Whether to Upgrade from Cash-Based to Accrual-Based Accounting

Minimally, the day you decided to sell your business you triggered the need to produce a complete set of financial statements. If you've been using a cash-based, checkbook-like bookkeeping system, you may have also triggered the need for an accounting upgrade. That'll be the case if your business has accounts receivable and accounts payable, because such outstanding commitments aren't shown on cash-based statements, but a buyer will want to see them.

Business accounting methods fall into two categories, cash-based accounting and accrual-based accounting. Until the day you decided to sell your business, managing your money by monitoring cash in and cash out probably worked just fine, especially if your business is a small sole proprietorship that isn't reliant on inventory or customers who buy on credit. Most small businesses that can use cash accounting do so because it's easier to understand and less time-consuming to manage than accrual accounting. Accrual-based accounting, however, is the preferred accounting method, especially for most businesses that stock inventories for sale or have significant amounts of receivables, payables, or debt.

Here's a quick explanation of the two:

- ✔ **Cash accounting** records income when it's received and expenses when they're paid. In cash accounting no entry is made until cash trades hands, and each transaction is entered once — when money comes in or goes out — just like in your checkbook, which is the primary record of many small businesses.

- ✔ **Accrual accounting** records revenues when they're earned and expenses when they're incurred. With accrual accounting, each transaction involves several entries. All sales except cash sales are recorded as accounts receivable at the time they're invoiced, even though the business may not receive payment for 30 days or longer. When the customer payment arrives, the amount is credited in accounts receivable and added to a cash account. Expenses are recorded when materials are purchased or expenses are authorized, even though the business may not actually pay the bill until some day in the future. Until that time, the amount is held as an account payable and added to the *current liabilities* of your business. When an outstanding expense is paid, the payment amount is subtracted from a cash account and removed from the accounts payable and current liability accounts. In accrual accounting, businesses don't record cash; they record commitments.

As you know, how you keep your books depends on decisions you made with advice from your bookkeeper or accountant. How you present your books to prospective buyers, however, depends on what buyers want to see. And sophisticated buyers want to see not only what money your business has received and paid, but also what money it has committed to pay (your accounts payable) and what money others have committed to pay you (your accounts receivable). Accrual-based accounting is an essential part of creating a balance sheet that accurately reflects the financial condition and financial obligations of your business.

Preparing Financial Statements

Your buyer wants to see (or better yet, to scrutinize) four financial statements: An income statement, which is also called a profit and loss statement; a balance sheet, which states the financial condition of your business; a cash flow statement, which shows how money moves through your business; and a seller's discretionary earnings statement, which shows how much cash your business generates annually for the benefit of you, the owner. Of these four statements, you'll include the seller's discretionary earnings statement in your selling memorandum (explained in Chapter 8). The other statements will be necessary as you summarize financial information in your sale offering. They'll also be essential during the due diligence investigation that will follow acceptance of a buyer offer.

The upcoming sections describe each of the four statements in detail. Along with the explanations are forms you can use to create the statements. As I've said previously, consider creating working versions of the statements by using the forms in this book or by using business accounting software. Then take your self-produced statements to an accountant to have your work reviewed or used as the basis for professionally produced financial records.

Before finalizing your statements, double-check that the numbers synch with the numbers on your tax returns, bank statements, and other documents. This isn't just important — it's imperative. Your buyer will likely insist, through legal clauses inserted into your sale documents, that you *warrant* (or offer your personal assurance of) the accuracy of the financial information you provide, especially if your financial statements aren't formally audited prior to presentation. If, after buying your business, a buyer were to learn that you misrepresented or provided erroneous facts, nothing but trouble follows.

Cash versus accrual: Why it matters

As an example of why an accrual-based balance sheet matters, consider the case of a printing business that produced a large catalog order and delivered it to a customer on December 1. Here's how the job looked on paper, when recorded as a cash transaction:

✔ The print shop purchased the paper for the order in early November, and to avoid late charges had to pay for the paper in early December: Cash out

✔ The printer also had to pay considerable shipping charges to get the printed catalogs delivered by the early-December client deadline: More cash out

✔ Immediately following the early-December delivery, the print shop invoiced the client for the job. The printer's customary terms require payment within 30 days, so the bill won't be due until early January: Revenue in limbo

On a cash-basis statement, as of December 31 the print shop looks like it's spending more than it's making. Here's where an accrual-based balance sheet comes to the rescue.

By preparing an accrual-based balance sheet, the printer can bring the story into balance by showing the catalog client's outstanding bill as a business asset in the form of an account receivable. To a buyer's eyes, the print shop's financials just came into focus.

The income statement

Your income statement is used to calculate your *net profit*, also called your *pretax net income* or your *bottom line*. When completed, your income statement shows how your company performed financially by showing how much money it made or lost over recent years. Your income statement is the basis of your *seller's discretionary earnings*, or the amount of money your business actually generates annually for you (which I cover later in this chapter). It's also the basis for projecting future performance based on past experience. A later section has more on that topic.

What it contains

The income statement shows:

✔ **Gross sales** — also called *gross revenue* — reflect all income from sales generated by your business before any costs are deducted.

✔ **Gross profit** — also called *gross income* or *gross margin* — reflects how much your business actually earned from gross sales after paying the *cost of sales*, which is also called the *cost of goods sold*. Your *cost of sales* includes all the costs associated with producing, assembling, or purchasing the product or service that you sold to generate revenue.

✔ *Operating profit* — also called *operating income* or *EBIT*, which stands for earnings before interest and taxes — is what remains of gross profit after you subtract operating expenses and depreciation expenses. *Operating expenses* are the costs involved to operate your business, including rent, utilities, salaries, benefits, marketing, travel, entertainment, and any other necessary day-to-day business expenses. *Depreciation expenses* cover the amount of money you subtract each year to account for declining value of major items purchased previously by your business, such as automobiles, computer systems, or even buildings. You're allowed to spread the cost of such items over the number of years they'll be in service by expensing a portion of the cost each year under the category of depreciation.

✔ *Profit before taxes* is the number you arrive at after you adjust your operating profit to account for non-operating income or expenses such as interest earned from business investments or interest paid for business loans.

✔ *Net profit* — also called *net earnings*, *net income*, or *the bottom line* — is what's left after the very last expenses are backed out … like taxes. If you run a sole proprietorship or partnership, profit before taxes is passed personally to the owners, who treat it as personal taxable income. Therefore, sole proprietors or partners don't need to calculate net profit because they don't have business taxes to subtract. But other business types are responsible for taxes, and those obligations have to be subtracted before the business can calculate its net profit or bottom line.

How to complete it

Figure 5-1 shows an example of an income statement. Form 5-1 on the CD-ROM includes a blank multi-year income statement that you can complete by filling in your business numbers. If you use business accounting software, the program you use will include an income statement form that you can use instead. To use Form 5-1, follow these steps:

✔ Open the form, which contains an Excel worksheet.

✔ Customize the form by typing in information that presents your business financial facts.

• Begin by replacing the column headlines to define the years your statement covers. For instance, if you're producing your form in 2009, then the most recent annual figures available will be for 2008. Therefore, click in the cell titled *Last Year* and change it to read 2008. Then replace the next column headline with 2007, and the far-right column headline with 2006. If you're offering your business for sale in the middle of a year, if more than one quarter has passed you should also present year-to-date performance.

- Enter financial data for your business in all the shaded cells. Begin by clicking your cursor in the shaded left-hand cell of the Sales line, then type in your annual sales for last year. Then click in the center cell and enter that year's sales. Click in the far-right cell to enter your sales for three years ago. Continue this process for each row, until all the shaded cells contain your business numbers.

- The form will automatically calculate Gross Profit, Operating Profit, Profit before Taxes, and Net Profit. If your business is structured as a sole proprietorship or partnership, profit passes through as income to owners and so you have no business taxes to subtract. If that's the case, you can simply delete the lines for *Taxes* and *Net Profit*, and end your Income Statement at the line titled *Profit before Taxes*.

In addition to the short-form income statement shown in Figure 5-1, you and your accountant will probably create a longer-form version that shows how your cost of sales and your sales, general, and administration costs are allocated to expense categories, which are usually referred to as your *chart of accounts*. You'll want to have this longer-form version available during due diligence, when the buyer will want to learn all the details about how your business runs. Almost any accounting software includes a chart of accounts; take a look at the following sample.

Sample Income Statement Chart of Accounts

Cost of Sales
Refunds
Collection Expense
Operating Expenses
       Salaries
       Advertising
       Auto Expense
       Business Promotions
       Computer Expense
       Depreciation and Amortization
       Dues and Subscriptions
       Meals and Entertainment
       Travel
       Insurance
       Interest
       Legal and Accounting
       Licenses
       Office Expenses
       Outside Services
       Retirement Plans
       Postage
       Repairs and Maintenance
       Taxes: Payroll
       Taxes: Other
       Telephone
       Uniforms
       Utilities

INCOME STATEMENT

Enter your numbers in shaded cells.
Boldface categories calculate automatically.

As of December 31			
	Last Year	Previous Year	Previous Year
Sales			
Cost of sales			
Gross Profit	0	0	0
Sales, general, & administration costs			
Depreciation expenses			
Operating Profit	0	0	0
Interest & other non-operating income			
Interest & other non-operating expenses			
Profit before Taxes	0	0	0
Taxes			
Net Profit	0	0	0

Figure 5-1: Creating an income statement.

The cash flow statement

Your cash flow statement shows how much money came into and went out of your business over the statement period and how your business's assets changed as a result. Your cash flow statement is essential in running your business because cash is your business lifeline, and you need to verify that dollars are coming in at a rate to offset what's going out. Even if your business prepares no other statements, you probably keep a cash flow statement, prepared annually or more frequently, in order to monitor finances and prepare for tax preparation.

What it contains

Here's what your cash flow statement shows:

✔ **Total funds in,** including all money you received from sales, dividends or interest from business investments (such as money market deposits), and any other revenue made by your business.

✔ **Total funds out,** including every cent that was paid out of your business over the statement period for cost of goods acquired, operating expenses, interest, taxes, payments on your building or equipment, payments for long-term loans, and payments to yourself in the form of distributions.

✔ **Net change in cash position,** which shows the difference between the amount of money that came into and went out of your business over the statement period. This is the bottom line of your cash flow statement.

✔ **Changes in liquid assets,** which show how cash and investment accounts changed as a result of the net change in your cash position.

How to complete it

On the chance that you don't already have a cash flow statement, Figure 5-2, included as Form 5-2 on the CD-ROM, shows what's involved. To use the form, follow these steps:

✔ Open the form, which contains an Excel worksheet.

✔ Customize the form by typing in information that presents your business financial facts.

  • Begin by stating the time period the cash flow statement covers. The sample form is set up to cover a calendar-year period.

  • Replace the column headlines to define the years your statement covers.

  • Enter financial data for your business in all the shaded cells.

  • The form will automatically calculate the Available Cash and Total Cash Out of your business over the specified time period. By subtracting Cash Out from Available Cash, the form then calculates your net cash flow.

To make the form even more useful as a management tool, create a longer-form version that expands the row titled "Other operating expenses" to show how payments are allocated to expense categories, called a chart of accounts. Almost any accounting software includes a chart of accounts; to see a sample, refer back to "The income statement" section.

The statement of seller's discretionary earnings

The statement of *seller's discretionary earnings* (or SDE) combines information from your income statement and balance sheet with adjustments that back out certain expenses, including owner benefits, one-time non-recurring expenses, and expenses that are considered *discretionary,* meaning another owner may choose not to incur them, and such a decision wouldn't greatly harm the business. The result is a report that shows how much your business has earned annually for you. You can bet the SDE statement is one a buyer studies carefully. It's also a key factor that you'll use when pricing your business, which is the topic of Chapter 6.

CASH FLOW STATEMENT

Enter your numbers in shaded cells.
Boldface categories calculate automatically.

As of December 31			
	Last Year	Previous Year	Previous Year
Source of Funds			
Beginning cash (bank accts, petty cash)			
Income from sales of products/services			
Income from sale of assets			
Income from customer deposits			
Loans			
Available Cash	0	0	0
Use of Funds			
Payroll			
Other operating expenses			
Purchases of capital equipment			
Tax payments			
Total Cash Out	0	0	0
Net Cash Flow	**0**	**0**	**0**

Figure 5-2: Creating a cash flow statement.

Why it's important

Earnings aren't the same thing as profits:

- ✔ *Profits* are the amount of money that remains after covering all business expenses, including all money paid to you and all funds spent on discretionary items. Business buyers want to see that a business generates a profit, but they understand that most owners don't want to generate high profits because profits are taxable.

- ✔ *Earnings* reveal how much money your business actually generates annually for the benefit of its owner. That's why before you offer your business for sale you need to work with your accountant or broker to recast your financial reports to present an accurate indication of your SDE.

How to complete it

The form in Figure 5-3 (available on the CD-ROM as Form 5-3) gets you started on calculating the SDE for your business. To use the form, follow these steps:

✔ Open the form, which contains an Excel worksheet.

✔ Revise the right-hand column heading. Replace the words "Last Year" with the year for which you're stating your business earnings.

✔ Replace numbers in all shaded cells with figures that represent the financial facts for your business.

- Be careful to see that figures you enter into the SDE statement correspond to figures for the same categories on the same-year income statement and balance sheet for your business. Get advice from your accountant if you're not completely sure of the numbers.

- The form will automatically calculate your business earnings before interest, taxes, depreciation, and amortization, referred to as your business EBITDA.

- Adjust your EBITDA by listing all business expenses that benefit you personally or that reflect discretionary expense decisions that you make. When you fill in the shaded cells, the form will automatically subtract the adjustments to arrive at the pro forma SDE for your business. Use the rows currently labeled "Other" to insert labels of non-cash expenses such as depreciation or amortization that your accountant may advise you to add back into your earnings. Also, if your buyer isn't assuming any of your loan payments, you can add loan expenses back as well.

Some businesses set their sale prices based on earnings from the most recently ended year. Others — especially businesses with earnings that have fluctuated over the past few years — base their sale price on an average of earnings over the past few years, weighing more recent years more heavily. Still others (though only a few) sell based on forecasted earnings that differ greatly from recent past earnings due to completion of a new product introduction, a production process breakthrough, or some other business accomplishment that has strong potential to greatly and positively affect future earnings.

Recasting your numbers for a sale

Anyone selling a business will get advice about *recasting financials* for the sale. Your first reaction when you hear the term may be that someone's telling you to cook the books, but recasting financial statements is as legitimate as legitimate gets. It's such a normal procedure that sometimes you'll hear *"recasting"* referred to as *"normalizing"* your financials.

In running your business, you deduct every possible allowable business expense as a fair way to minimize profits and resulting taxes. When it's time to sell, though, you want to quickly show how much cash your business actually generates for a full-time owner/manager, so you recast your financials to create a pro forma or projected statement showing how much money your business earns for you. Figure 5-3 shows what's involved to create this statement, called a statement of seller's discretionary earnings.

SELLER'S DISCRETIONARY EARNINGS STATEMENT

	2007
Sales Revenue	$630,000
Cost of Sales	$355,000
Operating Expenses	$195,000
Net Income	**$80,000**
Add-backs for Interest, Depreciation, Taxes, and Amortization Deducted	
as Operating Expenses Above	
Add-back for Interest Paid on Loans	$3,500
Add-back for Depreciation	$15,000
Add-back for Taxes Paid	
Add-back for Amortization	$240
EBIDTA* (Earnings before interest, depreciation, taxes, and amortization)	**$98,740**
Add-backs for Personal, Discretionary, and One-Time Expenses	
Owner's Salary	$84,000
Owner Payroll Taxes	$6,000
Family Member Wages/Payments/Benefits	
Owner Employee Benefits	$6,000
Owner/Family Benefit for Personal Auto Use	
Auto Insurance for Personal Auto Benefit	
Contributions and Donations	$2,000
Fair Market Rent Adjustment	
Owner's Health, Life, Other Insurance Premiums	$4,000
Professional Legal, Accounting, Tax Services	$1,000
Owner Retirement Plan Contribution	$2,800
Travel & Entertainment Expenses	$3,500
Subscriptions and Memberships	$3,500
Nonrecurring Expenses (such as leasehold improvement)	$6,000
Other	
Other	
Other	
Pro Forma Seller's Discretionary Add-backs	**$188,800**
Pro Forma Seller's Discretionary Earnings	**$217,540**

Figure 5-3:
Calculating your seller's discretionary earnings.

The balance sheet

Your balance sheet shows the value of everything your business owns — its *assets* — minus everything your business owes — its *liabilities* — as of a certain moment in time, usually year-end or month-end. The statement shows cash transactions along with outstanding commitments that others have made to your business (accounts receivable) and that your business has made to others (accounts payable and other liabilities). Your balance sheet is important, complicated, and best created by your trusted accountant.

In a few cases, some businesses may not need a balance sheet. If your business operates entirely on a cash-transaction basis — with no accounts receivable or accounts payable — and if your business has absolutely no debt (for instance, if your furnishings and equipment are owned in full and your business has no liabilities), you can probably explain your finances to a buyer using your income statement and a list of the assets you're selling. But most businesses for sale have finances that are a bit or a lot more complicated, and therefore, almost all buyers require a balance sheet along with the other necessary financial statements.

What it contains

Here's what a balance sheet shows:

- ✔ **Current assets** include the most liquid asset of all: cash. In fact, current assets are also called *liquid assets* because you can liquidate them for cash rather quickly if you need to. Current assets also include investments in money markets or other safe securities, accounts receivable, the cash value of your inventory, and any prepaid expenses for items you haven't yet received, such as insurance premiums or a fee prepaid to retain an attorney.

- ✔ **Fixed assets** are large, costly items that may take a while to liquidate should you need to do so. Fixed assets include the purchase price or reasonable value of land, buildings, and major equipment owned by your business, minus any depreciation you've already written off to reflect the decline of each asset's value over its useful life span.

   Be aware that you can depreciate any major item that wears out over time, but you can't depreciate land.

- ✔ **Intangibles** are assets of value that you can't actually see or touch. The benefits of valuable contracts, a franchise ownership, or a rarely granted license or permit are examples of intangible assets. So are patents that protect technologies or processes your business invented. Intangible assets are usually only carried on a balance sheet if you paid to acquire them.

   The intangible asset most frequently owned by a small business is *goodwill*, which is another way to say the positive value of your business name and reputation in your marketplace. Goodwill is important to sale pricing (see Chapter 6), but it isn't reflected as a value on the balance sheet unless your business acquired it as part of a previous business purchase.

✔ **Total assets** show the total value of all your current, fixed, and intangible assets.

✔ **Current liabilities** include bills, loans, or other debts your business owes for which payment is due within the coming year. Your current liabilities include your *accounts payable* for everything from utilities and rent to supplier invoices, and your *expenses payable* for obligations such as salaries, insurance premiums, and taxes due at the time your balance sheet is prepared.

✔ **Long-term liabilities** include your business's major long-term financial obligations, such as a loan to purchase major equipment or a mortgage on the building your business owns and occupies.

✔ **Owners' equity** is the line on your balance sheet that shows what part of your business you actually own. *Equity* takes two forms: *Owner-invested capital*, which is money you've invested in your business (either your own money or money you borrowed personally to put into your company); and *retained earnings*, which are earnings generated by business profits that you've left in your business rather than paid to yourself or other owners. Your equity is called your *net worth* in your business.

✔ **Total liabilities and equity** is the sum of everything your business owes to creditors, vendors, and banks (these are your current and long-term liabilities), plus money your business owes to its owners (shown as owners' equity on your balance sheet).

The balance sheet is called a balance sheet because the statement's two categories — *Total Assets* and *Total Liabilities and Equity* — must equal or balance each other. If they don't, something's wrong, and you need to correct your entries until the totals match.

How to complete it

Figure 5-4 (Form 5-4 on the CD-ROM) shows a blank balance sheet. To use the form, follow these steps:

✔ Open the form, which contains an Excel worksheet.

✔ Revise the column headings by replacing the words "Last Year" and "Previous Year" with the years for which you're presenting your business financial information.

✔ Replace numbers in all shaded cells with figures that represent the financial facts for your business.

✔ The form automatically calculates totals for each balance sheet category.

✔ Be sure the figures in the rows titled *Total Assets* and *Total Liabilities and Equity*, shown in bold type on the form, equal each other. Also be sure your accountant checks your work.

BALANCE SHEET

Enter your numbers in shaded cells. Boldface categories calculate automatically to replace zeros with your balance sheet totals.

As of December 31			
	Last Year	Previous Year	Previous Year
ASSETS			
Current Assets			
Cash			
Investments			
Accounts receivable			
Inventories			
Prepaid expenses			
Total Current Assets	0	0	0
Fixed Assets			
Land			
Buildings			
Equipment			
Accumulated depreciation			
Total Fixed Assets	0	0	0
Intangibles (Goodwill, patents, etc.)			
TOTAL ASSETS	0	0	0
LIABILITIES AND OWNERS' EQUITY			
Current Liabilities			
Accounts payable			
Accrued expenses payable			
Total Current Liabilities	0	0	0

continued

Long-term Liabilities			
Loan			
Mortgage			
Other			
Total Long-term Liabilities	0	0	0
Owners' Equity			
Owner-invested capital			
Retained earnings			
Total Owners' Equity	0	0	0
TOTAL LIABILITIES & OWNERS' EQUITY	0	0	0
Note: TOTAL ASSETS equal TOTAL LIABILITIES & OWNERS' EQUITY			

Figure 5-4: Creating a balance sheet.

Calculating Financial Trends and Ratios

Informed buyers scan your financial statements for success indicators or red flags. When they're looking to buy a restaurant, for instance, they know to check food, labor, and rent costs as a percentage of sales. In service businesses, they check whether the net profit margin is holding steady to see if costs of sales and operating expenses are growing at a pace that's eating up the bottom line. Different types of businesses have different average net profit margins, and astute buyers know what to look for.

You can strengthen your sale offering by helping buyers see the positive financial trends and ratios of your business, rather than making them dig through your financial statements to arrive at the calculations on their own. In this section, I outline some financial interpretations you may want to prepare, depending on the kind of business you're selling.

From running your business over the years, you know which indicators to watch as monitors of your success. Those indicators are the same ones that will matter to buyers, so be ready to present and discuss your performance in each area that's important to your business success.

When you compile trends or ratios to present to buyers, be sure to use numbers from the financial statements that you'll be presenting in your sale memorandum or during due diligence. Don't make the mistake of picking up numbers from working versions of your statements — perhaps statements that don't reflect input from your accountant's review, for example.

Otherwise, you may end up showing one number in one place and another number in another place, and the effect will be buyer confusion rather than confidence.

Also, don't share financial statements, trends, or ratios with prospective buyers until they've signed a confidentiality agreement, which I explain in Chapter 8.

Sales and expenses growth trends

No matter what kind of company you're selling, a buyer wants to know how your sales and expenses have trended.

Buyers will start by studying the recent history of your revenues. A business can't deliver a decent bottom line unless it delivers a decent top line first. If your sale revenue is declining, a buyer will assume that either your product or service has lost appeal in the marketplace or your business has lost marketing effectiveness, or both. If sales are increasing, the buyer will have confidence that your business is doing something — or a lot of things — right. Either way, your sales tell the story.

Next, buyers will look at your expenses — both for your cost of sales and for your operating costs. Mainly, the buyer wants to see that costs aren't rising faster than revenues.

If your sales for the past few years have been on an upswing and your expenses are in check, show buyers a chart that makes the positive trends of your business apparent at a glance. Use Form 2-1 on the CD-ROM for charting your recent sales growth, cost, and profit history as part of your assessment of the sale-readiness of your business. That same chart is a good addition to your selling memorandum, as explained in Chapter 8.

Sales and earnings growth rate

In addition to understanding the recent sale and profit trends for your business, a buyer wants to get a sense of what's in store for the next few years. The most reasonable, defensible way to forecast your business future is to base projections on past experience, using information from the sales and profit chart you assemble using Form 2-1 and the Seller's Discretionary Earnings Statement you prepare using Form 5-3.

Figure 5-5 (Form 5-5 on the CD-ROM) shows a sample that you can update to calculate the three-year average growth rate of your business. To use the form, follow these steps:

✔ Open the form, which contains an Excel worksheet.

✔ Revise the column headings by replacing the words "Last Year" and "Previous Year" with the years for which you're presenting your business financial information.

✔ Replace numbers in all shaded cells with figures that represent the financial facts for your business.

✔ The form automatically calculates the annual and three-year average growth rate of your business sales and earnings.

When you know the three-year average growth rate for your business, you have credible information on which to base future growth projections. Simply, if your business keeps doing what it's doing, then based on the past four years' experience it will continue to grow at a similar rate.

✔ **If the three-year average growth rate for your business is positive,** your projected growth rate is positive, which is what buyers want to see. (Chapter 8 helps you present these findings in your selling memorandum.)

✔ **If the three-year average growth rate is negative,** your projected growth rate is negative — and unattractive to a buyer. If that's your case, do one of two things:

- Delay your sale while you turn your business growth around.

- Spend extra time with Chapter 7, which helps you prepare business and marketing plans you can present to a buyer to show the untapped opportunities that await a buyer who applies additional resources to the business.

THREE-YEAR AVERAGE GROWTH RATE

	Last Year	Previous Year	Previous Year	Previous Year
Sales	630,000	570,000	522,000	495,000
Seller's discretionary earnings	157,000	140,000	135,000	165,000
Growth over previous year (%)				
Sales	9.52%	8.42%	5.17%	
Seller's discretionary earnings	10.83%	3.57%	7.41%	
3-year average growth rate (%)				
Sales	7.71%			
Seller's discretionary earnings	7.27%			

Figure 5-5: Calculating the three-year average growth rate for your business.

Inventory turnover

Inventory turnover is an important indicator of efficiency in manufacturing, distribution, and retail businesses. You don't want to reveal your inventory turnover rate in your sale offering or selling memorandum because it's a confidential aspect of running your business. Do be prepared, however, to present facts about your inventory to your buyer during due diligence.

To calculate how many times your inventory turns in a year, take these steps:

1. **Look at how much your inventory was worth at the beginning of the statement period (January 1 on a typical annual statement) and how much it was worth at the end of the statement period (usually December 31). Add those two numbers and divide by two to determine your average annual inventory.**

2. **Divide your annual cost of goods sold (also called cost of sales) by your average inventory for the same period. If your result is 2.5, for example, then your inventory turns over — which means you sell your inventory — two and a half times a year. If your rate is 52, then your inventory turns over weekly.**

Inventory turnover rates vary depending on the type of industry you're in. No one rate serves as a target for all businesses. Retail businesses and businesses with a low average product price expect a far higher inventory turnover rate than the rate expected by, say, a manufacturing company that sells equipment priced at tens of thousands of dollars or more. What's more important to your buyer is how the inventory turnover rate for your business is trending. Over the past few years, has your inventory turned at an increasingly more rapid rate? Generally, a high turnover ratio is better than a low ratio because it means inventory is well-managed and selling quickly.

If your inventory turn has slowed because you've intentionally stocked up on materials that are going up in cost or getting harder to acquire, you want to present those facts to the buyer. You can include the information in your selling memorandum — if you feel it provides a business advantage that you're comfortable sharing with prospective buyers — or you can share the information after you receive a buyer offer and are into the process of due diligence.

Number of days in receivables

If your business operates on an all-cash basis, you won't have any accounts receivable to manage. However, if you bill customers and allow payment on, say, a 30-day schedule, then one way that a buyer assesses the strength of your business is by reviewing how long credit sales remain in accounts receivable before they're paid. The results reveal two things: how efficiently your business manages its receivables and the strength of your clientele, based on how able or willing customers are to pay their bills.

If you use billing software, information on the status of your accounts receivable is probably a few keystrokes away. To make a manual calculation of the number of days bills remain in receivables, take these steps:

1. **Divide your total annual sales by 365, the number of days in a year. The result shows your average daily sales.**

2. **Divide your current accounts receivable balance (from your balance sheet) by your average daily sales. The result shows the number of days average sales remain uncollected, or the average length of time it takes you to get paid for a product or service after you sell it.**

Most businesses aim to collect credit sales within 30 days, with accounts receivable that stretch to 45 days indicating a reason for caution, and longer periods representing a reason for real concern. Why? Because the chance of collecting delinquent accounts drops dramatically as the time between the due date and the current date expands. Credit agencies will tell you that after three months, you have less than a 75 percent chance of collecting a past-due bill, a number that drops to nearly 50 percent after six months.

Current ratio

Your current ratio is also called your *liquidity ratio*, because it shows whether your business has enough short-term, fairly liquid assets to pay short-term debt obligations and accounts payable over the next year. Even if you operate your business on a cash basis, with customers paying you on-the-spot and suppliers paid in cash at the time of purchase, you'll likely still have accounts payable for utilities, supplies, and services required to keep your business going.

To calculate your current ratio, divide current assets by current liabilities (both figures are on your balance sheet).

If current assets are double current liabilities, your business is in good short-term financial health, and it's worth your while to promote your strong liquid position when presenting your balance sheet. If your assets-to-liabilities ratio is closer to 1, Chapter 3 provides steps for strengthening your financial position prior to a sale.

Assembling Backup Information

To verify that the numbers you're presenting are legitimate, you need to have some backup information ready to present to your buyer. Some of this information goes into your selling memorandum (see Chapter 8) and some won't be shown until the buyer starts doing research as part of *due diligence* (see Chapter 12). Have the following information handy:

✔ Income statement and cash flow statement for the current year

✔ Projected seller's discretionary earnings statement for the current year

✔ Income statement, seller's discretionary earnings statement, and balance sheet for the past three years

✔ Schedule C from personal tax returns or corporate income tax returns for the past three years

✔ Depreciation schedule from your most recent tax return

✔ Current list of major equipment and furniture, including value (Chapter 6 includes a form you can use)

✔ List of any existing liens

✔ Aging of account receivables report

✔ Employee list, including salaries, benefits, and length of employment

My advice on how to present the fact that your business generated unreported income is simple: Don't even try. Unreported income is income that isn't reflected on business reports and tax forms, which means it's fraudulent. Trying to hide such income for tax purposes and then to reveal it for sale purposes is like asking to have your cake and eat it, too. If you tell a buyer you do a brisk business in unreported income, the buyer should have a more pressing question than how you can prove the unreported income — the buyer will wonder what else you're hiding.

Forms on the CD-ROM

Form 5-1	**Income Statement**	Enter numbers for your business in shaded cells; form automatically calculates your income statement totals
Form 5-2	**Cash Flow Statement**	Enter numbers to show funds in and funds out of your business and to arrive at the net change in your cash position over the statement period

continued

Form 5-3	**Seller's Discretionary Earnings Statement**	A form for recasting your income statement to reflect how much your business actually earned for the benefit of you, the owner
Form 5-4	**Balance Sheet**	Enter numbers for your business in shaded cells; form automatically calculates your balance sheet totals
Form 5-5	**Three-Year Average Growth Rate**	Enter your business sales and earnings for the past four years and the form automatically calculates your average growth rate, which can be applied to future projections

Chapter 6

Pricing Your Business

. . . .

. . . .

The burning issue as your sale launch nears is to determine how much your business is worth so you can decide how much to sell it for. Obviously, you don't want to price it too low and essentially leave money behind, but you also don't want to run buyers off by asking a price they find terribly out of line. This chapter helps you strike the balance.

The most commonly used approach for pricing small businesses is the multiple-of-earnings approach discussed throughout this chapter and book. To use this approach, you assess the attractiveness of your business — mainly in the areas of financial strength, health of your business sector and market area strength, and the likelihood that your business will transfer easily and successfully into new hands. Then you adjust for risks that accompany your business and for the attractiveness of the sale terms you'll be offering. Based on the outcome of your assessment, you rate your business sale offering on a scale of one to five. This rating becomes what's called the *earnings multiple* that you use to price your business. A business with growing earnings and a strong operation that's likely to transfer easily to a new owner tends to win a higher earnings multiple than a similar business with significantly lower earnings, a weaker operation, and seller-to-owner transition snags. By the time you wade through the upcoming pages, you'll have a good sense of the earnings multiple that fits your business situation.

After you set your earnings multiple, you apply it to the amount of money your business earns annually to come up with a reasonable price for your business. Most buyers pay one to four times annual earnings, with the average small business sale price set toward the middle of that range, at two to three times earnings. Chapter 5 includes information on determining your annual business earnings, called your *seller's discretionary earnings*, or SDE. The rest of this chapter walks you through the pricing process.

After you use the information in this chapter to arrive at an estimation of what your business is worth, enlist the help of your accountant and broker (if you use one). They may use different valuation approaches to verify your estimation and assist with your pricing decision. If your business has a high value derived from assets that involve complicated appraisals, or if you seek SBA or bank loans that require appraisals, consider hiring a business valuation firm or a valuation consultant (Chapter 4 gives you advice on hiring these sale team members).

With that, let the pricing process begin!

Making a List of the Information You Need

You won't find any shortcuts when it comes to assessing the value of your business. You can't pull best-guess numbers out of your head. Following is the list of the information you need:

- **Financial statements.** To value and negotiate the price of your business, you need financial records that reach back three to five years, or since inception if your business was founded only in the past few years. Chapter 5 includes information on the financial forms you'll need. If your records aren't in formal order, use the advice in Chapter 5 and work with a bookkeeper or accountant to properly assemble your information before taking any further steps in the sale process.

  Of the statements detailed in Chapter 5, the one that's most important to the pricing process is the *statement of seller's discretionary earnings* (SDE). This statement recasts the taxable profits of your business by adding back in all expenses that benefited the owner or that reflected decisions for discretionary purchases that another owner may not make. The result is a bottom line that shows how much money your business generates annually for the benefit of its owner. Be sure you, along with your accountant and broker, are clear about this number before you go further in the pricing process, because most small business sale prices are set by multiplying earnings by what's called an *earnings multiple*. The earnings multiple is usually a number between one and five, based on business strength and attractiveness, with higher numbers reflecting stronger, more attractive businesses.

- **The value of business assets.** Assets fall into two categories — tangible or physical assets, and intangible assets, which include assets of your business you can't actually see and touch, such as the value of your client lists, intellectual property, and brand name, to name a few. This chapter includes advice you can follow when putting a price on the assets of your business.

✔ **The sale price of comparable businesses** in your industry and market area. This information isn't always easy to find, but this chapter tells you where to look.

✔ **An assessment of business strengths and risks.** If you need help in this area, turn to Chapter 2 for advice. Then use the form in this chapter as you assess how your business strengths and weaknesses create attributes and risks that will affect your sale price and attractiveness to a buyer.

✔ **A description of the sale terms you're willing to offer.** Financing is necessary in most small business purchases. If you can offer a seller-financed loan for part of the purchase price, or if you're willing to accept part of the price through deferred payments that the buyer doesn't have to make until some defined point in the future, you'll enhance the attractiveness of your sale offering to most buyers, resulting in a higher earnings multiple and sale price. Some studies have shown that seller-financed deals earn multiples nearly one-third higher than those of businesses that require all-cash payoffs. How the buyer ends up paying depends on the outcome of buyer-seller negotiations regarding the deal structure and payment approach, which are described in detail in Chapter 13. For now, though, know that your business offering will appear more attractive to most buyers if you indicate your willingness to offer favorable sale terms including seller financing.

With these facts in hand, you and your sale team will be ready to determine a reasonable earnings multiple for your business, which is the basis for setting your sale price.

Getting Clear about What You're Selling

Think in residential real estate terms for a minute. Say you want to sell your home. If you sell it fully furnished, you price it differently than if you sell it cleared out down to the carpet and fixtures. If it has outstanding features that go with the deal — amazing landscaping, brand-new wall-mounted flat screen TVs, and top-of-the-line appliances, for instance — you add something to your price to cover those assets, unless you decide to sell them separately.

If your home's in a highly desirable location, you charge more. If the home's in dire need of repair, you charge less. In other words, what you sell and the condition it's in determine how you price it. In that way, pricing a home and pricing a business involve similar considerations. The more attractive the offering, the higher your earnings multiple and, therefore, the higher your asking price.

The one big difference between selling a home and selling a business is that when you sell your home, you sell the *home* — including its structure, fixtures, the land it sits on, and maybe even its furnishings and equipment. When you sell a business, you may sell the whole works through what's called an *entity sale* or a *stock sale*, or you may sell business assets through what's called an *asset sale*. An asset sale, which is the structure of 99 percent of small business sales, is more like selling the *contents* of a home, and even the address, but not the structure itself. The difference between asset sales and entity sales is complicated and affects how sale proceeds are taxed and how liabilities are held by the seller or transferred to the owner. It's an important issue that's covered in Chapter 13, which contains information on structuring and negotiating your deal.

Your prospective buyers want to know whether you're offering an asset sale or an entity sale, because they want to know what the sale price covers.

Selling your business assets

In most small business sales, the seller keeps the actual, legal business structure, called the *business entity*, and sells the *assets* of the business, including tangible assets such as furnishings, fixtures, equipment, accounts receivable, and inventory; and intangible assets, such as the business name and its reputation. (I cover both types of assets later in this chapter, in the "Valuing Your Assets" section.)

In an asset sale, the buyer moves the purchased assets into a newly formed business entity.

If your business is a sole proprietorship, your only choice is to structure your deal as an asset sale, because your business has no stock to sell. After the sale is completed and the assets are transferred to the buyer, your sole proprietorship ceases to exist and automatically closes down. If your business is a corporation or LLC, after business assets are transferred to the buyer, your business entity will likely have no remaining value, and you'll work with your attorney to dissolve and close it down.

Selling your business through an entity sale

A very few small business sales take the form of *entity sales*, which are also called *stock sales*. In an entity sale, the owner of a corporation sells its stock to a new owner, and the owner of an LLC sells its membership shares. Because the assets and liabilities of the business are owned by the stockholders (or by the LLC members), when the shares are transferred from the seller to the buyer, everything the business owns and owes — assets and liabilities — goes with them, unless some are specifically excluded from the deal. For that reason alone, sellers typically prefer entity sales and buyers typically don't. With an asset sale, buyers know what they're getting. With an entity purchase, they can't be sure of what kinds of liabilities or legal hot potatoes may appear in the future, which makes due diligence a far greater challenge.

If you're selling a corporation or an LLC, the decision to sell assets or entity is one that involves negotiation between the buyer and the seller, both because of the transfer of liabilities and also because of tax implications, which you can read about in Chapter 13.

Valuing Your Assets

You want to value your business's assets for two reasons. First, you want to know the value of everything you own so you can compare that total asset value to the sale price you arrive at through the multiple-of-earnings pricing approach. By comparing the two numbers you can confirm that your price, in fact, covers the value of what you're selling. Second, by understanding the value of your assets you're better able to determine and justify the earnings multiple that you set to price your business.

To value your business assets, you create an inventory of all the assets of your business and assign a value to each based on what it would cost to create or replace that asset in similar condition. Before you get started, you need to understand the two forms of assets, tangible and intangible:

- ✔ *Tangible assets* include business furnishings, fixtures, equipment, lease-hold improvements, inventory, real estate, automobiles, and other major physical assets.

- ✔ *Intangible assets* include intellectual property such as copyrights, trademarks, and patents. Intangible assets also include *goodwill*, a term used to express the economic advantage a buyer receives above and beyond the value of the other assets being purchased. Goodwill includes the value of your business name and reputation (also known as your *brand*), customer relations, trained employees, and other intangible assets that give your business a competitive edge and the ability to succeed in the future.

You need to understand the difference between tangible and intangible assets, because at sale time (or in the sale contract), the IRS requires you to break the price down into asset categories, which are taxed at varying rates. Chapter 13 includes information on allocating the purchase price.

To prepare for an asset-based valuation, read the next sections for advice on assigning a value to each of the assets you sell, beginning with a valuation of your tangible assets.

Pricing your tangible assets

Tangible assets are probably the easiest part of your business to value, because by their very definition, tangible assets are ones you can see and touch. You can often even find comparable items on the market (through eBay and other online shopping sites, through equipment distributors, and through other used-equipment outlets) to help you determine current market values. When valuing your tangible assets, also talk with your accountant, who can help you figure the depreciated value of items you've held for multiple years.

Following are steps to follow when valuing the two major tangible-asset categories in a business sale: furnishings, fixtures, and equipment; and inventory.

Furnishings, fixtures, and equipment

A buyer wants to see, at a glance, every asset you're selling and what each item is worth.

To simplify how you create your asset list and how buyers view it, itemize assets by grouping them into categories. You may categorize by asset type, such as office furniture, leasehold improvements, computers, production equipment, automobiles, and so on. Or you may find it easier to categorize assets by the way they're used in your business — for example, front office, information systems, production, and so on. Or many small businesses find it easiest of all to categorize by listing assets as they're physically placed in your business — for example, reception area, conference room, showroom, executive offices, sales offices, and so on — making it easy for a buyer to walk through and connect the listed asset to the physical item.

Figure 6-1 shows a portion of a form where you can list your furnishings, fixtures, and equipment, along with the replacement and fair market values for each asset. This worksheet, which is Form 6-1 on the CD-ROM, allows for multiple pages of asset entries, with totals calculated automatically.

To use the form, follow these steps:

- ✔ Replace the category description with a description that reflects the way you're categorizing assets. For instance, if you're categorizing by asset type instead of location, instead of *reception area,* you might type *office furniture*, under which you'd list such items as desks, chairs, tables, file cabinets, and so on.

- ✔ Add categories simply by typing a new heading in bold type.

- ✔ Under each category, list items owned by your business, including the date and price of acquisition, what it would cost you to replace the item in like condition, and what you believe the item could be sold for in its current condition in the current marketplace.

✔ Continue to type in categories and assets until all the assets to be sold by your business are listed. The form is set up to automatically total the replacement and fair market value of all items on your list.

FURNISHINGS, FIXTURES, AND EQUIPMENT LIST

Asset Description	Date/Price Acquired	Replacement Value	Fair Market Value
Category: Reception Area			
2 iMac Computers	2006/$3,000	$3,000	$1,500
Reception Desk	1999/$2,400	$3,000	$1,200
2 Desk Chairs	1999/$400	$500	$300
4 2-drawer file cabinets	1999/$600	$600	$500
Category: Sales Offices			
4 iMac Computers	2006/$6,000	$6,000	$3,000
4 Executive Desks	1999/$6,000	$6,000	$3,000
4 Executive Chairs	1999/$800	$800	$500
4 2-drawer file cabinets	1999/$600	$600	$500

Figure 6-1: This worksheet helps you value your tangible assets.

Inventory

If your sale includes inventory of raw materials, work in progress, or finished goods, use your existing, working inventory list as a starting point to determine the current replacement value of your inventory. Then work with your accountant to remove inventory items that are slow-turning or obsolete before arriving at an inventory valuation for pricing purposes. During due diligence, your buyer will confirm your inventory, and at the time of closing you need to present a final inventory value.

Valuing your intangible assets

In businesses with well-known names, products, and reputations, up to half the business sale price often covers the purchase of intangible assets — things buyers can't hold in their hands.

Intangible assets fall into two general categories:

✔ **Intellectual property rights assets,** including trademarks, patents, licensing agreements, and trade secrets.

✔ **Other intangible assets,** including business name and reputation, processes, strategies, and general know-how, which together contribute to business value over and above the value of tangible assets. These intangible assets comprise what's called the *goodwill* of your business. They include

- Your business name and brand identity

- A trained workforce

- Loyal clientele

- Strong and durable supplier and distribution networks

- Phone numbers and Web sites

- Proprietary technology, systems, and processes

✔ *Brand equity,* which is the value of the competitive advantage of your name and reputation in the minds of consumers and business and industry partners.

Appraising intellectual property assets

If your business owns trademarks, patents, or other intellectual property assets, and if they give your business a marketplace edge that competitors or others would pay money to acquire, seek professional assistance to put a value on those assets. Valuing intellectual property is a complicated process that usually involves formulas to determine the degree of innovation involved, the marketplace or industry applications, and the length of time the intellectual property asset has had and will continue to have value.

Valuing the goodwill of your business

In small businesses outside the service sector, goodwill isn't usually valued separately because it's automatically reflected in the income statement. If the income statement shows strong and increasing sales, margins, and profits, then it shows good brand strength and valuable goodwill. Without a good product, reputation, service, and image — without a good brand — a business can't achieve strong, profitable sales year after year.

Within the personal service business sector, however, goodwill often contributes a major portion of the sale price. For instance, much of the value of a business owned by a hairdresser, veterinarian, dentist, or marketing consultant is based on how well the business is known and regarded. If the brand is strong, the business has high goodwill value the owner can use to justify a business price based on a higher-than-average earnings multiple.

To put your brand to a quick brand strength test, use the form in Figure 6-2 (available on the CD-ROM as Form 6-2). Follow these steps:

✔ Answer all ten questions, rating your responses from 1 to 10, reflecting answers ranging from rarely to frequently.

✔ Review your responses. If most of your answers are in the range of 9 or 10, your brand has strong marketplace presence, consumer influence, and economic value. Based on that knowledge, you want to reflect your brand strength as you set the earnings multiple you use to price your business.

What's worth more — your business or its tangible assets?

After tallying up the value of physical assets and inventory items, some business owners decide they're better off liquidating their businesses and selling tangible assets rather than undergoing the time, effort, and resources it takes to sell tangible and intangible assets through a business sale. Unless your business is in a downward spiral in a down-trending industry or market area, that likely won't be the case in your situation. Still, it's good to know your options. Take this test:

1. Add the current market values you assigned to all inventory, furniture, fixtures, and equipment to arrive at the total market value of your business's tangible assets.

2. Compare the total market value of your tangible assets to the price you think someone would pay to buy your business, based on the multiple-of-earnings approach described in this chapter. Your comparison will lead you in one of two directions:

If the sale price you arrive at through the multiple-of-earnings calculation is lower than the value of your assets, then the parts of your business are worth more than the whole of your business. That's a strong sign that you may be better off liquidating and selling your assets separately instead of proceeding with a business sale.

If your tangible asset value is significantly lower than the sale price you estimate, continue your asset valuation by calculating the worth of your intangible assets to get a sense of the full value of your business assets so you have all the facts when you set your earnings multiple and asking price.

Either way, you'd be wise to continue the pricing process outlined in this chapter so you have the information you need to decide whether to sell tangible assets on their own or to sell your business, including its name, through an asset sale.

ASSESSING BRAND VALUE	
Circle responses and add up your score. Totals closest to 100 indicate high brand value.	
Customers are willing to pay a premium to purchase your offering over a similar solution.	Rarely Frequently 1 2 3 4 5 6 7 8 9 10
Customers typically return for additional purchases without promotional incentives.	Rarely Frequently 1 2 3 4 5 6 7 8 9 10
Customers arrive at your point of purchase with confidence in your brand and consistently follow through with a product selection and purchase.	Rarely Frequently 1 2 3 4 5 6 7 8 9 10
Your customers and business associates refer new customers to your business.	Rarely Frequently 1 2 3 4 5 6 7 8 9 10
Customers change their minds and choose not to purchase upon close consideration at the point of sale.	Frequently Rarely 1 2 3 4 5 6 7 8 9 10
Customers abandon your business for another in your market area, either due to discontentment or better deals.	Frequently Rarely 1 2 3 4 5 6 7 8 9 10
Your sales have increased consistently over past years, with equally strong increases in profits.	Definitely Not Definitely 1 2 3 4 5 6 7 8 9 10
Your brand is presented positively in industry reviews, business coverage, and other publicity.	Rarely Frequently 1 2 3 4 5 6 7 8 9 10
When you raise prices, purchases by established customers decline.	Frequently Rarely 1 2 3 4 5 6 7 8 9 10
Your highest-priced or highest-profit offerings are among your best selling items.	Definitely Not Definitely 1 2 3 4 5 6 7 8 9 10

Figure 6-2: Assessing the economic strength of your brand.

Especially if your brand is strong, you may want to come up with a brand value that you can add into the overall asset valuation that you use to justify your earnings multiple and verify the validity of your sale price. To value your brand, you can take the following two steps, both from the book *Branding For Dummies* (published by Wiley), which I authored with branding expert Bill Chiaravalle:

- ✔ **Assess the replacement cost of your brand** by adding the costs involved if you or a new owner have to rename your business and rebuild the level of awareness and loyalty you currently have in the marketplace. To arrive at this cost estimate, include costs to develop and register a new name, to design and trademark a new logo and slogan, to register and create traffic to a new domain name and Web address, and to develop new marketing, advertising, and promotional materials.

- ✔ **Assess the economic value of your brand** by calculating the extra money consumers are willing to pay, or how far out of their way they're willing to go, in order to purchase your product, which they know and trust, over a lesser-known or lesser-valued offering. One easy way to perform this calculation is to determine how much more your business charges for products or services than your lesser-known competitors, and then to multiply that difference by the amount of product or service you sell each year, arriving at an indication of the economic advantage your brand delivers through premium pricing, which is the economic value of your brand.

While you won't charge for your brand directly, based on the economic value of your brand and what it would cost to re-create your brand identity and image, you'll set an increased earnings multiple and allocate a greater portion of your sale price to cover the goodwill of your business.

Assessing the Comparable Market Value of Your Business

A *market-based valuation* — also called a *comparable-sales* method of pricing — is a valuation approach that helps you set your earnings multiple based on what businesses similar to yours in the same or a similar industry and market area have sold for. This approach is widely used as a pricing standard by almost all commercial and residential realtors. With businesses, though, it isn't as widely used, because information on comparable business sales isn't always available or accessible. With some sleuthing, though, you may be able to come up with earnings multiples that similar businesses in your industry sector or market area have used to establish their sale prices. This chapter tells you where to look and what to ask. It also describes the typical earnings multiples for businesses comparable to yours in earnings and in type of business.

Gathering info from those in the know

The fastest way to learn how businesses similar to yours have been priced is to turn to those whose livelihoods depend on advising businesses like yours as they ready for the sale process. To research comparable sales information:

- **Contact a business broker in your market area,** who likely has information on recent business sales and average sale prices for businesses in various industries. Ask if the broker has handled or has access to information on recent sales of businesses of your size and type. Then ask if the broker would be willing to share generalities about how the businesses were priced. If you're not ready to reveal your sale plans, you can couch your questions in terms of a general fact-finding mission, saying you're working on some long-term exit planning and that you'd like to know what kind of earning multiples businesses similar to yours in your market area have sold for.

- **Contact your industry association** to obtain information on selling trends and average sale prices within your industry. While a local broker can help you with pricing trends in your market area, representatives of your industry may be able to provide you with national and possibly regional business sale trends specific to your industry sector. You don't have to tell your personal plans — you can explain that you're trying to access information about business sale and pricing trends. Ask if the industry keeps such statistics or knows of brokers who specialize in selling businesses in your industry.

- **If you're selling a franchised business,** turn to your franchisor, who likely has and can share current information on sale prices and pricing approaches. If dozens or hundreds of franchises that share your brand name sold last year, access to information on their sale prices will provide you with valuable, credible pricing information. For more information on selling a franchise, see Chapter 1.

Relying on market trends

Market experience indicates that certain kinds of businesses are more attractive to buyers, and those businesses tend to be priced using a higher-than-average earnings multiple. The following summary of sale trends helps you begin to set your earnings multiple based on the experiences of businesses like yours:

- Businesses with higher earnings sell at higher earnings multiples:
  - **Businesses with earnings in the range of $150,000** tend to be priced at around two times earnings
  - **Businesses with earnings greater than $150,000** are often priced at multiples of two and a half times or above, with multiples that rise with the size of the earnings

- The nature of your business also tends to affect your earnings multiple:

- **Businesses in the manufacturing arena** go for earnings multiples of four or even higher, so long as the product being manufactured is competitive and forecasted to have a strong and growing market that won't be negatively affected by workforce or globalization issues

- **Distributorships** with strong earnings are priced on the higher end of the scale, often at as much as four times earnings

- **Equipment-intensive businesses** with current, attractive, tangible assets and positive sales and earnings trends win prices on the high end of the scale

- **Service and retail businesses** are priced on the lower end of the scale, with businesses facing stiff competition priced at earnings multiples between one and two

- **Restaurants and food service businesses** are priced in the middle of the scale if they're profitable, with struggling businesses going for far less

Adjusting comparable market information to fit your business situation

While the prices of comparable or similar businesses can influence your asking price, you need to base your final pricing decision not on the price of other businesses but on the attractions and risks of *your* business. Use comparable pricing as a starting point, and then adjust your earnings multiple upward or downward to account for the particular attributes or weaknesses of the business you're selling.

The worksheet in Figure 6-3 (available on the CD-ROM as Form 6-3) helps you assess the attributes and risks of your business. To use the form, follow these steps:

1. **Begin in the left-hand column, checking each statement that applies to your business.** The statements you check reflect the attributes of your business.

2. **Then go to the middle column and check each statement that applies to your business.** These are your risks.

3. **Review your responses in the first two columns of the form.** If your business has many attributes and few risks, you'll probably be able to price your business on the high end of the earnings multiple scale, which typically ranges from one to four. If risk far outweighs attractiveness, you'll be lucky to come in on the low end of the scale.

4. **Finally, review the factors in the right-hand column, which deals with sale terms.** You may be able to adjust your earnings multiple upward if you offer the favorable sale terms listed in the form.

FACTORS THAT AFFECT SALE PRICE

✓ *conditions that apply to your business*

Most small businesses sell at 1–4 times seller's discretionary earnings.
If nearly all your checkmarks are in the "attractive aspects" column you may be
able to ask a price on thehigh end of that scale. If you place many checks in the
"risks" column, your price will need to be on the low-end of the scale.
You may be able to adjust your price slightly upward if you present
favorable sale terms, as shown in the right hand column.

✓ Attractive aspects that contribute to business value		✓ Risks that detract from business value		✓ Terms that improve purchase decisions	
High annual earnings that allow healthy owner income and cash flow	☐	Low annual earnings	☐	You're willing to accept a down payment and provide seller financing to the buyer	☐
Increasing revenues and profits	☐	Declining revenues and profits	☐	You're willing to sign a non-compete agreement that stipulates you won't compete with the business you're selling	☐
Increasing revenues and profits	☐	Declining revenues and profits	☐	You're willing to sign a non-compete agreement that stipulates you won't compete with the business you're selling	☐
Experienced staff that will remain with the business after a sale	☐	Business success relies almost entirely on owner's expertise and presence	☐	You're willing to train the buyer and assist with the business transition	☐
Well-known business name with good reputation	☐	Low business name awareness and weak or poor reputation	☐		
Desirable business location with long and transferable lease	☐	Business is in non-transferable location, a poor location, or a location with an expiring or problematic lease	☐		
A strong and growing industry and market area	☐	Heavy competition with little competitive advantage	☐		

Valuable tangible and intangible assets	☐	Few assets of value	☐	
Unique and preferred products and service	☐	Products and services lack distinction or customer demand	☐	
Strong clientele and customer database	☐	Business is heavily reliant on a few clients	☐	
Good future potential	☐	Business lacks or has unprofessional financial records	☐	

Figure 6-3: Determining the attributes and risks that affect sale pricing.

Determining Your Earnings Multiple and Pricing Your Business

Get ready to answer the final question: What's your price?

Setting your asking price involves two steps:

ON THE CD

1. **Start with the annual seller's discretionary earnings for your business, a topic that's explained in Chapter 5 and shown in Form 5-3.**

2. **Multiply your annual seller's discretionary earnings by an earnings multiple of 1 to 5, as calculated by using the form in Figure 6-4.** To use this form, which is Form 6-4 on the CD-ROM, follow these steps:

   • Go down each row of the form, replacing the sample ratings in the shaded cells with ratings between one and four for your business, with one indicating weakness and four indicating high strength.

   • The form automatically computes your estimated earnings multiple by averaging your ratings.

After you have an idea of the multiple you think fits your business situation, you just do the math — multiply your annual seller's discretionary earnings by your earnings multiple — to arrive at the price you think you can charge (and what a buyer may be willing to pay) for your business. With a few calculator keystrokes, you've established your pricing starting point. It'll likely be adjusted by your accountant or your broker — who may help you revise either your seller's discretionary earnings or your multiplier — and almost certainly it'll be a point of negotiation with your buyer. But for now, you have a good idea of what to charge for your business and how to defend your price.

The number you arrive at using the multiple-of-earnings approach usually covers the selling price of all tangible and intangible business assets excluding liquid assets such as cash and accounts receivable minus accounts payable, and non-operating assets such as your car. You can either isolate liquid or non-operating assets from the sale offering (and from your balance sheet) or sell them separately. Chapter 13 is full of information on structuring your sale.

EARNINGS MULTIPLIER CALCULATOR

Factors That Affect Earnings Multiple	
High annual seller's discretionary earnings ($100,000=2; $150,000=3)	2
Revenues and profits have increased steadily over past 3-5 years	2
Experienced staff will remain with business after sale	2
A well-known name and good reputation	2
Located in a desirable region	2
In a strong and growing industry	2
Serves a strong and growing market area or areas	2
A strong competitive position within marketplace	2
Well-located facilities with a long and transferable lease	2
Valuable furnishings, fixtures, and equipment	2
Broad-based clientele and good customer database	2
Distinct and preferred products and services	2
Operation is easy to assume and run	2
Management and clientele will easily transition to new owner	2
Attractive sale terms (such as seller financing, earning contingencies)	2
Estimated Earnings Multiple for Your Business	2

Figure 6-4:
Figuring the earnings multiple for your business.

Forms on the CD-ROM

Form 6-1	**Furnishings, Fixtures, and Equipment List**	A form for listing assets and their replacement and fair market values
Form 6-2	**Assessing Brand Value: Worksheet**	A form for rating the strength of your brand on a scale of 1-10
Form 6-3	**Factors That Affect Sale Price**	A worksheet for weighing your business attributes, risks, and sale terms that affect sale pricing
Form 6-4	**Earnings Multiple Calculator**	A form for determining how well your business rates in the areas that affect sale pricing, ending with an estimation of the earnings multiple to use to price your business

Chapter 7

Telling Your Business Story — Succinctly!

. . . .

In This Chapter

▶ Preparing a quick introduction of your business and sale offering

▶ Summarizing your business and marketing plans

▶ Explaining your operations

. . . .

*W*ith a large number of businesses expected to be for sale over the next few years, you can be sure of one thing: A buyer considering your business has plenty of alternatives. As the old saying goes, so many choices, so little time. Though many aspects of a business sale are flexible, the window of opportunity you have to grab a buyer's attention and gain the chance for a closer look isn't.

Quickly, you need to announce your offering, convey what your business is, and tell how well it performs financially and operationally. After you have the buyer's attention, you need to be ready to deliver the fuller story of your business in a way that carries the buyer's initial interest to the next phase of the purchase decision.

This chapter helps you craft an attention-getting snapshot of your business and offering as well as create a compelling message to present the fuller picture. It also helps you describe how your business works — how it does what it does, who it serves, and how it has succeeded and will continue to succeed in its marketplace. You'll use some of this information when you're preparing your selling memorandum, which you give to serious buyer prospects (more on that in Chapter 8), and you'll use other information when a very serious buyer signs a letter of intent and begins the purchase process (Chapter 11 helps you with this step).

For now, the upcoming pages help you get your story together. Because your time is precious and you're likely eager to get the sale process underway, you certainly don't want to waste time doing tasks that won't really add much value to your business as a sale prospect. For that reason, I begin by helping you decide which areas you'll benefit most from enhancing so you can head straight for the sections that yield the most benefit for *you*.

Strategizing Your Storytelling: Where to Invest Your Energy

All business owners will benefit from the beginning part of this chapter, because everyone needs to be ready to make a powerful business introduction when a prospective buyer appears. From there, owners can direct their attention to different parts of this chapter:

- ✔ **If you have a financially healthy business that's likely to sell for under $200,000,** your business's financial health will be the primary strength your buyer focuses on, so you probably won't need an elaborate presentation of your business strengths. Your buyer will, however, want to know how your business runs, and, especially if you're the only key operational player, how it can be easily transferred to a new owner. Head to the sections on the business and marketing plans, later in this chapter, to summarize how your business works and how your marketing efforts generate and keep customers. Then spend some time with the section on creating an operations manual so you can show the buyer how your shoes can be filled.

- ✔ **If you have a business that's in good financial and operational condition with an asking price well above $200,000,** visit the "Updating and Summarizing Your Business Plan" and "Updating and Summarizing Your Marketing Plan" sections to prepare a summary of your business plan and your marketing program. Then, because your asking price is significant and your buyer may be considering a number of alternatives, spend extra time with the "Highlighting business strengths" and "Describing your business model" sections, which contain advice for highlighting your strengths and explaining how your business makes money. If you think buyers will hesitate because they're concerned about how your operation will transfer to a new owner, consider the advice in the "Presenting Your Employment and Operations Policies" section, which focuses on presenting employee and operation plans.

✔ **If your business has financial, operational, or transferability weaknesses and you don't have time to fix them,** you'll probably have to lower your earnings multiple and asking price to accommodate for the risks a buyer will be taking on. You'll also have to lay out an easy-to-follow turnaround plan. To do so, spend time updating and summarizing your business and marketing plans to show the steps that will overcome the situation your business faces. Then, to prove that your business's strengths outweigh its weaknesses, spend time with the "Highlighting business strengths" and "Describing your business model" sections, which highlight and define revenue streams and strengths.

✔ **If you're using a broker,** he or she may follow a different approach for assembling your business story. Even so, at least scan this chapter because it will be useful as you assemble supporting information and prepare for upcoming buyer conversations and negotiations.

Briefly Introducing Your Business

Whether in person or in an ad, you have only a few seconds to grab a buyer's attention and convey what your business is and why it's worth further consideration. Amazingly, many business owners are left tongue-tied when it comes time to describe their businesses. You may be able to stumble through a meandering explanation at a networking event or over a business lunch, but a buyer — especially a buyer who's looking at a long list of business offerings — wants the facts in a quick, easy-to-grasp statement. To give your sale offering a second thought, a buyer needs to know the basic ins and outs of your business — the simple *who, what, where, when, why,* and *how.*

This quick introduction usually takes place in one of two ways:

✔ **A one-minute verbal introduction,** which you present when telling prospects about your business (or your broker presents on your behalf, if you're using a broker). This brief introduction is the one you'll include in the overview section of your selling memorandum.

✔ **A 20-word written advertisement,** which is just a condensed version of your verbal introduction. This will usually take the form of an online posting that prompts prospective buyers to request more information.

In this section, I take you through the two-step process of whittling your business scope to a conversational sales pitch, and then I help you trim back even further, so you end up with a tight, 20-word print ad that's capable of luring prospective buyers by the hundreds (having dreams isn't so bad, right?).

Introducing your business in 60 seconds or less

You need a quick, inspiring introduction of your sale offering that you or your broker can deliver in 60 seconds or less, which is about how long prospective buyers will take to decide whether they want more information.

The following list shows you what a one-minute introduction needs to cover and gives you tips for distilling your business down to an easily digestible, enticing preview for potential buyers. When writing your introduction, here's what you need to consider:

- **Your business description:** Here, you want to explain what your business does in a way that leaves the prospective buyer thinking, "Now this sounds interesting ..."

- **Your product or service:** Keep this statement to one sentence.

- **Your customer and market:** Describe the location and nature of your market and the kind of customers you serve.

- **Your business's edge over the competition:** Basically, just describe how your business is unique and successful. Mention such factors as location, staff, systems or processes, marketing approach, and special (and transferable) licenses, permits, relationships, or contracts.

- **Why you're selling:** If possible, combine the reason for your desired exit with a positive point about why your timing is right for the buyer.

- **Positive business trends:** Provide a statement that gives a snapshot view of gross sales and financial trends for your business.

Introducing your business with an elevator pitch

Sometimes you'll hear short business introductions referred to as *elevator pitches*, because they last about the length of an elevator ride.

In case you're curious, the term *elevator pitch* became popular in the 1990s, when founders of high-tech start-up companies learned to use chance meetings with venture capitalists, often during elevator rides, to quickly introduce their businesses as part of their efforts to gain funding.

You'll probably never stand in an elevator with your prospective buyer. In fact, if you use a broker, you won't even be the one to introduce your buyer to your prospect. But sooner or later your business needs to be introduced, either by you or by an intermediary. When that time comes, you'll have just seconds to convey what your business is, where it's located, why it's successful, and how it's a good deal. The information in this chapter prepares you for that moment.

✔ **Your asking price:** Just tell 'em how much you're asking for your business, simply and directly. In fact, the buyer will care more about your business sales and earnings, which the buyer will use to decide what he or she thinks your business is worth, but you'll also want to name the price you're seeking.

After you figure out what to say for each point, combine your statements to create a short script that you're comfortable delivering in person or in writing.

Before you say that all those points can't be covered in less than a minute, consider this example:

> *Our casual, upscale restaurant, located in a growing and affluent suburb of Seattle, is a local institution in the community. Known for fresh Northwest fare and a vibrant setting, the restaurant, bar, and three group dining rooms draw customers year round from 11 a.m. daily. Since opening in 1988, we've been praised in numerous national travel features, and we consistently rank as a local favorite in news reviews and reader polls. I'm selling the restaurant because I want to retire and move closer to my adult kids and their families, and because the business is in such good condition, with a loyal clientele and a recently renewed long-term lease. I'm asking $400,000. Year-to-date, gross receipts were $450,000, with 2007 sales of $800,000 and 2006 sales of $750,000.*

Shrinking your 60-second intro to a 20-word classified ad

After you get your business introduction down to a minute-long description, the next step is to shrink it to a 20-word ad. That's not a typo; your first introduction to most of your prospective buyers will take the form of a 20-word online listing.

Though your ad has to be short, you control how short or long you make it by deciding how much you're willing to pay to the Internet site or newspaper advertising department. Want some advice? When given the choice, don't take the cheapest option. If you say too little in your ad, you may as well say nothing at all. As an example of a good online ad, look at this example:

> *Casual, upscale restaurant located in affluent Seattle suburb. A local institution for 20 years. 2007 Gross $800,000. Asking price: $400,000.*

Years ago, when buyers had a greater tolerance for advertising, *teaser ads* that told just enough to pique interest worked to inspire requests for more information, but those days are gone. Today's buyers don't want to work to obtain information. Either they'll see what they're looking for as they quickly scan your ad, or they'll move right past your ad to the next one that looks more interesting.

Your advertising needs to give prospective buyers the information they want and need, including

- Enough information to decide if your business sounds attractive and like what they're looking for

- Enough about the nature and price of your business to allow buyers to pre-qualify themselves, so only those who have the qualifications necessary to buy and run your business respond with requests for more information

According to Sunbelt Business Brokers CEO John Davies, approximately 90 percent of initial buyer inquiries for businesses with an asking price of under $1 million are responses to Internet business-for-sale listings. Nine times out of ten you'll introduce yourself online, and many of those listings give you just 20 words to work with to make the first impression on a prospective buyer.

In boiling down the essence of your offering to 20 words or fewer, you need to cover these important points:

- **Tell what you're selling:** Is it a restaurant, a beauty salon, an accounting practice, a software manufacturer, or what?

- **Tell where you're located:** To announce your offering while keeping your business identity confidential so you don't tip off clients, competitors, or staff about your sale, you might choose to give an indication of your location, such as "in an affluent and growing Phoenix suburb," rather than pinpointing where you are. Chapter 9 has more information on weighing how confidential you want to keep your sale intentions.

- **Tell why you're successful:** Explain how your business is distinctive and preferred over competing choices and why it's an attractive purchase option.

- **Tell your sales figures:** Buyers want to know not just what you're charging, but what you're making. By stating your gross sales revenue you give them the information they need to determine whether the size of your business fits their purchase criteria.

- **State your asking price:** Nothing more to say here!

Chapter 9 offers more information on how to write ads that present your sale offering. For now, use the preceding tips to write a 20-word first-draft version. This version will keep you focused on the essence of your offering as you use the rest of this chapter to prepare your longer story.

Updating and Summarizing Your Business Plan

After you catch a buyer's eye, you need to be ready to show how your business works. Your business probably matches one of two conditions:

- ✔ **If you already have a business plan and your business is in good condition for a sale,** telling your business story will be easy. When the time's right (after a prospective buyer has signed the confidentiality agreement described in Chapter 8), all you have to do is share your existing business plan and financial statements.

- ✔ **If you don't have a business plan, and if your business isn't in prime condition for a sale,** you have some work to do. Refer to Chapter 2 and/or the CD-ROM and consult Forms 2-2, 2-3, and 2-4 to assess the pre-sale condition of your business. Then turn to Chapter 3 for advice on improving your business prior to a sale. When you know your weaknesses and how to address them, you'll be ready to write or update your business plan. The upcoming section shows you how.

Don't be put off by the term *business plan*. For a small business, you may be looking at nothing more than a few pages that summarize your company, your business environment, and your operations and finances, along with an action plan that details how your business intends to meet its goals and objectives.

Your effort will pay off twice during the upcoming sale process. First, you can pick information straight from your business plan as you assemble your selling memorandum. Second, after a serious buyer signs a letter of intent and begins the research and negotiation steps of the business purchase, your business plan will be a key document that you can share as you answer questions and detail opportunities and growth plans.

Creating a brief business plan (or shrinking your existing one)

Business plans can run up to 100 pages long, but not the plan you'll share with your buyer. In fewer than 10 pages (way fewer if yours is a business with only a few employees and a straightforward, easy-to-run operation), you can create a business plan summary that provides the key facts that buyers want to see. The form in Figure 7-1 (Form 7-1 on the CD-ROM) shows you what to include. Use the form as a checklist to keep yourself on track as you assemble your plan.

For many of the items listed on Form 7-1, a sentence or two will provide enough description. But in the "Business Strategy" part of the plan (described in the following sections), you'll probably want to go into more detail, especially to highlight areas where your business is very strong or where it faces challenges that an infusion of time, energy, and investment can overcome.

SHORT-FORM BUSINESS PLAN CHECKLIST	
Business Overview	☐ Business introduction ☐ Mission statement ☐ Key products or services ☐ Business model (how you make money) ☐ Business goals and objectives
Business Environment	☐ Industry overview ☐ Market area overview ☐ Customer description ☐ Major competitors and your competitive advantage ☐ Business advantages (such as licenses, permits, proprietary processes, and so on) that create barriers to entry that new competitors will find difficult to match or overcome
Business Description	☐ Products and services offered ☐ Operation overview including location, equipment, labor, and processes ☐ Marketing overview including marketing communications (advertising, promotions, publicity) and sales approaches ☐ Distribution overview including description of sales channels (retail, direct, wholesale, online) ☐ Customer service overview including how customers are served; how customer data is collected, kept, and used; and how loyalty is developed and maintained ☐ Management overview, including profiles of key staff, salaries, and employment policies ☐ Organization overview, including an organization chart and a description of how the business will transition to a new owner and continue with strength after a sale
Business Strategy	☐ Summary of strengths and opportunities ☐ Plan for overcoming weaknesses and addressing threats ☐ Plans for generating future growth ☐ Short-term marketing plan

Figure 7-1:
An outline for your business plan.

Highlighting business strengths

Where your business is very strong, highlight your capabilities in your business plan, and then go further by referring the prospective buyer to more information contained either in, or as an addendum to, your selling memorandum. (See Chapter 8 for an in-depth discussion of the selling memorandum.)

For instance:

- ✔ **If your location is a strong selling point,** assemble information that presents the business, recreation, and lifestyle advantages of your surroundings.

- ✔ **If your production processes are a strong suit of your business,** detail how you do what you do to prove to the buyer that your strengths are ready for seamless transfer. Reference that an operations manual is available, if you have one. You won't include details of your production processes in your selling memorandum, as it's too confidential to share with multiple buyer prospects, but you'll want to have the information ready to share during the due diligence process.

- ✔ **If your business benefits from licenses, permits, or relationships that provide an advantage and curb competitive threats,** describe how those advantages will transfer with the business to add strength after your departure.

- ✔ **If your sales are on an upward curve,** then marketing is a strength of your business and a strong purchase motivation. Show how your business attracts and will continue to attract customers by including a summary of your marketing plan (follow the steps in a later section of this chapter).

Pretend you're selling a car

My father-in-law, who was best friends with a man who sold more used cars than any of his many competitors, never tired of telling how his friend did it. "It's amazing! He advertises every last feature on the car, even that it has an ashtray." (Back then, all cars did!)

Simply, this very wealthy car dealer didn't allow a single car attribute to go unnoticed. His used-car ads noted if the car had new windshield blades, tinted glass, seatbelts, and so on, while adjacent ads told the make, model, mileage, and color, period.

Business buyers have always faced a large selection of opportunities, but over the next few years that selection will grow exponentially. Businesses that look like the best bets will get to the sale closing room. Showcase your strengths — every single one of them — to make it to the sale finish line.

Overcoming weaknesses and threats

Where your business needs to overcome weaknesses or address looming threats, don't cower. Hit the issue head-on in the "Business Strategy" section of your business plan, with descriptions of ready-to-go (or in-the-works) turn-around plans. Especially:

- ✔ **If your sales are declining,** show the proposed marketing plan that can be implemented to reverse the situation.

- ✔ **If the market your business serves is facing declining numbers,** present a plan for how your business is prepared to tap into new markets, either by:

  - Promoting in new geographic areas

  - Marketing to new target customer groups within your established geographic area

  - Using direct and online marketing approaches to reach beyond the confines of your current, troubled marketplace

- ✔ **If you face new, aggressive competitors,** outline your plan for retaining and growing your customer base.

- ✔ **If your business struggles to address the current wants and needs of your marketplace,** describe an action plan for updating or adapting your offerings to match current interests and trends.

- ✔ **If you think a buyer will be fearful that your business faces transferability issues** — such as difficulty transferring clients or production processes from seller to buyer — be prepared to address the issue, either by a transition period during which you're willing to remain available to assist the new owner, by the ongoing presence of key staff, or by other plans that you're ready to put in to smooth the transfer. You don't want to highlight the problem, but by stating your transition plans you may allay potential buyer concerns.

Describing your business model

You may call it something else (like your revenue stream or your method of doing business), but in case the term comes up, you should know what it means: Your *business model* is how your business makes money. Most small businesses make money simply and directly by producing a product or providing a service and selling that product or service to customers directly through the business office or retail setting. Other business models involve sales through distributors, online marketing, auctions, licensing arrangements, subscription services, or other channels.

However your product reaches your customer, a buyer wants to know how your sales occur. You'll include pieces of this information in a number of places within your selling memorandum. The selling memorandum guidance in Chapter 8 and the template in Form 8-3 on the CD-ROM help you put information in the right places. To describe your business revenue stream, explain the following:

- ✔ **The main sources of revenue for your business.** Detail how sales are generated by key product or service categories. Also show how your business generates other streams of revenue — for instance, from the sale of accessories, service agreements, installation services, or any other products or supporting services.

- ✔ **What portion of sale revenue pays for *cost-of-sales* or *cost-of-goods sold*** — the out-of-pocket expenses you incur to purchase the materials or services necessary to create your product or service — and what portion remains in your business as your *operating profit* or *gross margin*.

- ✔ **How much you charge for your products or services.** Present a list of your product prices or services fees.

- ✔ **How (or if) you charge different prices for different customers.** Describe your customer groups and how pricing inspires purchases from each segment.

- ✔ **Your sale distribution and pricing strategy.** Are sales distributed fairly evenly throughout the year, or do they occur seasonally or around major events? Do market conditions affect your pricing strategy?

- ✔ **Your payment arrangement with customers/clients.** In short, how do people purchase your products or services? Depending on your business type, some questions to consider in this category include:

  - Do they buy on cash or credit?

  - Do you send once-a-month invoices?

  - Do you charge for work-in-progress or only upon delivery of the purchased product or service?

  - Do they pay retainer fees?

  - Do they purchase subscriptions?

  - Do they sign bulk-purchase contract agreements?

- ✔ **Your price increase policy and schedule.** Include details about the last time you raised prices.

- ✔ **Areas within your business model that have experienced strong growth.** For instance, if Internet sales have grown strongly, or if client activity has shifted away from one-time purchases toward bulk contracts, note these changes and describe how they'll likely affect your business future.

When presenting your summary of revenue streams, point out strengths by highlighting products or market niches that perform well, along with how your business can further capitalize on these growth areas. Also point out areas of untapped revenue-growth opportunity such as:

✔ Price or rate increases

✔ Increased use of contract sales, subscription sales, bulk sales, or other ways to lock in customers and reduce sale transaction costs

✔ Increased emphasis on revenue channels that have shown the greatest growth in the recent past, such as online, direct sales, or wholesaler agreements

Updating and Summarizing Your Marketing Plan

A business can't generate strong earnings without first generating strong sales. Because marketing is the key to sales, a description of your marketing approach is an essential component of the selling memorandum that explains your business sale offering. Additionally, you want a copy of your marketing plan (or at least a summary) to show the buyer during the due diligence phase of the business sale process. The marketing plan summary for a service business that recruits customers primarily by word-of-mouth and directory ads will likely fit on a single page, while a business with a marketing budget that reaches into the tens of thousands of dollars or more will probably need to create a longer document.

If your business already has a marketing plan, you can either present that document during due diligence or, if you feel it reveals confidential approaches that you want to share only after the sale is closed, you can create a summary version of your full plan, following the outline shown in Figure 7-2.

Whether your business has a large or small marketing program and budget, if your sales are strong, a summary of your marketing plan will serve as a welcome game plan for your buyer to adopt and follow. If your sales are declining, your summary may be the key that opens your buyer's mind to the opportunities that can result from the infusion of a new owner's energy and investment.

This section details what to include in your marketing plan summary.

Getting a glimpse of what you should include

As you assemble a summary of your business marketing plan, you may find it helpful to use the checklist in Figure 7-2, which I also include on the CD-ROM (as Form 7-2).

The following sections provide more in-depth information about what you should discuss in each section of the summary.

SHORT-FORM MARKETING PLAN CHECKLIST	
Market Situation	☐ Customer description ☐ Market segments served by your business ☐ Market size and growth trends ☐ Market growth opportunities ☐ Competitive environment ☐ Competitive advantages ☐ Business climate overview
Market Position and Brand Statement	☐ Market niche filled by your business ☐ Unique benefits or values provided by your business ☐ Brand image, or what customers believe about your business
Marketing Strategy	☐ Product strategy ☐ Distribution strategy ☐ Pricing strategy ☐ Promotion strategy ☐ Advertising approaches and samples ☐ Marketing literature samples ☐ Professional resources list ☐ Advertising and promotion calendar
Marketing Budget	☐ Annual marketing expenditures ☐ Existing marketing materials that eliminate the need for new investment

Figure 7-2: An outline for your marketing plan.

Providing a picture of the market

This section describes your market, including your customers, your market area, and your competitive environment. This information is essential to buyers, who want a definition of the customers your business serves, whether the number of potential customers is growing or declining, and whether competition for the customer's purchase is moderate or stiff. Include the following information, providing a statement that summarizes the information and then going into more detail if you feel the strength of your marketing program will be a key to your buyer's decision:

- ✔ **A description of your customers,** including your customer profile (if you need help creating your customer profile, Chapter 8 includes a form for use when preparing the selling memorandum), how your customers divide into market segments that your business serves, the size and growth trends of your market, and how you plan to cultivate market segments that best present growth opportunities

- ✔ **The business climate** in which your business operates, including how your business responds or is prepared to respond to such outside forces as changing economic and competitive conditions, increasing labor or supply costs, new rules and regulations, and shifting customer preferences

Pinpointing your market position

A buyer wants to understand how your business fits in its competitive environment and how its name and reputation are regarded in the marketplace. Especially if you've justified a business price based on a higher-than-average earnings multiple due in part to the strength of your business name and brand, describe the following attributes in your marketing plan summary:

- ✔ **Your market *position*** — the niche that your company fills in your competitive marketplace and in your customers' minds. For example, if your business is the only one among similar businesses in your market to offer home delivery, that service would be part of your position. If you're known to have the highest quality product, or the fastest turnaround, or any other distinction, highlight your unique differentiating aspects in your marketing plan and sale materials.

- ✔ **Your *value proposition*, or the unique benefits or values your business delivers.** For example, if a shoe repair shop is known for doubling the life of favorite old shoes, that's its value proposition. If a Web site is known for consistently and quickly finding car rental rates that are half the price otherwise available, that's its value proposition.

- ✔ **The image of your business, or your *brand*.** Whether you call it your reputation or your brand image, the set of beliefs or promises that customers associate with your business name can be an important asset. Include a sentence that details what promises customers believe they can count on from your company. This section is especially important if you plan to price your business using a higher-than average earnings multiple in part due to the strength of your business name and brand reputation. To assess the value of your brand, follow the advice in Chapter 6.

Sharing your four-part marketing strategy

The marketing strategies your business employs are the heart of the marketing plan. They tell how your business competes and succeeds in four areas:

- **Your product strategy** describes how your business prices its products, how it bundles products as part of a pricing strategy, how it plans pricing as a competitive strategy, and how it presents prices to customers.

- **Your distribution strategy** describes how your business gets products to customers and how it uses various marketing channels (direct sales, retail, wholesalers, online sales, and so on) to enhance product availability.

- **Your pricing strategy** describes your business pricing philosophy. It details whether your prices are set with an intention to be the high-end price choice, low-end price choice, or mid-market price choice in your competitive arena; how you set prices to achieve trial and repeat business; whether you offer financing or credit; whether your prices are set or flexible; whether you reward bulk or contract purchases with pricing incentives; and how prices fluctuate seasonally or increase annually.

- **Your promotion strategy** describes how you get your marketing message to customers. In your marketing plan summary, convey whether your business relies most heavily on advertising, promotions, sales presentations, or publicity. Specify whether you rely on one-to-one marketing using direct mail, phone calls, and e-mail messages or whether you use mass media advertising to reach your market. If you use advertising, describe the types of media, ads, and messages that work most effectively for your business. If you use sales literature as a key marketing component, list and include samples of recent materials. If you contract with advertising or media-buying professionals, share the names and details of those resources as well.

For help developing or enhancing your marketing strategies, refer to Chapter 3, which includes a section on strengthening weaknesses and building strengths in key capabilities, including marketing.

Stating your marketing budget

Present your marketing budget so a buyer will have a sense of how much your business spends annually to attract customers, generate sales, and inspire customer loyalty. Your full marketing plan should include an itemized breakdown of marketing costs, but in your plan summary you can simply state your annual marketing budget without revealing your line-by-line allocations, which you may want to hold as confidential. In your budget, include costs that your business incurs to

- ✔ Create and place ads
- ✔ Create and send direct mailers
- ✔ Create and print sales and promotional literature
- ✔ Host events and promotions
- ✔ Host and design Web sites
- ✔ Participate in trade shows
- ✔ Create displays

If your business has a good supply of sales literature, and if it has standing formats for ads, promotions, trade show displays, and other marketing items that don't require new investment by the business buyer, note this advantage in your marketing plan.

Presenting Your Employment and Operations Policies

You may think it sounds like overkill, but you'll enhance the attractiveness of your business by putting your operation policies into writing, if you haven't already done so. If your business has a team of employees, be ready to present your buyer with your employment policies. If your business produces a unique product or service, be ready to show how you do what you do, in a step-by-step manner that the new owner can review and adopt as part of an easy business transition.

If your business has only a few employees, or if your operations are uncomplicated and very straightforward, outlining your policies should take only a few hours and a few sheets of paper. If your staff is larger, and if your procedures are more complex, the effort will be more extensive. Either way, invest the time necessary to follow the advice in the upcoming sections. After you're done, you'll be able to include a statement in your selling memorandum explaining that outlines of employment policies and operational procedures will be available for review during due diligence. With that single statement your business will appear well-managed, more attractive, and less risky to a buyer.

Employment policy manual

An employment policy manual protects employees and employers by clarifying policies and procedures, describing expectations, and detailing how business is conducted. If you have employees and don't have a manual or handbook outlining your employment policies, you need to create a docu-

ment that summarizes for your employees and for your buyer how your business addresses employment issues. Most manuals include two sections. One section covers general policies, such as policies for attendance, dress, use of company property, confidentiality of business and personal information, performance reviews, and so on. The other section covers compensation and benefits.

Employment policy manuals are legal documents that require experienced legal input and advice. To create one, either hire a human relations consultant or do it on your own using one of the many available software programs (search online for "employment policy manual software" and you'll reach countless resources). No matter how you create yours, have your attorney review the draft before you consider it finalized.

Operations manual

An operations manual shows how your business runs. It puts what's inside your head into writing so key employees or a new owner can keep your business running the way it should, even if you're not there to oversee the operation. Every business needs a document that outlines how the business is run, though not all businesses need a full-on manual. Look at the following list and decide whether you can explain everything a new owner needs to know on a page or two. If so, that'll be the length of your document. On the other hand, if you need a tabbed binder to hold the information, get ready to create a binder full of details. The complexity of your operation will determine the outcome. You pass along the operational overview to the buyer of your business during the due diligence phase of the sale process, unless your systems are very innovative and confidential, in which case you might share an outline and hand the manual over after the sale closes.

An operations manual includes the following types of information, as well as outlines of other policies or procedures unique to your business:

- Business opening and closing hours and procedures
- Cash and checkbook handling procedures
- Cost estimate and job order and processing procedures
- Product production procedures
- Billing procedures and procedures for credit, returns, refunds, discounts, gift certificates, special orders, and other purchase transaction issues
- Shipping and receiving procedures
- Building operations, including maintenance, alarm systems, and emergency procedures
- Equipment handling and maintenance policies

✔ A HIPPA manual, MSDS (material safety data sheet), and an OSHA manual, if required by law

✔ Sales procedures and sales staff policies, including quotas and commissions

✔ Customer service procedures

✔ Web site, e-mail, and online usage procedures

No two operations manuals are the same, but most follow similar formats. Search online for "creating a small business operations manual" and you'll find resources such as advice, software, and templates.

Forms on the CD-ROM

Form 7-1	**Short-Form Business Plan Checklist**	A checklist to use when compiling a short version of your business plan
Form 7-2	**Short-Form Marketing Plan Checklist**	A checklist to use when compiling a summary of your marketing plan

Chapter 8

Preparing Your Selling Memorandum

In This Chapter

▶ Outlining a selling memorandum

▶ Using your selling memorandum to make a good first impression

▶ Putting together all the parts of your selling memorandum

▶ Getting a signed confidentiality agreement before showing your selling memorandum

As soon as you and your broker (if you're using one) start to market your business, expect requests for more information. In the business sale process, "more information" isn't delivered in bits and pieces but in a bound document called a *selling memorandum* (sometimes called an *offering memorandum*, a *confidential description book*, or just a *selling book*), which you hand to serious prospects after they sign a confidentiality agreement. Whether the business you're selling is very small or impressively large, if you're trying to sell to an unknown third party — that is, anyone who isn't a business insider, family member, or pre-identified buyer — you need to create a selling memorandum to give prospective buyers a tantalizing look at what your business is all about.

This chapter serves as your selling memorandum blueprint and construction plan. The upcoming pages tell what's involved, the outline to follow, what to include and not to include, how to present facts in the best possible light, and how to get signed confidentiality agreements before distributing your selling memorandum and the sensitive business information it contains.

Demystifying the Function and Form of a Selling Memorandum

A selling memorandum is a booklet that provides a buyer with an initial look inside your business. By creating a single document that you can present to all prospective buyers, you not only save yourself the time of assembling the information over and over again, but you're also assured of telling each prospective buyer the same story. Plus, by compiling all the information into one convenient source rather than sharing information verbally or through various mailings or deliveries, you don't have to deal with as many buyer questions because buyers will have one source of information to refer to, again and again.

You have a choice regarding who will prepare your memorandum:

- ✔ **If you're using a broker to help sell your business,** your broker will either create a selling memorandum for you or guide you through the preparation process. The broker's outline may differ from the one shown in this chapter, but the content should be similar.

- ✔ **If you're selling your business on your own,** you can follow the basic outline and tips throughout this chapter. If you need further help, you may be able to contract with a broker to help prepare your selling memorandum even if you're not listing your business with the broker. See the section "Tips for Making a Good First Impression" for more on this option.

Make sure an attorney reviews your selling memorandum before you print the final copies. If you don't already work with an attorney, most brokers will share names of attorneys with experience in business sale transactions. Your attorney can also prepare or review the confidentiality agreement (which is the topic of the last section of this chapter) that you need to be sure to obtain before distributing your selling memorandum to prospects.

The purpose

A selling memorandum is part business plan and part marketing brochure; it answers the questions buyers have when they find out your business is for sale while also previewing the reasons your business is a good purchase opportunity. In a single document, your selling memorandum gives buyers a snapshot of your business history and purpose, its products and customers, its operations and management, its financial history, its future prospects, how much it makes for the owner, how much you're asking for a sale price, and why you're selling.

John Davies brings the purpose of the selling memorandum into focus by reminding his Sunbelt clients that the intention is simply to get buyers to take the next step. It's not the final step — just an important step along the way. He compares the selling process to a more familiar matchmaking process — dating. "If we got into all of our likes and dislikes, or our hopes and problems, on the first date, there probably wouldn't be a second date. Too much information delivered too soon isn't good."

A selling memorandum is full of enough facts to whet interest and enough description to help a buyer see your business strengths and opportunity.

Here's what a selling memorandum does and doesn't do:

- ✔ **It provides facts, but it's not a just-the-facts document.** It also describes the attributes that make your business attractive, along with ideas for how it can be improved and expanded in the future by a new owner.

- ✔ **It emphasizes the attractiveness of your business, but it doesn't ignore weaknesses.** It shows how shortcomings can be addressed and turned around.

- ✔ **It provides a good overview of what your business is and how it works, but it doesn't try to tell everything a buyer will ever want to know about your business.**

- ✔ **It presents earnings and asking price information without disclosing complete financial information.** Think of it as a summary that gives buyers enough information to decide whether they want to take the next step.

The selling memorandum features facts about your business that are presented in a favorable light — you are trying to sell your business, after all — but every piece of information must be true and verifiable. The buyer will carefully check the facts during due diligence, and you'll likely need to warrant the accuracy of the information you provide.

After compiling the facts of your business and seeing your successes all detailed in a single document, you may decide the advantages of your business are greater than the ones you projected when you arrived at the earnings multiple used in your pricing determination. If you think that may be the case, go to Chapter 6 to figure out how to adjust your asking price. Remember, this isn't a time to start over-pricing, because a business priced too high will scare buyers away. If your advantages clearly justify a higher multiple of earnings, though, now's the time to make the adjustment, because your price is likely to come down during buyer-seller negotiations (but it almost never goes up from the number presented in your selling memorandum).

Conversely, as you describe how a new owner can address any deficiencies in your business, you may decide to practice what you're preaching — to implement the changes and turn weaknesses to strengths on your own before announcing that your business is for sale. The alternative is to account for weaknesses by setting a lower sale price, risking that the price adjustment may not be compelling enough to offset the risks your business weaknesses represent.

The basic blueprint

Selling memorandum booklets differ from business to business, varying by length and content depending on the size and complexity of the business being sold and the type of buyer being courted. This section gives you a run-down of all the sections that comprise your selling memorandum so you have a global view of the memorandum's potential contents. One quick note: You need to include a table of contents so readers can quickly reach the infor-mation they're seeking only if your selling memorandum runs longer than four pages (not counting the appendix). The summary is also optional, but because it's a bit more in-depth than the table of contents, I briefly cover it in the next section.

Figure 8-1 (available on the CD-ROM as Form 8-1) provides a checklist of the possible content you can include in a selling memorandum. Notice that most of the sections are necessary for all buyers to include. The variable is how much detail you need to include. Under each section heading, look at the notes included in parentheses for advice regarding whether the section is nec-essary or optional in your selling memorandum.

The summary

After you create your selling memorandum, you may find that you need to create a summary of the memorandum to give buyers an at-a-glance overview of your sale offering. Your selling memorandum summary serves three purposes:

✔ If your business is easy to explain and likely to sell at a price under $200,000, the summary may be all you need to share with prospects to get the sale process started. Flip ahead to the "Summary of business and offer" section, later in this chapter, for guidance.

✔ If your selling memorandum is longer than ten pages (not counting the appendix), include a summary at the beginning to give readers a quick overview of the memorandum contents.

✔ The selling memorandum summary is especially useful as a first response to ad inquiries, because it allows you to provide a rapid response without revealing all the details of your business offering before you have time to learn more about the prospective buyer's inter-est level and ability to buy your business.

SELLING MEMORANDUM CHECKLIST	
Table of Contents *(Sellers with documents longer than 4 pages not including appendix)*	
Summary of Business and Offer *(Sellers with documents longer than 10 pages)*	
Business Description *(All Sellers)* ☐ Business history, ownership, and structure *(Necessary)* ☐ Overview of sales and earnings *(Necessary)* ☐ Overview of product/service and growth trend *(Necessary)* ☐ Key strengths and attributes *(Necessary)* ☐ Reason for sale *(Necessary)*	☐
Location *(All Sellers)* ☐ Geographic location *(Necessary)* ☐ Building description and address *(Necessary)* ☐ Lease information (Include if business success is reliant on building and location)	☐
Operations *(All Sellers)* ☐ Operating hours and seasonal information *(Necessary)* ☐ Major equipment and furnishings *(Necessary)* ☐ Inventory *(Include if business is selling inventory)* ☐ Production or work processes *(Include if production or distribution is a unique attribute)* ☐ Staffing overview, organization chart, information on staffing policies *(Include if business has more than a few employees)* ☐ Workforce trends and issues (Include if business has more than a few employees	☐
Product or Service *(All Sellers)* ☐ Description of product or service *(Necessary)* ☐ Sales, growth trends, and projections *(Necessary)* ☐ Product/service opportunities *(Include if business faces good growth opportunities)*	☐
Market Environment *(All Sellers)* ☐ Industry information, including demand and growth trends *(Include if industry growth is a strength; or if industry is facing challenges that your business has or is prepared to address)* ☐ Geographic market description and growth trends *(Include if business serves a specific geographic area)* ☐ Customer profile and purchase patterns *(Necessary)* ☐ Description of marketing approach *(Necessary)* ☐ Competition, including major competitors and competitive trends *(Include especially if competition is stiff and likely to concern buyers)*	☐
Future Plans and Projections *(All Sellers of businesses with Unresolved Weaknesses or Not-Yet-Addressed Opportunities)* ☐ Near-term business development goals and plans ☐ Market expansion potential and development plans	☐
Financial Information *(All Sellers)* ☐ Accounting method *(Necessary)* ☐ Summary of recent earnings and near-term forecasts *(Necessary)*	☐

(continued)

Offering and Price Terms *(All Sellers)*
☐ Asking price and pricing approach *(Necessary)*
☐ Information on terms *(Necessary)*
☐ Contents of sale *(Necessary)*
☐ Buyer qualifications *(Include if owner must possess professional expertise or meet certain requirements such as financial or loan qualifications)*
☐ Seller's transition plan, including non-compete agreement *(Include especially if seller is key driving force in the business)*
☐

Appendix *(All Sellers)*
☐ Seller's discretionary earnings statement *(Necessary)*
☐ Asset list *(Necessary)*
☐ Seller's disclosure statement *(Necessary)*
☐ Market area information *(Include if buyer is likely to come from outside the area where business is located)*
☐ Photos of business location and equipment *(Include so long as photos don't reveal business identity)*
☐ Marketing materials *(Include if marketing materials represent business well)*
☐ Other _____
☐

Figure 8-1a:
Use this outline as your selling memorandum checklist.

The CD-ROM has a template that guides you as you write the whole memorandum (see the next section for details). The form in Figure 8-2 (Form 8-2 on the CD-ROM) gives you a checklist to follow as you prepare the summary.

SELLING MEMORANDUM SUMMARY CHECKLIST	
☐ **Business's Name** ☐ **Owner's Name** ☐ **Contact Information**	☐
Business Description ☐ Introduction ☐ Business overview including type of business, legal structure, date founded, short history, sales and earnings ☐ Geographic area and business location	☐
Outstanding Features ☐ Strengths ☐ Market position ☐ Financial performance	☐
Asking Price and Information on Terms ☐ Asking price ☐ Information on terms, including cash required at closing and financing information ☐ Contents of sale (business entity or assets, asset value, inventory value, other inclusions or exclusions) ☐ Summary of necessary buyer qualifications	☐
☐ **Reason for Sale**	☐

Figure 8-2:
Checklist for a selling memorandum summary.

Tips for Making a Good First Impression

In some ways, the selling memorandum is to your business sale what an ad or brochure is to your product sale. It's completely factual (it has to be, because you have to warrant its accuracy, and it will become the basis for the legal agreements that will close your sale), but it also describes your business offering in a way that makes prospective buyers want to visit your business and meet you personally — before anyone else snaps the opportunity away. Done correctly, your selling memorandum will pre-sell your business. Here are some tips to follow:

✔ **Pay attention to aesthetics.** If you use your selling memorandum summary as your first response to buyer prospects, be sure it's packaged to make a good and professional first impression for your business. The look of your selling memorandum makes a quality statement about your business to prospective buyers. Make even the shortest selling memorandum look distinguished and professional by printing the entire document using a high-quality laser printer and good paper. If you have stationery, print your selling memorandum cover on your letterhead and use matching blank sheets for the rest of your document. Print the summary on your business letterhead and second sheet (or on high-quality paper) and enclose it in a nice-looking folder. Just because it's a short document doesn't mean you should neglect its appearance.

If your business has pocketed presentation folders with your name and logo printed on them, use them for this presentation. If not, consider attaching a copy of your overview to a copy of your best-looking marketing material — a brochure or menu, for example, along with your business card and a short, personally signed cover letter. Chapter 10 includes information on what to include in your initial and follow-up communications.

✔ **Make sure your document is professionally written.** If you're not a writer (or typist or proofreader), then get help in writing your selling memorandum. If you're working with a business broker, he or she will either help you prepare it or will do it for you. Even if you're selling your business on your own, you may be able to get a broker's help preparing your selling memorandum. Some brokers will prepare it for a fee, usually somewhere between $1,500 and $2,500. They may even agree to credit this document preparation fee against the sale commission should you change your mind later and decide to list with a broker after all. Especially if you're strapped for time or light on writing and presentation skills, the investment is well worthwhile. Not all brokers offer this help, but it can't hurt to contact a local broker and ask. Just remember to request confidentiality from the broker before disclosing your sale plans.

✔ **Use widely understood language,** avoiding jargon and insider business language. The exception is technical terminology. If you need to use technical terms to explain your business and its products, and if a buyer needs to be familiar with the terms to be successful at your business, use the terminology, though sparingly and with descriptions.

✔ **Be honest and accurate.** Your selling memorandum isn't a formal legal document, but prospective buyers will view it as a statement of facts, so be sure the information it contains is completely accurate. Have your accountant review all information that deals with finances, and be sure your attorney reviews the full document before it goes to a prospective buyer.

The statements and data in your selling memorandum typically get incorporated into the legal documents of your purchase/sale agreement, so take great care not to make false, inaccurate, or overly optimistic statements that may be misleading to the prospective buyer.

✔ **Don't reveal confidences.** Only one prospect will end up buying your business, and that buyer won't want the others to have sensitive inside information. Also, in spite of your best efforts to maintain confidentiality, you have to assume that people other than the ones you hand the document to will see your selling memorandum. Don't tell trade secrets, confidential pricing information, information on client contracts, customer names or details, or other information that you or the new owner wouldn't want divulged to competitors or others. Instead, explain customers, staff, suppliers, distributors, and business partners in general terms that describe the nature and strength of your organization without naming names or sharing confidential details.

✔ **Don't turn your selling memorandum into a sales pitch.** Present facts and strengths and let prospects draw their own positive conclusions. When you present forecasts, be realistic and steer clear of guarantees or false claims. Highlight the features of your business that give it a unique advantage in its competitive marketplace, then let sales and earnings charts speak for themselves — an approach that's far more powerful than hard-sell language.

✔ **Number each selling memorandum you produce.** Repeat the number on every page of your book and keep track of which prospect was given which numbered edition. Your effort will alert buyers that you're serious about maintaining the confidentiality of the document contents.

Compiling the Contents for Your Selling Memorandum

What follows is a description of each portion of the selling memorandum, along with some advice on what to include and what not to include, depending on the size and nature of your business. Your selling memorandum officially begins with the business description. The table of contents and summary introduction precedes it, if your document is long enough to need those parts, but this is where your memorandum officially begins.

Form 8-3 on the CD-ROM includes a template to work from as you assemble your document. The template follows the time-tested selling memorandum structure used by Sunbelt in hundreds of U.S. and dozens of international business brokerage offices. To customize the template, simply delete sections that aren't relevant to your business, insert your own business facts and descriptions at the prompts, and update the table of contents when you make changes to the template (I provide instructions for updating the table of contents in the corresponding section that follows).

If the creation of a selling memorandum still feels overwhelming, even with the advice in this chapter and on Form 8-3, consider asking a business broker to prepare the document for you — either as a normal part of a listing agreement, or for a fee if you're selling your business on your own.

Cover

The cover of your selling memorandum makes the first impression for your business sale offering, so be sure it's printed on a good-quality printer on your stationery or other high-quality paper. Here's what to include on the cover:

- ✔ **Your business name.** If you use stationery, you don't need to print your business name on your cover, because your name and logo, if you have one, are already printed on your letterhead. If you print your cover on paper other than your stationery, feature your name in the logotype and logo used in your business marketing materials.

- ✔ **The title of your document.** Present the title of your document in large type, along with the word "Confidential." For example: CONFIDENTIAL SELLING MEMORANDUM, or CONFIDENTIAL BUSINESS OFFERING, or whatever other name you use for the document.

✔ **Contact information.** If a broker is presenting your business, this part is easy. The broker will add a box to your cover sheet that says something like, "Offered by Sunbelt of Anytown," followed by the broker's phone number, e-mail address, and business logotype and logo.

If you're presenting your business for sale directly, this part of the cover preparation gets a little tricky. If you use your letterhead for your cover sheet, it already includes your business contact information. However, for confidentiality reasons, you probably don't want prospects calling your business phone number, unless you're the one who always answers the phone. So you may want to add a box that says, "To discuss further, please send a confidential e-mail to `bobjones@confidential address.com`," using your personal e-mail address or a separate e-mail address you establish for sales inquiry purposes. Don't use your business e-mail address because mail to that address may be seen by others in your business. If you'd rather receive inquiries by phone, your instructions may read, "To discuss further, please place confidential calls directly to Bob Jones at 555-555-5555." If the number you provide on your selling memorandum cover is your cellphone number, be sure you answer the phone with a businesslike greeting, and record an appropriate message in case the buyer's call reaches your voice mail.

Table of contents

If you use the selling memorandum template in Form 8-3 on the CD-ROM, a table of contents is already included. You need to update it, however, as you add, delete, or retitle sections. If your memorandum is very short and doesn't need a table of contents, delete it by clicking your mouse at the beginning of the table of contents title, dragging through to the end of the contents section, and then hitting the delete key. To update the table of contents after you complete your document, follow these steps:

Macintosh:

1. **Press the *control* key and click your cursor in the left margin of the first page of the table of contents. A menu will appear.**

2. **In the menu, select *update field* and a dialog box will open.**

3. **In the dialog box, select *update entire table*, which will update both the page numbers and any changes you've made to headings. Click *OK*.**

Windows:

1. **Right click the cursor in the first page of the table of contents and select *update field*. A dialog box will open.**

2. **In the dialog box, select *update entire table*, which will update both the page numbers and any changes you've made to headings. Click *OK*.**

Summary of business and offer

Before you create a summary, first determine whether you need one (see the section earlier in this chapter called "The summary"). Then follow whichever of the following bullets applies to you:

✔ **If you include the summary as an addition to a full-blown selling memorandum,** first write the rest of the memorandum (following the Form 8-3 template on the CD-ROM and the guidance throughout this chapter), and then select a few key sentences from each part to create your summary (Form 8-3 includes a template for the summary as well).

✔ **If your complete selling memorandum doesn't require a summary,** just select and delete this section from the Form 8-3 template.

Business description

Because this is the first official page of your selling memorandum, begin by identifying your business, street address, and asking price. For example:

THE GREATEST BUSINESS

123 Ideal Street

Anywhere, USA 00000

Price: $500,000, including assets and inventory

Now describe your business, following the time-tested format of *who, what, where, when, why,* and *how.* A prospect wants to know who you are, what kind of business you run, where it's located, and why you're selling. Don't make a buyer search for these key facts — tell the buyer early, and if the facts match with the buyer's interests, the sale process will be off and running. Here's some specific guidance outlining what you need to include in the business description:

✔ **One-sentence introduction:** Begin this section with a single statement that defines and explains your business. Chapter 7 helps you whittle your description down to a 20-word ad, and you can use that statement here.

If your memorandum is long enough to include a summary, you can use the same exact introductory statement in both your summary (described in the previous section) and in this section.

✔ **Business history, ownership, and structure:** In this section, tell when your business was founded and by whom, list its current ownership and business structure (sole proprietorship, LLC, partnership, C corporation, or S corporation), and include a positive summary of its current condition.

✔ **Overview of sales and earnings:** This is what a buyer *really* wants to know. Give an indication of whether your business is growing and how much it earns. Make a simple, straightforward statement such as, "Business has grown at an average rate of X percent over the past ten years, with most recent annual sales of $630,000 and net profit (seller's discretionary earnings, as reflected in Exhibit A) of approximately $158,000."

✔ **Key strengths and attributes:** Highlight your company's strengths, including the staff's skills; work environment and hours; location and setting; unique and easily transferred processes; strong, growing, and loyal customer base; and well-regarded name and reputation.

✔ **Reason for sale:** State your reason for selling and how long you'll remain available to assist in the business transition. This can be the same exact statement as the one in the preceding "The summary" section.

Location

This section contains information describing your regional setting, business location, and building and lease:

✔ **Geographic setting:** Geographic information is essential to include if your buyer is likely to live outside your market area, but it's important in all sale offerings because you can't be sure where your buyer will come from. Use this section to introduce your geographic setting to provide a regional profile and highlights of the livability, recreation, employment advantages, business environment, and growth trends of your region, and — if your geographic setting is home to your business *and* where your customers come from — to present an overview of the local population in terms of income, education levels, and population growth rates.

Your local chamber of commerce and economic development offices likely have materials that describe regional population profiles and growth trends, educational opportunities, seasonal visitor counts, and other descriptions of your market area. Another good resource is the U.S. Census Bureau. Go to www.census.gov/, type the name of your city and state into the search box, and you'll reach pages of information containing population, business, and geographic highlights.

✔ **Business location:** Highlight the advantages of the physical location of your office, shop, restaurant, or retail setting, including information about the town or suburb in which you're located, the business or residential area that surrounds your location, growth patterns, major access roads and ease of access, and other factors that contribute to the attractiveness of your location.

✔ **Building and lease information:** Describe your business building, including square footage and building attributes such as décor, recent leasehold improvements, access, signage, building services, group meeting rooms, parking, and other building strong points. Include building photos in the selling memorandum appendix, and in this section refer readers to the appendix photos. Also in this section, explain your monthly or annual rent or other fees.

Most important — especially if your business success is reliant on your building and location — describe the terms of your lease. Explain your lease initiation and termination dates, renewal option, rate escalation clause, and any security deposits or fees that will become the responsibility of the new owner.

Be aware that many restaurant buyers won't even consider a business unless the lease for its location is secure for at least the next five years, and most lenders will require a lease term of at least five years. If necessary, work with your building owner to renegotiate your lease before offering your business for sale.

Operations

This is where you tell a buyer how your business runs. This is a meaty part of your selling memorandum and a part that benefits from photos, which you can include in your selling memorandum appendix and refer to in this part. Begin with a sentence or two that defines what your business does, how it does it, and how it generates revenue. For example: "A restaurant with a vibrant and year-round lunch, dinner, and evening business, group meeting rooms that host up to 100 guests, and a catering division that serves more than 300 remote events annually." Then, break this part into the following sections:

✔ **Operating hours and seasonality:** This section is a straightforward statement of the days and hours your business is open and the seasons or times of year when it does the bulk of its business. Figure 8-3 shows a chart that's included in Form 8-3 that you can use in this section.

Figure 8-3:
This chart helps you present seasonality of business sales.

Annual Sales by Season 2007			
Jan–March	**April–June**	**July–Sept**	**Oct–Dec**
XX%	XX%	XX%	XX%

✔ **Major equipment and furnishings:** In this section, include a paragraph or two that describes the furnishings, fixtures, and equipment your business owns, including the lump sum fair market value of the assets included in the sale. For an itemization, refer readers to the asset listing that you include in the appendix.

✔ **Inventory:** If your business has an inventory, describe the approximate value of inventory to be included in the sale and how it's priced (for example, "at seller's cost"). Because inventory fluctuates until the date of sale closing, state that "A detailed accounting of inventory items will be provided during the buyer's due diligence."

✔ **Production or work processes:** Summarize how your business creates and distributes its product or service.

- If your production process is unique or complicated, tell whether a production manual or outline exists or how you otherwise plan to transition the process management to the new owner.

- Detail how the business uses distributors or wholesalers and the transferability of those relationships.

- Describe other unique and advantageous supplier relationships and strategic alliances.

- Note whether your business has an operations manual (outlined in Chapter 7) that will help the new owner take over management of policies and procedures.

✔ **Staffing:** A buyer wants to know how your business is organized, managed, and staffed. If your company has a large staff or a lot of departments and managers, you may include an organization chart in this section. If not, you should at least describe how your organization is structured and managed, and if you're the main force in the business, explain how easy it will be for a new owner to step in and assume the position you're vacating.

If you have staff, include the following information:

- Introduction of your key managers or employees — if not by names, then at least by titles, along with a description of their responsibilities, expertise, and length of service with your business.

- An employee list, including each one's title, salary, and year hired, so a buyer can get a sense of the payroll, experience, and loyalty of your team. Figure 8-4 shows a chart that's included in Form 8-3 that you can use in this section.

Employee Information				
Employee	**Title**	**Part-Time (PT) / Full-Time (FT)**	**Annual Wage**	**Years of Service**
Owner				
Employee #1				
Employee #2				
Employee #3				
Employee #4				
Employee #5				

Figure 8-4:
This chart helps you describe your staff.

✔ **Workforce trends and issues:** Summarize any workforce issues that will affect a new buyer, including

- Employee benefits package
- Employee recruitment, training, retention, and reward programs
- Current or imminent labor union problems
- Employee contracts
- * Employee litigation cases

If your employment policies are outlined in a manual, explain that the manual will be available during the due diligence process.

Product or service

In this section of your selling memorandum, describe the following information:

✔ What product or service your business sells.

✔ What makes your product or service unique and valuable to customers.

✔ A breakdown of how sales fall into product categories, if they do, and how each category contributes to total sales.

For example, Figure 8-5 illustrates how a landscaping business shows sales by business or corporate clients, residential contract clients, residential on-demand services, and developer model-home contract clients. If your business realizes sales from multiple product lines or client types, display your information in a similar chart, using the sample included in the Form 8-3 template on the CD-ROM.

TIP

✔ If your business has experienced problems with certain product lines, or if it has recently introduced products or services that have boosted sales or opportunities, include a "product/service opportunities" section to point out how you're working to address problems or build on strengths.

Figure 8-5:
This chart helps you present product lines, sales, and growth.

Annual Sales by Season 2007		
Revenue Stream	**% of Past Year Annual Sales**	**% Change from Previous Year**
Business/corporate landscaping contracts	27%	+7%
Developer model-home landscaping contracts	18%	−12%
Residential yard contracts	38%	+12%
Residential on-demand landscaping services	17%	+6%

Market environment

REMEMBER

Buyers are willing to pay most for businesses with good opportunity and low risk. Because your market provides your business with its opportunities, this section of your selling memorandum will get special buyer attention. The upcoming sections tell what to cover.

Industry information including demand and growth trends

This section of your selling memorandum is important if your industry is strong and growing, in which case it's an attractive aspect of your business, or if it has problems, in which case you need to show how your business is poised to address the issues your industry faces.

To fill out this section, head to Chapter 2 for advice on how to assess your industry's condition and its growth trends. Then compile a short overview of your industry situation to include in your selling memorandum. You should include the following information:

✔ The size of your industry

✔ Current market demand for your industry's offerings

✔ How your business has adapted to reflect industry changes

✔ How your business is positioned to compete well in your industry

✔ How your business is configured to address challenges your industry faces

Geographic market description and growth trends

If your business serves a specific geographic area, describe how the customer base within your market area is growing or changing and how your business will benefit as a result. Show population statistics and trends for the past three years, and show growth of the portion of the market served by your business — for example, growth of business start-ups, or growth of the population aged 55+, or growth of the population with interests in the products your business offers, and so on.

If your market is shrinking, describe how your business has begun or is prepared to open new and promising market areas, or how it can appeal to new groups within your current market area to build sales. Note that a marketing plan is available for review at a later stage in the purchase process.

Customer profile and purchase patterns

In your selling memorandum, include a profile of your typical customer and the customer's buying pattern:

- ✔ **If your business serves individual customers or consumers,** describe your typical customer in terms of gender, age, education level, household information, income, and ethnic and language information. Also describe how customers decide to buy products like the ones you sell, whether they buy on impulse or after careful consideration, how they pay (cash, charge, buy on credit), and their price- and quality-consciousness. The checklist in Figure 8-6, available as Form 8-4 on the CD-ROM, will help you arrive at a customer description. You may have to rely on best-guess information in some areas, and in other areas you may not be able to come up with an answer. Review the full checklist, though, because even if you can complete it only in part it will help you come up with your customer description.

- ✔ **If your business serves business clients,** describe the size and industry of businesses you serve and the reasons businesses buy from you. Also describe how purchase decisions are made, whether your company is the exclusive provider of your kind of products or services to your clients, and whether your relationships are protected by signed contracts (use the checklist in Figure 8-7, which is available as Form 8-5 on the CD-ROM).

CUSTOMER PROFILE
GEOGRAPHY Where are your customers? Do they live or work in specific neighborhoods, regions, states, or countries?
DEMOGRAPHY **Gender** __% Male __% Female **Age** __% Children __ % Teens __% 20–30 __% 31–40 __% 41–50__% 51–64 __% 65+ **Education** __% Current students __% High school diploma __% University degree __% Post-graduate **Household Information** Are customers predominantly single, married, divorced, widowed? Are they parents with children still at home, couples without children at home, grandparents, and so on? Do they rent or own their homes? What kinds of homes do they live in? **Income** What income category do most customers fall under? What are their professions: Are they retired, self-employed, professionals, students, and so on? **Ethnic Information** Is your customer base of a specific nationality? What languages do they speak?
BEHAVIORAL PATTERNS **Interests** What are the recreational interests of your customers? What magazines do they read, programs do they watch, music do they listen to? Do they use the Internet? **Beliefs** Do your customers participate in particular groups, organizations, churches, political parties, or other associations?

BUYING PATTERNS

Do your customers decide to purchase on their own or upon the advice of others, and whom?

Do they buy on impulse or after careful consideration?

Do they pay cash, charge, or buy on payment plans?

Would you say they're more price-conscious or status-conscious?

Do they put greater value on quality or service than on price?

Figure 8-6a:
Creating a
customer
profile.

BUSINESS CLIENT PROFILE

Types of Businesses Served

Industry: _____

Size/Annual sales: _____ Size/# Employees _____

Location: _____

Are your clients in industries that are growing, holding steady, or declining?

Other typical characteristics:

Client Purchase Preferences

What major benefits do clients receive from your business?

What qualities of your business do clients value?

Client Purchase Patterns

Are purchase decisions made by owners, operations managers, or marketing people?

Do purchases require several levels of approval?

Are purchases made through a central office?

Do clients work exclusively with your business or do they use multiple suppliers for products like yours?

Do clients sign contracts with your business?

Figure 8-7:
Creating a
business cli-
ent profile.

Description of marketing approach

Tell how your company markets itself, including

- Whether your business uses mass media advertising, Internet advertising, one-to-one (direct mail, phone, and e-mail) marketing, or networking to communicate its marketing message, and the emphasis or weight you place on each communication approach

- A list of the organizations in which your business participates to develop market awareness and contacts

- Information on your Internet presence, including your Web address, how you use the site, and site traffic information

If your business invests heavily in marketing, mention that a complete marketing plan and budget is available for review during the due diligence process.

Competition including major competitors and competitive trends

First things first: Don't even think of saying that your business has no competition. Every business has competition, and your prospective buyers want to know what kind of frying pan they're about to jump into.

- Describe your market-area competitors, which are the nearby businesses that customers consider as alternatives when buying products or services like the ones you sell. For each competitor, list the business name, location, competitive attributes, competitive weaknesses, and, if possible, how your business excels.

- Describe indirect competitors such as online sites that compete for your customers' business.

- If you know that new major competition is about to come on line, don't bury the fact. Your buyer will learn the truth soon enough, and when that moment comes, your credibility could go down the drain if you haven't been candid. Be frank about competition heating up, but offset the information with your plan on how best to respond.

End this section with a summary of how your business is positioned with a clear point of difference that helps it win customers and excel in your competitive environment. Follow this example: "In our competitive environment, Abacus Accounting is the only regional accounting firm that caters exclusively to small businesses, whose owners choose our service because of our experienced understanding of their needs and our ability to link them to a network of small businesses within our clientele."

Future plans and projections

Include a list of actions you believe can propel further growth, or, if growth is weak, recommend actions that can reverse declines. To create this list, ask yourself this key question: If you had more time and money, what would you do to improve your business?

You don't have to highlight weaknesses, but you do need to honestly represent the condition of your business. This is the place in your selling memorandum where you can present areas of your business that would benefit from improvement and expansion, along with preliminary plans for how current business deficiencies or opportunities could be addressed. Also, detail pending legal, financial, or regulatory issues, along with how you plan to deal with them.

Be aware that you'll likely have to "represent and warranty" the information in your selling memorandum, so honesty isn't just a good policy, but a requirement.

Financial information

You should save the full set of your financial statements (including year-to-date statements and statements for the past three years) to share after you have a letter of intent and have entered the buyer's homework process called *due diligence*, but you need to share an overview of your finances in your selling memorandum. Otherwise, the buyer won't know what kind of money your business generates, whether your price is in the ballpark, or whether your company's size matches the buyer's objectives and abilities. For that reason, include your statement of seller's discretionary earnings in your selling memorandum.

In the financial section of your selling memorandum, plan to provide an overview of the information contained in the memorandum appendix, including the following:

- **Accounting method.** Tell whether
  - Your books are kept on a cash or accrual method (see Chapter 5 if those terms sound foreign)
  - Your statements follow the calendar or a different fiscal year
  - Your books are kept in-house or by a bookkeeping or accounting firm
  - Your books are reviewed or audited periodically by an independent CPA

✔ **Financial overview.** Provide buyers with a summary of your sales, earnings, and growth trends by including the following:

- The chart from Form 2-1 on the CD-ROM, which presents your business sales and profit trends for the past three years.

- The chart from Form 5-5 on the CD-ROM, which displays the three-year average growth of sales and earnings.

- State that a statement of seller's discretionary earnings is included in the appendix to present recasted income statement results in order to reflect the actual cash flow of your business.

- State that full financial records for a specified number of recent past years will be provided during the buyer's due diligence, at which time the owner and the business accountant will be available to explain adjustments and provide supporting documentation.

Price and terms

This is a just-the-facts section that every buyer wants to see. Include the following information, which should be exactly the same as the pricing information in your selling memorandum summary (if your document includes one):

✔ **Asking price.** For example, "[Name of business] is a California Subchapter S Corporation with all shares held by the owner. Asking price is $575,000."

✔ **Terms.** Include this section if you're offering seller financing, for instance, "Seller requests $275,000 cash at closing and the balance financed by SBA note or by seller financing to qualified buyer at 7 percent over 5 years."

✔ **Contents of sale.** For example, "Business sale includes assets. Furnishings, fixtures, and equipment have a fair market value of $275,000, detailed in the appendix. Inventory will be included at owner's cost with schedule available during due diligence."

✔ **Buyer qualifications.** For instance, you can stipulate that the buyer must qualify for SBA financing.

✔ **Business transition plan.** Include information on the amount of time and training included in the selling price to provide for a smooth transition of the business to the new owner, and information on whether you'll be available for further assistance at a fee, if required.

✔ **Non-compete agreement.** This is the part where you state that you agree not to compete with the buyer for a certain period of time and within a certain market area. The template in Form 8-3 includes a statement you can customize for your selling agreement. The actual non-compete agreement is a legal document that's prepared as part of the sale process.

✔ **Seller's disclosure statement.** Your selling memorandum should end by noting that a detailed disclosure statement regarding the business and the information presented in the memorandum is included in the appendix.

In this final section, convey your attempt to be accurate by including a statement such as, "All information herein has been prepared by the seller, and to the best of the seller's knowledge, it is accurate."

Appendix

The appendix includes the backup information that supports your selling memorandum. The appendix will always include your financial data, the assets being sold, and the seller's disclosure statement. Other appendix exhibits depend on your sale offering and preferences. This information should be bound into the back of your selling book. It requires no description other than section titles such as Exhibit A, Exhibit B, and so forth.

Either number the contents of your Appendix with lower-case Roman numerals — i, ii, iii, iv, v, and so on — or arrange the contents behind labeled tabbed divider sheets for easy access.

Include the following information:

✔ **Financial data.** Include your statement of seller's discretionary earnings (see Form 5-3 on the CD-ROM), as well as other financial statements that you, your broker, and your accountant feel are necessary to convey your financial condition.

✔ **Assets.** Include your asset list and values, as assembled in Form 6-1 on the CD-ROM, reviewed for accuracy by your accountant.

✔ **Seller's disclosure statement.** Ask your broker or attorney to help you compile and complete a seller's disclosure statement that provides prospective buyers with an accurate assessment of your business condition, all licenses and regulations that apply to your business, and all pending legal issues or considerations. Your buyer will conduct a complete inspection of your business during due diligence, but this form provides answers to preliminary questions.

✔ **Market area information.** Resident, business, and regional growth profiles and publicly available market data and materials.

✔ **Photos of business location and equipment.** Include captioned photos of your business, such as the building's exterior and interior, major work areas and equipment, and other photos that provide a sense of your business's setting to prospective buyers. Take these photos with a digital camera so they'll also be available for use in online business-for-sale postings.

✔ **Marketing materials.** End your appendix with samples of marketing materials that best represent your business and its offerings. Consider including one or several samples, such as brochures, menus, product sell sheets, packaging samples, or other relevant materials.

Trading Your Selling Memorandum for a Confidentiality Agreement

Letting the word leak out that your business is for sale is dangerous on both the home front, where your sale plans may cause employee and customer concerns or defections, and the marketing front, where competing businesses may use your sale news against you as they talk with your clients or suppliers.

For those reasons, never, ever share your selling memorandum with anyone who hasn't signed a confidentiality agreement (other than your attorney, who's legally bound to confidentiality). For everyone else, get a pledge of secrecy before sharing your sale offering information. Don't feel awkward about requiring a confidentiality agreement before releasing your information. Confidentiality agreements — also called non-disclosure agreements — are routine in the business world, and your request won't surprise a good buyer prospect.

You have a few options when creating this agreement: You can use a sample that your broker (if you have one) gives you, purchase one from a legal form shop or online site, or follow the very simple confidentiality agreement sample for a small business, provided by Sunbelt, included on the CD-ROM as Form 8-6. Regardless of where you get the form, make sure it includes the following information:

✔ **A clause that ensures mutual confidentiality,** which means that the non-disclosure agreement goes both ways:

- The prospective buyer will keep confidential the fact that your business is for sale, as well as any facts you provide about your business and offer

- You'll keep confidential the fact that the buyer is interested in your business, as well as any facts the buyer provides regarding his or her experience and financial capability

> ✔ **An expiration date for the confidentiality agreement,** usually no less than two years into the future so that you don't have to remain mum forever.

A confidentiality or non-disclosure agreement is a legal document, so get your attorney's input before finalizing the form.

Before you even share the confidentiality agreement (and, subsequently, the selling memorandum), determine the qualifications of the person inquiring about your business to assess whether the person is seriously interested and possesses the personal expertise and financial capability to buy and run your business. (Chapter 10 guides you through the process of prescreening respondents to your business-for-sale ads. If you use a broker, the broker will handle this task for you.)

When your selling memorandum and confidentiality agreement are ready, you're set to launch and navigate the active phase of the process. Turn to Chapter 9 as you put your sale announcement and buyer prospecting efforts into motion.

Forms on the CD-ROM

Form 8-1	**Selling Memorandum Outline Checklist**	An outline of the contents of a selling memorandum that you can use as a checklist as you customize your document to reflect the size and nature of your business
Form 8-2	**Selling Memorandum Summary Checklist**	An outline of a summary document that you can use both as an introduction to your longer selling memorandum and as an interim response to buyer prospects whom you want to further prescreen before sharing your complete selling memorandum and sensitive business facts
Form 8-3	**Selling Memorandum Template**	A template you can work from as you customize the outline and create the contents of the selling memorandum you'll present to prospective buyers
Form 8-4	**Customer Profile Checklist**	A form for describing customers of a consumer-oriented business
Form 8-5	**Business Client Profile Checklist**	A form for describing clients of a business-to-business company
Form 8-6	**Sample Confidentiality Agreement**	An example of a simple confidentiality agreement for a small business sale transaction, provided by Sunbelt

Part III
Launching and Navigating the Sale Process

The 5th Wave   By Rich Tennant

"Potential buyers of the company are coming through today. Tell everyone to look sharp and put out a few bowls of potpourri here and there."

In this part . . .

Snap on your seatbelt — your ride to the sale finish line starts here.

The chapters in this part help you steer the course from the moment you announce that your business is for sale to the arrival of a purchase offer.

Chapter 9 helps you plan your announcement and advertising strategy, write and place ads, and tap into the ever-growing strength of Internet business-for-sale sites. Chapter 10 guides the process of prescreening inquiries, sharing confidential information, and qualifying prospective buyers. Chapter 11 takes you through the final leg of the buyer-development marathon as you receive, evaluate, and accept a buyer offer.

Part III ends with the arrival of a letter of intent to buy your business. Chill the champagne!

Chapter 9

Planning and Launching Your Advertising Strategy

In This Chapter
▶ Creating your advertising strategy by identifying likely buyers
▶ Considering your advertising options
▶ Writing ads that get buyers' attention
▶ Responding to buyers' inquiries and refining your ads

*N*o one will tell you to post a *For Sale* sign in your business window, but other than that one taboo, your choices for letting buyers know your business is available run the gamut. The easiest way to announce your sale is by listing your business with a broker, but you can certainly proceed without one. If you intend to follow the for-sale-by-owner (FSBO) route, then this chapter is definitely for you. The following pages outline steps to take and examples to follow as you work to implement the right marketing strategy, write the right ads, advertise in the right places, and follow up with the right prospects. In other words, this chapter helps you simplify the job of offering your business for sale.

Considering Your Buyer Before Deciding Where to Advertise

In terms of advertising, selling a business is like selling anything else: You have to place your ads where your prospects are likely to look. In other words, fish where the fish are. To effectively target your efforts, you need to consider three things about your buyer: a basic description of who you think is likely to buy your business, what the buyer is looking for, and how the buyer is likely to look for businesses for sale.

Franchisee? Confer with your franchisor

If you're selling a franchise, you have less flexibility than the independent business owner, but you still have options. If your franchise permits you to sell to an outsider, request buyer referrals from your franchisor before you begin advertising that your franchise is for sale. Your franchisor may have a list of interested buyers to tell you about. If you're out of luck with franchisor referrals, move on to online postings. You'll come across many Web sites dedicated specifically to franchise sales, but as you look closely you'll see that they deal exclusively with *new franchise* sales. Franchise resales are offered online through the same sites that offer all other businesses for sale. *Remember:* Whether you seek a buyer through a broker or on your own, realize that you'll probably need to have your buyer, who will become a franchisee, approved by the franchisor. See Chapter 1 for more information specifically geared toward franchisees.

As you plan your marketing approach, keep your buyer profile in mind at all times. Even though classified and online ads may be dirt-cheap compared to other forms of advertising, the dollars still add up, so you want to be sure your advertising efforts are well-directed. Use the form in Figure 9-1 (Form 9-1 on the CD-ROM) to compile a description of the person you think just may buy your business. I take you through the process of filling out the form in the sections that follow.

Who's your buyer?

To figure out how to reach your buyer, start by creating a profile of the person you think will buy your business. By clearly defining who's likely to buy your business, you'll be in a better position to decide where to advertise and what to say in ads. Chapter 1 gives you a rundown of the most common types of buyers, but here I help you personalize your targeting efforts. To create your buyer profile, determine four things:

- ✔ Will your business buyer likely be an individual or a business?

- ✔ If the buyer is an individual, will that person likely have experience in your business arena and be looking for a business type that's specifically like yours? Or will the buyer be looking for a business in general — for instance, any one of a number of business types, so long as it fits the financial abilities and general interests of the buyer?

PROFILING YOUR LIKELY BUYER: CHECKLIST

Who is likely to want to buy your business? (Check all that apply.)

☐ An individual
☐ An investor or investor group
☐ Another business
☐ A buyer with specific interest in my business industry or arena
☐ A buyer with the specific education, licensing, or certification required to run my business
☐ A buyer who meets specific financial qualifications

What is your likely buyer looking for? (Check all that apply.)

☐ The buyer likely lives in the region where my business is located, or wants to live here, and therefore is shopping for businesses in this region
☐ The buyer is shopping for a business acquisition with no particular geographic emphasis
☐ The buyer is shopping for a business acquisition in no particular industry.

How is your buyer likely to search for business sale opportunities? (Check all that apply.)

☐ Online business-for-sale sites
☐ Industry-specific business-for-sale sites
☐ General business publications
☐ Industry-specific publications
☐ Local-market business brokers
☐ Industry-specific business brokers
☐ Local-market newspaper classified ads

DEVISING YOUR ADVERTISING APPROACH

How is your buyer likely to search for business sale opportunities? (Check all that apply.)

To reach the likely buyer of my business, I'll use the following advertising approaches:

☐ Online business-for-sale sites to reach computer-literate buyers or their advisors, regardless of regional or industry interest

☐ Industry-specific brokers, business-for-sale sites, and publications to reach buyers with specific interests in my industry

☐ General business publications to reach buyers with financial or professional backgrounds

☐ Local-market business brokers and local-market classified ads to reach buyers with specific interests in my market area

Figure 9-1:
A checklist and framework for defining how to reach your likely business buyer.

- ✔ Where does your buyer live? This isn't quite like *Where's Waldo?* but it's close. Online ads cast a very, very wide net, but if you decide to use print ads, you have to locate your buyer to know how best to reach that person. If your buyer is likely to be located in your hometown area or seeking to relocate there, local publications and brokers can help you get the word out. If your buyer is likely to read leading business and financial publications, you can place your ads in papers like the *Wall Street Journal*. Or if you know your region is experiencing an influx of residents from a major metropolitan area or a tech-savvy region, you can advertise in those locations.

- ✔ What qualifications, if any, does your buyer need? If your buyer needs a certain level of experience or a specific license or certification, you can advertise in journals and magazines — or even send direct mailers — to reach individuals with the required background. Also, you want to state the necessary buyer qualifications in your ads in a way that helps unqualified buyers quickly rule themselves out, saving both of you time and effort. Likewise, define the financial capability prospective buyers need to demonstrate.

What your buyer's looking for

Here are the most common reasons buyers seek to buy businesses:

- ✔ **As an investment** (in other words, someone who views your business as a way to earn a good return on the money required to make the purchase). Often, these folks are investors or small investor groups who look for profitable, easy-to-run businesses they can buy and pay someone to manage.

- ✔ **As a strategic move** (for instance, another business owner who sees the acquisition of your business as an efficient way to add a new business capability or to expand into your market area). Competitors or suppliers often look to make *strategic acquisitions* by buying a business like yours in order to extend the capabilities and opportunities of their existing businesses.

- ✔ **For personal reasons** (for example, a person who thinks your business looks like a fun or challenging way to spend time, be involved in the business community, and make some money). Typically, people with personal motives fall into one of three camps:

    - People who resemble your customers, particularly if your business serves affluent individuals who share a hobby or recreational interest

- Executives fed up with the corporate world who have enough experience and money to take on the challenge of owning and running their own business

- Change-of-heart retirees who realize they aren't ready to spend all their time on the golf course or with the grandkids and who are looking for attractive opportunities to stay involved in the business world (and maybe add some money to their retirement funds)

If your buyer fits into a couple of typical buyer categories — for instance, a person who resembles your customers and who is also a change-of-heart retiree, or a person from within your industry who is also fed up with the corporate world — focus on the category that's easiest to target. Anyone, anywhere could be fed up with the corporate world, for example, and so those people are hard to target and reach, but people within your industry are a more specific group.

Where your buyer's looking

To keep your budget intact, focus as much as possible only on the media outlets you believe your likely buyers will be reading or tapping into. If your buyers read every word of the local newspaper and have never heard of Google, then concentrate your advertising in print media rather than online (unless the buyer uses brokers or advisors who look for opportunities online). But if your buyers think Craigslist.org has eliminated the need for newspaper classified ads, don't waste your money down at the local paper.

Typically, buyers focus their search on one of the following aspects:

- **A specific market area:** If you think your buyer is looking to buy a business in your market area, chances are good the buyer has contacted a broker for help, and you should consider doing the same. Not only will the broker help match you up with buyer inquiries as they come in, you'll also gain access to a database of likely prospects.

- **A specific industry:** If you think your buyer is looking specifically within your industry for business offerings, use industry resources and publications to announce your sale. Also, network within your industry for buyer referrals, making confidential contacts with industry executives and posting your offering on industry-hosted Web sites that offer classified ad services.

To research industry-specific marketing opportunities, type the name of your professional field plus the term "for sale" into a search engine and check the results. For instance, if you search for "accounting firms for sale," among the top results is Accounting Practice Sales, "North America's leader in practice sales." Type in "law practices for sale" and you'll reach LawBiz Management Company, a legal practice sale resource.

✔ **The buyer's current locale:** If your buyer is most likely a local resident looking for businesses specifically in your area — especially if your business is very small and your community is small or rural — then your marketing plan will probably include quiet, confidential networking, local newspaper classified ads, and online postings, possibly placed by a broker who can also help you manage the issue of confidentiality (which is hard to maintain when you're instigating talk about your business right in your own backyard).

✔ **General interest:** If your buyer hasn't pinpointed your business location but is looking far and wide for the right business opportunity, then you'll need to cast your advertising net over a greater geographic area using Internet sites and possibly major business or industry publications. For example, if you feel confident that your buyers are readers of a particular publication, post classified ads there. And if you think your buyers go online, definitely use online business-for-sale sites. The "Taking advantage of the World Wide Web" section, later in this chapter, is full of information on tapping into the online marketplace to make your sale announcement to cyber-shoppers.

Getting Familiar with Your Advertising Options

Nearly all business sales are advertised in two ways: an online listing or a publication classified ad. This section tells you what you need to know as you head down either path.

Taking advantage of the World Wide Web

If you use a business broker, your broker will post your ad on the brokerage site and also on a number of high-traffic sites where buyers and brokers shop for business-for-sale offerings.

The biggest online for-sale sites include

✔ www.bizbuysell.com/ (see Figure 9-2), which describes itself as "The Internet's largest and most heavily trafficked business-for-sale marketplace, with more business-for-sale listings, more unique users, and more search activity than any other service." Ads placed at any subscription level also appear in the Wall Street Journal Online. BizBuySell is on nearly every listing of top business-for-sale sites.

✔ www.bizquest.com/, which describes itself as the Internet's oldest and most established business-for-sale marketplace. Business-for-sale ads that are placed at the premium subscription level are also placed on www.entrepreneur.com.

✔ www.businessesforsale.com/, a U.K.-based site that lists international and U.S. businesses.

If your business is geared toward a certain professional, also check out Web sites associated with national and regional groups that that person may be part of, especially associations that serve your business arena or industry.

Most online business-for-sale sites feature subscription-based programs that begin at about $40 to $60 monthly for the briefest listing, with costs climbing as you add more descriptive text and photos to your ad.

When given the choice, and if you can afford to, go for the lengthier online listing that allows you to tell more about your business and its strengths. Also, so long as they don't reveal your business identity, include photos if you can. Statistics from business-for-sale sites show that ads at higher subscription levels get more exposure and generate more leads. See Figure 9-2 for an example of BizBuySell's advertising options.

If you have any doubt about whether to list your business on Internet business-for-sale sites, take the word of a guy whose business handles more sale transactions than any other brokerage in the world. John Davies, CEO of Sunbelt Business Brokers, says that 90 percent of all initial buyer inquiries for businesses priced under a million dollars come from Internet business-for-sale listings. When a good nine out of ten business shoppers are looking online, online is the place to advertise your business.

To get your creative ideas flowing, log on to a few business-for-sale Web sites to see which ads catch your interest — and which ones don't. Look at the kinds of descriptions that grab you, the kinds of photos that cause you to take a second look, and the kinds of information that hold your attention.

If you're not sure where to look, go to a broker's site to see how the pros present business offerings online. For example, visit www.sunbeltnetwork.com/ and head to the "Find a Business for Sale" section of the home page. In the pull-down menu of locations, select "Nevada" to look at a region with lots of for-sale activity, and therefore lots of listings to study. Click "Search Businesses" and examine the results. Notice how businesses are described by a pro — you can use the examples as models for your own description. Also notice the columns of information presented on the site — city, state, asking price, revenue, and cash flow (also called *seller's discretionary earnings*, described in Chapter 5). These columns represent the fields that buyers can search as they try to narrow their purchase options.

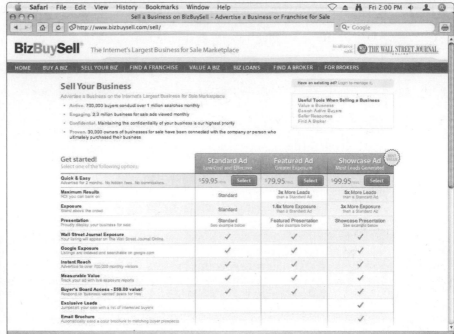

Figure 9-2:
The
advertising
structure for
BizBuySell.

Be ready to submit information for each field when you post online, or your business won't appear in many buyer searches. For instance, on the Nevada Sunbelt site, some buyers will be interested only in Las Vegas businesses, or businesses with asking prices of around $250,000, or businesses with cash flow of $150,000.

Placing ads in newspapers and industry magazines

Most business-for-sale ads in newspapers take the form of small-print ads placed in Sunday classified sections, either in your local area or in newspapers in other areas where you think your prospects will be reading.

If your business is likely to be purchased by a professional in your field, also consider classified advertising in magazines or newsletters that serve your trade or industry. Begin by looking at the industry publications you subscribe to. If they carry classified ads for businesses for sale, and if they have impressive circulation numbers, call to ask about ad rates. Be hesitant about advertising in a publication you've never heard of. If you've been in business in your field for a number of years and haven't come across the publication, it probably isn't prominent enough to warrant your ad investment.

When you advertise your business in print publications, you use one of two kinds of classified ads to tell your story:

✔ Small-print classified ads are typeset by the publication, which means that they all look alike except for the words they contain.

✔ Classified display ads feature headlines, illustrations, and whatever typestyle the advertiser chooses, so they're more visually distinctive and attention-getting.

Small-print classified ads are the most frequently used form of business-for-sale print ads, because they're easy to produce and place, and they cost the least amount to run. They're also workhorses. They aren't glamorous, they include no photos or logos, but they convey the information you're trying to spread. To make your ad stand out amid a sea of similar ads, follow these tips for a head start, and then be sure to check out the next section for important details:

✔ Begin your ad with a statement — in bold, capital letters — that conveys the most important thing you want readers to know. Example: **PROFITABLE FURNITURE MANUFACTURER FOR SALE.**

✔ Write your ad to talk directly to the person you think will buy your business (refer to Form 9-1).

✔ Feature as many business highlights and attractive features as you can afford to include.

✔ Don't use abbreviations or jargon unless you're sure all prospects will understand exactly what you're trying to say.

✔ Tell how to contact you.

Writing Ads That Work

Good ads streamline the buyer qualification process, which I cover in Chapter 10, in two ways:

✔ **They provide a good description of your business,** so prospects understand enough about the nature and size of your offering to rule themselves out if your business doesn't match up with their interests, abilities, or financial capabilities.

✔ **They ask each prospect to provide background information,** so you can rule out those whose interests and financial capabilities don't match up with your business and its sale price.

By basically swapping information in advance — you sharing information in your ad and your prospects sharing information in their ad responses — you save time following up with shoppers who aren't ever going to buy a business like yours. You also keep the more detailed information about your business confidential until you're sure you're dealing with a legitimately interested and able prospective buyer.

It may seem counterintuitive to run ads with the intention of shooing off prospects, but when nine out of ten shoppers never buy, you're wise to do everything possible to tip the long odds in your favor by attracting inquiries from only the most likely buyer prospects.

Whether you advertise your business for sale primarily on the Internet or in newspaper or industry magazine ads, you have to tell your story and whet buyer interest quickly for these two reasons:

- ✔ In Internet business-for-sale postings or in print media classified ads, you don't have much space to work with. You're often literally paying by the word.

- ✔ Whether online or in classified ads, readers form quick opinions. Either your ad will sound like a good fit for their interests, or it won't. Usually, the facts don't tip the balance between interest and rejection; *how* you present the facts does.

Watching your words

Your test is to write a short ad that tells a compelling story about your business. When writing small-space ads, weigh your words in two ways.

- ✔ **Be sure every word is true.** You'll respond to ad inquiries by sharing your selling memorandum, which you have to warrant for accuracy, so don't set up a bait-and-switch story.

- ✔ **Be sure every word pulls its weight** by contributing to the explanation of your business as an attractive purchase prospect.

As an example, which of the following two ads would grab your attention, if you were a buyer in the market for an advertising agency?

Advertising agency for sale

or

Profitable and growing 15-year-old advertising agency for sale, with clients throughout the Southwest and offices in fast-growing metropolitan area

The second example provides information that will get a second glance, because it doesn't leave readers with questions.

In a matter of a few lines or sentences, let your ad answer a prospective buyer's questions, including *what*, *where*, *when*, *why*, and for *how much*:

- *What* **are you selling?** If you're selling a landscaping business, say so right upfront. Better yet, instead of saying you're selling just any landscaping business, say that you're selling "a profitable landscaping business with a solid list of commercial, residential, and developer contracts."

- *Where* **is your business?** Ideally, especially in online ads where buyers search for businesses in specific locations, you want to state the city in which your business is located. In other ads, you may want to avoid stating your hometown if you think your location will tip off clients or competitors who notice the ad. For instance, you may not want to say, "Located in Laguna Beach, CA" if yours is one of only a handful of businesses that fit your business description in Laguna Beach. Instead, you can say something like, "Located in a small beach community in Southern California."

- *When* **was your business founded,** or, more quickly stated, how long has it been in business. You can put this fact into your business description ("a profitable 10-year-old landscaping business"), add it to your growth statement ("with a solid list of commercial, residential, and developer contracts that has increased steadily since 1997"), or state it elsewhere in your ad. The point is to let a buyer know that your business has already passed the test of time.

- *Why* **is your business an attractive deal?** You may never win a second glance from buyers unless you tell them, in the first ads they see, that your business is a particularly good deal. Flip back to Chapters 2 and 6 for details about the factors that contribute to a strong business — and therefore a good business opportunity. If your business is profitable and growing, if it generates good earnings, and if it benefits from a good employee team, a well-known and well-regarded business name, a terrific location, unique and desirable products and services, loyal clients, and good growth potential, say so, so long as every statement you make is true and verified in your selling memorandum.

- *How much* **are you asking?** Whether to list your price is a point of debate among folks selling businesses. If you don't tell your price, you open yourself to inquiries from people without the financial qualifications to buy your business, wasting your time and theirs. On the other hand, if you do tell your price, you run the risk of scaring off people who gulp and walk away. The consensus among business brokers and sale advisors is to take the risk and tell your price, along with your most recent annual sales figures, so buyers can put your price in perspective. Online, buyers shop by searching price categories. For instance, they look for businesses priced between $250,000 and $350,000. If you don't tell a price, your business doesn't appear in the buyer's search, and that's a huge opportunity loss.

Be aware that many buyers view your asking price as a starting point from which to negotiate. Sometimes the buyer pays the full price, but more often your closing price will be less (sometimes 15 to 30 percent less) than what you originally asked. Chapter 6 offers pricing advice and tips.

Requesting responses that help you pre-screen inquiries

After you grab a buyer's attention and interest with your ad, the buyer will want to know how to get more information. If you buy online ads that allow you the space, at the end of each ad invite buyers to request more information by submitting

✔ Why they want to buy a business

✔ Their approximate purchase timeline

✔ Their experience in business and in your business arena

✔ Their financial capability

For example, your ad may end with a statement such as, "Please reply with a statement describing your business background, the type and size business you seek to acquire, and your interest in this business." Put differently, your ad could read, "Please respond with a statement describing what interests you in this type of business, what you expect in terms of business earnings potential, and when you plan to purchase a business."

As you craft your response invitation, remember that your purpose at this stage is to collect the information you need to cull the serious and able buyers from the wannabes and information sleuths. (If you're using a broker, the broker will shield your identity and handle the process of screening responses to cull unqualified buyers. If you're not using a broker, you'll have to handle these tasks on your own.)

Avoid revealing any of the following points in your ads:

✔ **The name of your business.** Instead, focus on what your business does and how well it does it — buyers care more about the nature and strength of your business in this initial phase anyway.

✔ **An e-mail address that reveals your identity.** Instead, take advantage of the following offerings provided by many publications and business-sale Web sites:

- **The ability to place *blind ads*,** in which the business identity isn't revealed and responses are funneled to you through a media-provided P.O. Box or e-mail address. This option keeps your business sale plans confidential and allows you to follow up only with leads that seem to come from serious prospects who are qualified to buy and own your business.

- **Identity-protecting features on business-for-sale Web sites,** many of which allow you to request buyer information on a screen that appears when shoppers click a reply button to "Contact the seller." For example, when using `www.bizbuysell.com/`, the inquiry-response screen can be set up to read: "Confidentiality agreement required. Before releasing further details, the party offering this business for sale requires a signed confidentiality agreement. Click the button to view and print the form."

On the same inquiry-response screen, you can include a request for additional information. Again using `www.bizbuysell.com/` as an example, the screen can be set up to read: "The party offering this business for sale asks you to please include the following information...," followed by a request for information on the amount the prospective buyer is able to invest in a business and the preferred purchase time frame.

✔ **The location of your business,** especially if your town is small and yours is one of the few businesses that fit your description in your geographic region. Instead, describe the nature of your location with enough detail that buyers can determine whether it's the kind of place they want to own a business.

Tracking Your Ad Responses

If you use a number of advertising outlets (newspaper classified ads, a couple of online sites, and an industry-specific newsletter, for example), track which ads produce which responses. When you start to see what works — which media outlets deliver the most responses and which ads pull the best-qualified shoppers — edit or rewrite your ads and revise your ad schedule to put your money into the outlets that are performing most effectively.

You should track your ad responses in two ways:

✔ **According to number of respondents:** Keeping count of which publications or Web sites pull the most prospective buyer responses will probably be easy to do, because your ads will likely direct respondents to reply through the media outlet in order to conceal your identity. Simply by seeing where your responses are coming from, you'll be able to tell which outlets are working best. If some outlets aren't delivering responses, pull your ads and put the money into those that are.

✔ **According to qualifications of respondents:** Chapter 10 helps you screen buyer responses, but note here that if you notice that some advertising outlets are doing much better at attracting buyers who are serious and who possess the capabilities to buy your business, look beyond the outlet to the wording of your ad. You may find that you've put forth a clearer or more complete message in the ads that pulled well-qualified inquiries compared to those that attracted tire-kickers or in-their-dreams shoppers.

A shared advantage of classified and online ads is that both can be updated on practically a moment's notice, so don't delay when you discover a way to make the ads work better. If you face writer's block, turn back to Chapter 7 for help putting your offering into words. If you still can't come up with a compelling message, consider getting help. You probably don't need an advertising copywriter, because you're not looking for a creative concept but simply a compelling description. Go to broker sites and read some of their listings to get inspiration from the pros. If you contracted with a broker to help with the preparation of your selling memorandum, see if that same broker can help you spiff up your ad.

Form on the CD-ROM

Form 9-1	**Likely Business Buyer Checklist and Profile**	A form for compiling a profile of your buyer

Chapter 10

Screening and Communicating with Ad Respondents

*I*f you opened to this chapter, you probably already placed your business-for-sale ads, and now you're preparing to deal with the responses they've generated. By this stage in the selling game, you should have your business story committed to words and bound into a good-looking selling memorandum to share with your most serious prospects. You should also have your confidentiality agreement ready for all interested parties to sign before you release your business sale information. Chapters 8 and 9 help you with those steps.

The one thing you probably aren't ready for, because it surprises most for-sale-by-owner business sellers, is the number of unqualified, even frivolous, responses you'll get to your ads. By most counts, 90 percent of the people who read and respond to business-for-sale ads never buy a business — and that figure climbs to 99 percent of responses to Internet ad postings. Many are "just looking"; others have champagne dreams and beer budgets; others aren't really shopping at all but just trying to collect information for their own purposes.

Of those who *do* buy a business, an overwhelming percentage don't buy the one whose ad triggered their initial interest and response. That's why you have to review ad inquiries with your eyes wide open. Otherwise, you could end up sharing your business facts and figures with people who have no intention or ability to actually buy *your* business.

If you list your business with a broker, he or she will handle the weighty task of sorting out unqualified inquiries and responding to valid ones. Otherwise, it'll be your job to rule out the idle shoppers, business owner wannabes, and information sleuths so you can respond only to serious, ready, and able prospects. In other words, if you're selling your business on your own, you have a significant amount of screening, qualifying, and communication work in front of you. The upcoming pages help you follow up with the right prospects — in the right way.

Recognizing Typical Business-Sale Ad Respondents

Your business-for-sale ads will attract responses from a variety of people who fall into the following groups. Lock these buyer types in your mind, because when responses to your ads start to come in, you'll want to quickly sort them into *Hot*, *Maybe*, and *Cold* categories, with plans to follow up with the first, wait and see about the second, and walk away from the third. I cover the three categories in the next section, but following are the highlights to remember about the buyer prospect types.

Dreamers

Dreamers are people who'd love to own a business but who lack the financial ability or business depth to make a business purchase. You'll recognize dreamers by the informality of their responses (for instance, hand-written or error-riddled responses) and by the lack of career depth or financial resources presented in their personal background statements or resumes. Unless you think the content of their responses overcomes the appearance of their inquiry, and unless you think the respondent may have a more capable backer, you won't even follow up with dreamers.

Idle shoppers

These people, known in the business-for-sale world as *tire-kickers,* may or may not be financially or emotionally ready to buy a business, but in either case, they lack urgency and are shopping more out of curiosity than with a serious intent to buy. Tire-kickers aren't easy to recognize until you can talk with them to find out how long they've been shopping for a business, what kinds of businesses they've considered, why they haven't yet purchased a business, and what kind of timeline they're on. If you can't figure out whether a financially qualified ad respondent may be a tire-kicker, follow the information in the upcoming section, "Confirming the Temperature of Warm Prospects." Tread slowly, giving yourself time to learn about the person's motivation before divulging confidential information about your business.

Sleuths

These are information seekers who include competitors and people from your industry who'd like to use the premise of a business purchase to learn more about the inner workings of businesses like yours. When you receive responses, cull the sleuths by doing some sleuthing of your own — go online to gather information about the respondent and the accuracy of the respondent's personal background statement. If you determine or sense that the buyer is just trying to get competitive information, you can ignore the request (that's the beauty of ads that don't include your business name). If you think the buyer may be legitimate, you can either send your selling memorandum summary as an interim step while you work to learn more about the prospect's motivations, or you can pick up the phone to have a real-time conversation that aims to answer your questions about the person's true interest, ability, and motivation to buy a business like yours.

Scavengers

You'll also hear this group called *sharks* or *bottom-fishers*. Scavengers look for businesses with sellers who are pressed by finances or life situations and who may be willing to let their businesses go at upset prices. They're not always easy to recognize, but if a buyer starts off focusing on your recent business problems or business debt or your need for a rapid sale, the person may be looking for the opportunity to drive down your price and seize a quick good deal. If you are, in fact, pressed to sell quickly because of finances or a life situation, a scavenger may be a prospect you'll want to pursue. Scavengers never make it into the top-priority pile of responses, but they're worthy of at least a second look if you're in a hurry and better prospects aren't panning out.

Ready, able, and un-aimed buyers

These buyers don't know what they're looking for other than the fact that they want to buy a business, period. They're willing to consider any offering that fits their price range, that's located in their targeted geographic area, and that requires personal abilities that match fairly well with their own.

These prospects are attractive because they're ready and able to buy. They're unattractive because they cast a wide net, and yours is likely one of many businesses they're considering. Put bluntly, they'll eat up your time with only a slim chance that the effort results in a purchase. Don't rule out these less-than-certain prospects altogether, but pursue them only if a prospect intent on buying a business in your industry, in your market, of your size, and on your timeline doesn't emerge.

Ready, able, and aimed buyers

The ready, able, and aimed buyers are people who know what they're looking for. In sales terms, they're known as *bluebirds*. If they respond to your ad, it's because they'd like to buy a business in your industry and of your size and because it matches their personal expertise and aspirations — for instance, an accountant looking to buy an accounting firm in your market area, or a hairdresser looking to buy a salon in your part of town. These are your best prospects and the ones who deserve your most immediate and intensive attention.

Placing Respondents into Follow-Up Categories

Each time you receive an inquiry to your for-sale ads, quickly scan the prospect's background information to determine whether the buyer has the personal and financial qualifications to buy and run your business.

I provide a checklist of respondent qualifications, shown in this chapter in Figure 10-1 and on the CD-ROM as Form 10-1, to aid you in this screening process. To use the form, first check the personal and financial qualifications you seek in the ideal buyer for your business. Those qualities are the standard against which you can test the qualifications of each prospect. As inquiries come in, you can quickly run down the right-hand column of the chart to see at a glance how well the prospect's interests and abilities align with your buyer profile.

Here's how to evaluate prospective buyers based on their responses to your business sale ads:

✔ **If the buyer didn't turn in enough information** to allow you to fill out the form, that alone probably tells you a lot; the buyer may be hiding personal information rather than admitting to being a never-gonna-buy dreamer, a tire-kicker, or a sleuth. Put the person in the "cold" pile unless, by reading between the lines of the scant information provided, you think the person may possess the qualifications to purchase your business. In that case, you may want to contact the person — without revealing your business or personal identity — and ask for the information you initially requested.

✔ **If none of the checkmarks align,** put the prospect into a pile you label "cold," "thanks, but…," or just "no way."

✔ **If some but not many checkmarks align,** leaving you concerned over gaps between your needs and the buyer's expertise and financial capability, the prospect may be somewhat but not ideally suited to buy your business. Consider him or her to be a "warm" prospect, requiring some immediate prescreening before moving into either the "cold" or "hot" inquiry pile.

✔ **If a prospect's background leads to checkmarks in critically important areas,** such as "necessary education, licensing, or certification" and the areas indicating financial ability, you'll know you landed a hot lead and a target for priority follow-up.

You may get a stack of responses to your ads, or you may get only a few. Either way, use Form 10-1 to help you assess the responses before you take the next important step, which is to seek a confidentiality agreement and reveal your business identity and the fact that you're selling. By undertaking this assessment, you increase your chances of following up only with prospects who are serious about and able to buy your business. After you put all the prospects into categories, immediately respond to hot prospects, and then follow up with warm prospects to gather more information about them.

PROSPECT QUALIFICATION FORM
Name of Prospect _____

	Ideal Buyer Profile (✓ all appropriate statements)	**Prospect Profile** (✓ all appropriate statements)
P E R S O N A L	☐ Buyer should have specific interest in my business industry or arena	☐ Prospect has specific interest in my business industry or arena
	☐ Buyer should have specific education, licensing, or certification	☐ Prospect has necessary education, licensing, or certification
	☐ Buyer should have previous business ownership experience	☐ Prospect has previous business ownership experience
	☐ Buyer should have previous experience in a small-to mid-sized business	☐ Prospect has previous experience in a small-to mid-sized business
	☐ Buyer should have previous experience in my business arena	☐ Buyer has previous experience in my business arena
	☐ Buyer should live in or want to move to the region where my business is located	☐ Prospect lives in or wants to move to in the region where my business is located
	☐ Buyer should want to work at and run my business	☐ Prospect wants to work at and run my business
U R G E N C Y	☐ Buyer has been seriously shopping for a business for the past __ months but not longer than __ months	☐ Prospect has been seriously shopping for a business for __ months and not longer than __ months
	☐ Buyer should want to make a purchase within the next __ months	☐ Prospect indicates interest to make a purchase with the next __ months
F I N A N C I A L	☐ Buyer seeks annual business earnings of approximately $_____	☐ Prospect seeks annual business earnings of approximately $_____
	☐ Buyer has ability to pay $_____ cash at closing	☐ Prospect has indicated ability to pay $_____ cash at closing
	☐ Buyer must be qualified for a seller or SBA loan of $_____	☐ Prospect has indicated solid qualification for a seller or SBA loan of $_____

Figure 10-1:
Weigh the qualities and qualifications of each prospect against your ideal buyer profile.

Hot prospects

Your most serious inquiries will come from ready, able, and aimed prospects who are looking to buy a business like yours. These are prospects with the financial capability to buy your business, expertise to run it, earnings expectations that your business can fulfill, and specific interest in a business like yours, rather than in any business, anywhere.

You'll recognize these hot prospects because their personal qualifications match the definition of your likely-buyer profile in terms of interest, business experience, and, perhaps most of all, financial ability to pay for your business. (If you haven't yet written a description of your likely buyer, see Form 9-1 on the CD-ROM.)

People who are seriously interested and able to buy your business are hot prospects. When you find one, jump straight to the "Responding to Hot Prospects" section, later in this chapter, to launch an immediate follow-up effort. Don't let the inquiry cool off while it sits on your desk. Brokers, who make a living selling businesses, respond to inquiries on the same day they arrive, so you should plan to do the same. Assume that the prospect has responded to a number of ads. If you wait several days to respond, the prospect may already be into meetings with some other broker-represented seller. You snooze, you lose.

Warm prospects

Warm prospects are iffy prospects, and iffy prospects require some prompt pre-screening efforts on your part. Warm prospects have some (but not all) of the qualifications you're looking for in a buyer, but they come with strings attached or backgrounds that trigger one or several flashing yellow lights. If serious prospects are hot, iffy prospects range from very warm to lukewarm to cool.

When you're ready to learn more about these respondents, pick up the phone or send an e-mail — using a special e-mail address or phone number that doesn't identify you or your business. Through this initial contact, gather enough additional information to allow you to either rule the prospect out or to move the prospect into — or at least in the direction of — your hot-prospect pile.

Warm prospects typically fall into one of the following categories.

Competitors

Inquiries from those who currently own or work for your competitors may or may not be serious, but either way, competitors are risky prospects. A competing business owner may be legitimately interested in buying a business like yours as a strategic acquisition. Or an employee of a competing company may be truly ready to dive into the field of business ownership. But in either case, the prospect could also be more curious than serious.

If you respond with a business introduction and the competitor is serious, the gamble could pay off in the form of a business sale. If the competitor's inquiry isn't serious, or if the negotiation doesn't conclude with a sale, you may come to regret that you gave a competitor inside information for nothing. That's why sellers proceed with caution when inquiries come from owners or top managers of competing businesses.

Unless you feel strongly that a competitor is a serious buyer prospect, put the inquiry aside and pursue it only if your top-priority hot prospects fall by the wayside.

If you feel a competitor is truly serious, follow the steps in the upcoming section, "Responding to Hot Prospects." Even then, proceed carefully. First, be sure to obtain a mutual confidentiality agreement (see the sample, provided by Sunbelt Business Brokers, in Form 8-6 on the CD-ROM). Then request buyer background information before sharing further information on your business. This information exchange allows you to determine whether the competing individual or business has the capability to purchase your business, and it also provides a good test of the competitor's true motivations. A competitor who's simply fishing for information about your business won't be interested in sharing confidential personal or business information, and that alone will provide the answer to your question about how to rate the validity of the inquiry.

Financially naïve respondents

Some respondents look qualified, except for the fact that their financial needs are backed by what appears to be little financing experience or knowledge. Those who state in their financial capability response that they'll get a loan to buy your business but make the statement in a way that looks naïve, with no mention of loan prequalification or solid collateral they'll commit to the deal, may turn out to be more trouble than they're worth.

For now, just be aware that if a buyer doesn't state his or her ability to buy with cash or to back a loan with solid collateral (like home equity or other real estate), that buyer is a warm prospect, at best.

Prospects with inadequate business experience or polish

If the prospect's response to your ad is full of typos and impossible-to-decipher answers, you may be seeing clues that the person lacks the necessary business ability to complete a purchase transaction. Even if your business doesn't require an owner with professional polish, you want to see some level of professionalism in your ad responses, either from the buyer or from whoever is advising the buyer during the sale process.

If a professionally weak prospect offers an all-cash payment for your business, the lead warms up considerably. But if you need to offer seller financing or rely on payments well into the future, a buyer like this goes from warm to cool in a hurry.

Cold prospects

One of the great things about placing ads without identifying your business is that you don't have to waste your time with cold prospects. So unless you really want to respond to these inquiries, set them aside — perhaps forever.

Cold prospects include

✔ People who neglect to divulge their purchase interests or capabilities.

✔ People who have little to no money to put down toward your business purchase and who are incapable financially of qualifying for loans.

✔ People who give answers that make you think they don't know what they want or when they want to buy.

✔ People who aren't interested in buying at all but are trying to sell you something — be it a business loan, consulting services, or an offering by a business broker to list your company should you decide over the coming weeks or months that it's too much to do on your own.

If you find that you're receiving way too many inquiries from unqualified buyer prospects, go back to Chapter 9 and rework your ads so they do a better job of helping buyers understand your business and price so they can rule themselves out if necessary.

Responding to Hot Prospects

When an information request from a hot prospect lands in your inbox, mailbox, or voice mail, your inclination will be to get the person information on your business — fast. Although you definitely need to follow up quickly, you also need to follow up carefully, making sure your assessment of the buyer's interest and ability is correct, and obtaining the buyer's confidentiality agreement before divulging your business identity information in your selling memorandum. The upcoming sections describe the process you should follow.

Calling to follow up

By this point, you should feel very confident that the prospect looks seriously interested and is capable of buying your business. Take these steps to quickly take the prospect's interest to the next level of involvement:

1. **Begin by placing a phone call to the prospect.** Make this call as soon as possible after receiving an inquiry from a serious and capable prospect. If you don't think it will reveal your business identity, identify yourself by name and explain that you're calling in response to the buyer's interest in acquiring your business. If your town is small and your prospect is local, hold off identifying yourself until after confidentiality is ensured.

2. **Thank the prospect for the response to your sale offering.** Convey how well you believe the person's experience and capabilities appear to match your ideal buyer profile.

3. **Exchange verbal information.**

   - Ask the prospect about his or her interests and purchase motivations. Use this portion of the call to confirm that your assessment of the buyer's capabilities is correct, and also to obtain new information about the buyer's purchase interests and timeline.

   - Answer the prospect's questions about your business, but be careful not to reveal your business identity.

   If either of you comes across information that makes you realize you don't have a match, you can end the conversation at that point. Otherwise, you should offer to share additional information.

4. **Offer to e-mail or fax a one- or two-page business overview** that the prospect can study to further confirm that your business appears to match the prospect's interests. This overview follows the same format as the selling memorandum summary (see Chapter 8 for information about how to create this document if you haven't already prepared it as part of your selling memorandum), but without any details that would give away your business identity.

5. **Ask to schedule a meeting,** during which you can each sign confidentiality agreements, exchange additional information, and discuss your offering further. Depending on the enthusiasm you sense, you can either schedule the first meeting during this initial phone conversation or offer to call back the next day to set the meeting. The latter option gives the prospect time to review the business overview you e-mail or fax before you call back the next day.

Meeting face to face

Unless great distance separates you and the prospect, aim for an in-person meeting instead of a phone conference. Simply by going to the trouble to be at the meeting, your prospect is making a commitment to the purchase process.

Schedule this initial meeting to take place in your accountant's or attorney's office, which accomplishes a couple of important objectives:

- ✔ You signal to the prospect that this meeting is more than just a get-to-know-each-other event — it's an important meeting between the prospect and you and your advisors.

- ✔ You can schedule the meeting without identifying your business.

If your prospect lives in a distant location and an in-person meeting isn't possible, schedule a phone conference to be attended by the prospect, you, and your accountant or attorney, as well as the prospect's accountant or attorney, depending on the prospect's wishes. (If the prospect asks that advisors attend this meeting, take that as a good sign that the prospect is a serious shopper.)

During the meeting, cover the following points.

Confirming the prospect's interest and purchase ability

First off, confirm that the prospect is interested in a business of your size and type and is prepared to make the kind of cash and financing commitment necessary to purchase your business.

If a prospective buyer doesn't give a clear picture of personal financial ability to purchase your business, request a financial statement before providing your selling memorandum. Almost any experienced businessperson will have a financial statement. If your business is quite small and doesn't require a buyer with a depth of business expertise, however, you may need to provide the buyer with a detailed request for the kind of financial information you require. You can get a personal financial statement form from the Small Business Administration (SBA) and give it to buyers who need assistance providing you with the financial information you want. To access a PDF file of the SBA form, go to `www.sba.gov/sbaforms/sba413.pdf`. Your bank likely has forms you can use as well.

Acquiring the confidentiality agreement

After you reconfirm the prospect's serious interest, obtain signatures on a mutual confidentiality agreement (your attorney should produce, or at least review and approve, this legal form; you can see a sample by looking at Form 8-6 on the CD-ROM). If the inquiry came in response to a business-for-sale Web site posting, it may be accompanied by the site-provided confidentiality agreement. If not, and if the prospect attends this first meeting by phone, obtain a signed confidentiality agreement before the meeting and before identifying your business.

This point deserves repeating: Never disclose that your business is for sale — and never share your selling memorandum — before you receive a signed copy of a confidentiality or non-disclosure agreement from the prospect.

In most cases, present the confidentiality agreement during your first meeting with a serious prospect.

If necessary due to distance between the prospect and your business, you may need to handle the confidentiality agreement request by phone or e-mail. When requesting the prospect's confidentiality agreement, use wording that sets a professional and friendly tone. Show your interest in ongoing discussions, but also be clear about the information required to allow you to take the next steps.

As an example, here's how a response to an inquiry may read:

> *Thank you for your interest in my business and sale offer. I look forward to providing more information as quickly as possible. First, would you please sign and return the attached/enclosed confidentiality agreement, which ensures confidentiality and agreement not to disclose confidential information obtained during our upcoming discussions? Also, please provide preliminary information on your business background, what interests you in this type of business, your desired purchase timeline, and your financial capability to provide cash and financing for a $X business purchase. I will treat your responses confidentially, and I sincerely look forward to our future discussions.*

Sharing your selling memorandum, in whole or in part

After the signed confidentiality agreement is in your hands, present the prospect with either your complete selling memorandum or your selling memorandum summary. Which one you share depends on how confident you feel about the prospect at this point.

If the conversation in your initial meeting leaves you with uncertainties about the prospect's motivation or capability, share only the summary. When doubt is present, you don't want to share the sensitive facts about your business that your complete selling memorandum contains. You may have already e-mailed or faxed this summary — in a version that doesn't include your business name — to the prospect. Even if that's the case, you can still pull it out again, this time with your identity in place, to refer to as you learn more information to either confirm or overcome your uncertainties about the buyer's interest and abilities.

When presenting the summary, take time to go over the document's facts, but don't just read it — use it to prompt conversation with the prospect. As you cover facts about your business, ask how they match up with the prospect's interests and capabilities. For example, as you discuss your business sales or earnings, move into a financial discussion about how much the prospect intends to pay for a business and how the purchase may be structured. As you end the presentation, ask the prospect to provide additional information in any areas that are causing you uncertainty. For instance, you may ask for more information on the prospect's desired purchase timeline, financial capability, or interest in owning a business of your size or in your business arena. Then schedule a second meeting, again to be held in the office of your accountant or attorney, to review the prospect's response to your request for additional information.

As soon as you're confident that the prospect is seriously shopping for a business, interested in a business like yours, ready to make a purchase, financially and personally capable of buying and owning your business, and committed to confidentiality, present your complete selling memorandum — but don't actually give a copy to the prospect at this point. Instead, present your book only for review during the meeting. If the prospect wants to review the contents privately and more carefully, offer to make a meeting room available.

If the prospect wants to take the selling memorandum from this initial meeting, provide a copy of the selling memorandum summary (or refer to the copy that you previously provided), explaining that the summary includes all the major points of your sale offering. Don't release a hard copy of your complete book until after you receive a purchase offer complete with a letter of intent. Turn to Chapter 11 for more on this step. You may make an exception if you're extremely confident about the buyer's motivation and ability to buy your business, in which case you can deliver the selling memorandum after you receive the signed confidentiality agreement and a copy of the buyer's financial statement.

Scheduling a tour of your business

If after reviewing your selling memorandum you and the prospect continue to see a good buyer-seller matchup, schedule a time for the prospect to visit your business. If you have a large manufacturing business or a business with lots of employees and customers, schedule the visit during a busy time of day when your sign is lit, your entry is unlocked, customers are coming and going, your staff is working, and your business looks vibrant. If you have a small operation or a professional business, you can schedule an after-hours meeting that allows the buyer to see your operation without risking that you tip off clients or employees about your sale intentions.

In the most successful business sales, this pre-purchase period is a time during which the buyer and seller work almost like partners. You'll share information back and forth and work together to resolve issues on both sides of the table as you seek to achieve a mutual objective — the sale and successful transition of your business.

The difference, of course, is that you're not partners — you're a seller and a prospective buyer — and you have to hold certain information about the ultimate price and terms you'll accept close to your vest, all the while keeping your relationship with the prospective buyer confidential from your employees and clients.

During this on-site visit, here's what will happen:

- You'll show the buyer your business. In previous conversations you've explained how it works, how it makes money, and how it's positioned for future success, but during the site visit you can not only tell, but show. You can also fuel the buyer's interest by pointing out features of your business that contribute to its strength and opportunity.

- The buyer will see your business firsthand, having the chance to ask questions and gain additional information. At the same time, based on questions you can put forth during the business tour, you can get the buyer to share additional career experience, more complete financial information, and purchase plans and timelines. The visit will also give you time to discuss how your business will transition and what the future may hold.

Make it your goal to schedule a business visit before your first meeting is over. When you're working with a seriously motivated, financially capable buyer, you want to keep the ball moving.

Confirming the Temperature of Warm Prospects

If an ad response appears to be from a valid prospect but you don't have enough information to qualify the prospect as hot, move quickly to find out more. On the chance that the prospect really is a serious buyer for your business, you don't want to lose the person's interest while you dither over whether to follow up. Contact the prospect quickly by phone or, if necessary, send an e-mail to request a phone conversation.

So long as you have unresolved uncertainties, don't share your business identity. Instead, explain that you're responding to the person's inquiry regarding the dog-training center in Albuquerque (or however you described your business in your ad). Later, when you receive enough information from the prospect to believe the person is, in fact, a serious and capable prospective buyer, follow the advice for responding to hot prospects.

Here are some other things you should do during this initial conversation:

1. **Thank the prospect for inquiring about your business.**

2. **Explain that you'd like to learn a bit more about the person to determine whether your business is a good fit before taking more of the prospect's time and attention.**

3. **Ask plenty of questions to develop a clearer sense of the prospect's motivations and capabilities to buy your business.**

   Glance back at Form 10-1, which has a lineup of factors you cited as important for your ideal buyer prospect to possess. Where you're not certain about how well the prospect aligns with your buyer ideals, use your initial conversation with the prospect to obtain more information.

   Avoid questions that can be answered with a "Yes" or "No" response so that the prospect does most of the talking. For instance, ask, "How do you feel about owning a four-person regional practice after your years with a major corporate firm?" Or, "From a glance at your financial statement it looks like you're just starting to build up capital. What kind of cash and collateral have you earmarked for purchasing a business like ours?"

4. **Probe to uncover the prospect's purchase motivation, again avoiding "Yes" or "No" answers.**

   Instead of saying, "Do you plan to make a purchase in the next four months?" say, "How has your business search gone so far?" Or, "How long have you been looking and what kinds of opportunities have you come across?" Follow up by asking, "What kind of purchase timeline are you hoping for?"

It's likely that during this initial screening phone conversation, the prospect will have some questions about your business size, location, price, operations, and other details. Don't give away your business name or facts that allow a buyer to put two and two together to identify your business. But do feel free to provide answers by basically reading from the one- or two-page business plan summary or overview that you've prepared to share with pre-screened prospects. (See Chapter 8 for information on preparing this summary.)

Your initial conversation with an iffy prospect will probably lead you to one of three conclusions and follow-up actions:

✓ **The prospect isn't ready or able to purchase your business,** in which case you should kindly but directly admit that it appears your interests and needs don't align. Offer your sincere thanks for the interest, extend your best wishes for the future, and bring the communication to an end. You never know if this person may know someone who may, in fact, be qualified to purchase your business, so be friendly and don't burn bridges. At the same time, don't waste your time or the prospect's time with additional meetings or conversation.

TIP

- ✔ **The prospect seems serious, but you still have doubts about financial capability or personal qualifications to buy and own your business.** If this is the case, ask the buyer for a personal background statement that includes a bank reference or a credit report before going further with purchase discussions. If the prospect balks or doesn't respond, you'll have the answer you need to move him or her into your stack of cold prospects.

- ✔ **The prospect is certainly serious but may not be a perfect match, due to a lack of ability in key areas such as financial capability or business experience.** In this situation, offer to share your business overview but without any identification of your business name. At the same time, ask the prospect to provide you with more information, such as a clearer idea of his or her purchase timeline, or more formal financial background, or other data that will help you determine the likelihood of a purchase. If the prospect responds with the requested information, you'll have what you need to rate the person's purchase likelihood as cold or hot. If the prospect doesn't respond to your request, you'll know that the communication has reached a dead end.

Form on the CD-ROM

Form 10-1:	**Prospect Qualification Form**	A checklist to help you evaluate qualifications of prospective buyers against an ideal-buyer profile

Chapter 11

Steering the Pre-Purchase Process and Accepting a Buyer Offer

Finding a serious and motivated person who wants to buy your business — and who has the financial capability to complete the deal in the near future — is almost enough to make you want to plan a celebration party. But hold your horses — you're not quite ready yet. Finding a buyer is kind of like getting a fish on the line — you still have to reel it in.

Between the moment that your prospective buyer emerges and the day a letter of intent to buy your business lands in your hands (which is the topic of Chapter 12 and which *still* isn't the end of the sale process!) lies an intensive period of information exchange, preliminary negotiations, and buyer-seller collaboration.

The process involves the sharing of sensitive information about your business, so don't invite a prospective buyer into your business — in fact, don't even introduce the name of your business — until you confirm the buyer's capability to purchase your business and obtain a signed confidentiality agreement, steps I outline in Chapter 10. If all looks promising after you accomplish those steps, then invite your buyer to see the inner workings of your pride and joy and to begin the next steps in the sale process.

If you list your business with a broker, the broker will guide you through the steps in the upcoming part of the sale process. If you're selling on your own, this chapter spells out all that you need to know. Either way, the goal is the same: to reach a point where the buyer is ready to make an offer and present a letter of intent to purchase your business. This chapter helps you prepare for the big show, present your business with confidence, and start pulling in your line, with buyer attached.

Preparing for the Buyer Tour and Your Business Presentation

Before your buyer steps through your front door, spend some time getting your business in top form — kind of like how you'd scour the house before the in-laws come for a visit. Following the advice in Chapter 3, you may have done a fair amount of work to improve your business appearance as you prepared it for sale. Now that the moment of a buyer's arrival is imminent, though, no detail is too small to notice:

- ✔ See that the door, entryway, windows, and even the floor mat are all clean and presentable.

- ✔ Check that light bulbs aren't burned out and that the place looks neat, clean, and as impressive as possible.

- ✔ Pull copies of your ads, sales literature, menus, newsletters, or any other promotional material or publicity items that you can show as indications of your business image.

- ✔ Be ready to give a whirlwind tour of your Web site.

- ✔ Have your presentation ready so you can flip through it quickly and effectively. If you have to rummage around to find things, you'll look disorganized — hardly a selling strong point.

The upcoming sections tell you what to expect as you do the walk-through of your business with a buyer. They also help you prepare for the kind of questions buyers usually have at this point, as well as for the kind of information you should try to obtain.

After you invite the buyer into your business, and as you're preparing for the visit, don't divulge to others the reason behind the visit. By now, you and the prospect have agreed to be candid and confidential, but you can't yet be candid with your employees or clients. This isn't yet a done deal, and if word leaks out, it could damage your business if employees feel insecure and decide to seek other jobs, or if clients who have great confidence in you personally decide to look for other business alternatives.

Presenting Your Business

When your prospective buyer arrives for the visit, introduce him or her as someone other than the possible next owner of your business so that you don't set off any gossip alarms among your employees. Your initial introduction, followed by your own casual attitude, should be enough to avoid stoking the rumor mill. Plan what you're going to say in advance so you and the prospect say the same thing. You can simply introduce the prospective buyer as a colleague or business associate, or a friend who you're showing around your business. Don't go into great detail — the more you say, the more you're apt to look like someone trying to make up a story. Also, if the person becomes the buyer — which is, after all, your objective — you want whatever introduction you gave to be true, though not necessarily complete.

Show your business to the buyer just as you'd show it to the director of your chamber of commerce, or to a drop-in visitor from an industry or business association. Don't try to hide the buyer from curious eyes, as that's likely to stir up questions.

As you go through your business, make the tour an overview of your operation, pointing out major equipment and various departments or work areas. Begin at the front door and show the buyer how either a typical customer or a typical job (depending on whether you sell consumer goods or produce products or services) goes through your business. You aren't trying to tell the buyer nitty-gritty details of how your business runs; you're just trying to share the size and scope of your business and provide a good sense of its culture, atmosphere, and inner workings.

During the walk-through, keep the conversation focused on the physical aspects of your business, not on its financial or other capabilities. Save those aspects of the conversation to be addressed during the more private portion of the buyer visit, explained in the next section.

Throughout your business tour and in all future meetings, be prepared and present with confidence. If you look jangled or disorganized, the buyer may read your signals as indications that you're nervous about the deal or that you're being less than frank about the information you're presenting. Whenever you're hesitant about facts, refer to your selling memorandum. It has all the important data about your sales, finances, operations, market environment, and future goals and plans.

Meeting Privately for Q&A

Following your business tour, go to a private meeting area to discuss your business offering and questions either of you may have for the other. If you don't have a private meeting area in your business building, consider going off site for this portion of the meeting, perhaps to the office of your accountant, where you probably held your first meeting with the buyer.

Each buyer-seller meeting will follow its own sequence, because each buyer situation comes with its unique set of questions to be answered. The next section deals with several of the questions nearly all buyers have in their minds. As you answer the buyer's questions, to make sure that everything you say is completely accurate, refer to your selling memorandum. You may feel that you're reaching for that document frequently, but by doing so you're also showing the buyer that not only do you have answers for the questions but that your answers are ones you've put in writing and stand by. What you don't want to do is to embellish facts or figures to make your business story look or sound better than it is. In the end, as part of the purchase and sale agreement, you need to *warrant,* or legally confirm, that the facts you provide relating to the sale of your business are accurate. Get your facts and figures right from the very start and stick with your accurate story throughout all conversations. Not only will this approach keep you out of legal hot water, it'll also increase the confidence with which you present your business.

Addressing the buyer's questions confidently

When presenting your business, remember the two key points on your buyer's mind:

- ✔ **Why are you selling?** You may have answered this question in one of the first conversations you had with the buyer, but at that time, your response was likely factual but brief. Most buyers want to know more about why you want out of your business. Be ready with an honest answer that helps the buyer realize that you're not just cutting and running. Explain why the time is right for you to sell. At the same time, explain why you believe that the time is right for your business to move into new hands, either because the business is in very strong condition and easy to transition, or because it's at a point where a few actions taken by a capable new owner can redirect the business onto a new growth track. Remember, honesty has to be your policy, because soon you'll have to warrant the facts you provide. If your business isn't strong and growing, don't say that it is. Instead, tell the truth — but accompany the facts with your honest assessment of the opportunities that await a new owner.

✔ **Where's the hidden opportunity?** The driving question on most buyers' minds — whether or not they ask it outright — is whether your business has untapped opportunities that make the price particularly attractive and, if so, why you haven't already seized them. Every buyer wants to pay a price that's a little less than the business is worth, but most buyers *also* want to know where upside potential is hidden so they can make their purchase even more profitable. The buyer may not come right out and ask this question, which makes it even more important that you be ready to raise the topic and address it frankly and with explanations that strengthen the buyer's interest in your business. You want to entice your buyer by providing information in the most favorable but accurate way while protecting your legal backside at the same time, following the upcoming advice.

Deepening the buyer's interest

As you lead your prospect through your business and meet afterward to answer any questions he or she poses, answer directly and specifically, but also take the opportunity to elaborate with explanations that emphasize your business strengths. Consider the following examples:

✔ **How long have you been in business, or at this location?** Give the length of time, but then go on to explain that over that period, sales have increased 48 percent, or cost of sales declined by 12 percent due to lower transportation costs, or you've expanded your production area to improve output by 10 percent, or whatever other business strength you can link to your location.

✔ **How many people work here?** Provide a number, but then explain how your business is staffed. You can talk about productivity per employee, or about how over the past few years you've shifted from part-time to full-time (or from full-time to part-time) staff and how that change has positively affected your payroll costs. You can also move into a short explanation about the quality of your workforce. For example, if training is a strength, mention it, along with the fact that your training program is detailed in a manual that will benefit the buyer. If the expertise of your staff gives your business an edge, you can discuss how key employees have signed employment contracts that will transfer to the new owner. This is also a good opportunity to mention that your business has employment and operation manuals that will make the buyer-to-seller transition efficient.

✔ **What challenges do you face or foresee?** Buyers often start with the easy questions and then move into the questions you may want to run from. But don't shy away — buyers need to know what they're getting into. Explain industry, market, or economic challenges that you've identified and successfully addressed. Also explain challenges on the horizon and how you intend to address them, or how a new buyer's investment may help your business avoid the challenge — for instance, by investing to introduce a new product, open a new market area, or retool operations to make the business more competitive. Don't be shy in discussing challenges — by discussing them, you have the perfect opportunity to present your business's potential for a new owner. It also gives you a good opportunity to mention that you've prepared updated business and marketing plans — a sure sign of a well-managed business — which you'll share during due diligence and pass along after the sale closes.

✔ **Does the business — or will a new owner — face any negative business or legal issues?** Don't dodge this question. Disclose problems that you're aware of now so they don't arise for the first time during the due diligence process, when they may come as a deal-threatening surprise to the buyer. To help you through this part, you can turn to your selling memorandum appendix (see Chapter 8), to the seller's disclosure statement that you created with the help of your attorney. This form discloses any problems you're aware of regarding business conditions, regulations, or legal issues. Where there's a problem, explain how it's being addressed.

Using discretion

As you answer questions, keep in mind that this buyer may not end up purchasing your business. Save your business secrets until after you receive an offer and a signed letter of intent to purchase your business, and don't reveal secrets or business information beyond what you'd feel comfortable sharing with a prospective new customer or business associate. If the buyer requests sensitive information — for example, copies of your business or marketing plans, or your employee handbook or operating procedures — explain that you'll be sure to have those materials ready during the due diligence process.

Until you have an offer in hand, avoid these two errors:

✔ **Don't share your proprietary processes,** secret formulas, client names and contact information, or financial details.

✔ **Don't negotiate the price of your business** or how the price may be structured — for example, with a portion coming from cash at closing and a portion coming from a seller-financed loan that you provide. It's too easy to agree to something that could end up costing you serious money in terms of tax implications, so don't venture into these discussions without your accountant's input. Instead, refer to the general price and terms stated in your selling memorandum and explain that as soon as the buyer proposes an offer, you'll involve your accountant as you work to make a deal possible.

Basically, don't let the cart get before the horse by talking about details of the deal before you have an offer in hand. Keep your eye on the immediate goal, which is to obtain an offer from the buyer.

Putting yourself in the interviewer's shoes

Use the business tour to not only show your business to the buyer but also to further develop your opinions about whether the buyer is capable of making the purchase. After you receive an offer, you'll probably take your business out of play for other buyers, so use this pre-offer period to assess whether you think the buyer has increasing or decreasing interest in buying your business. In your conversations, ask questions like these:

- ✔ **Have you purchased or started businesses in the past?** The point of this question is to find out whether the buyer's been part of successes or failed deals, and if there were challenges, what went wrong.

- ✔ **When would you like to complete your purchase?** This question helps you discover more about the buyer's timeline and urgency. It also helps you uncover buyer hesitancies, such as issues with the buyer's financial capability or with aspects of your business that the buyer views as obstacles to a purchase.

- ✔ **How long have you been looking for a business acquisition?** This question can lead into a conversation that reveals whether the buyer is looking at only your business or considering your business as one of several options. It also allows you to find out what other kinds of businesses the buyer is considering (and in what price range), whether the buyer has made offers on other businesses (and, if so, why they didn't close), and what the buyer found missing in other purchase opportunities.

- ✔ **What will be your source of funds for buying the business?** You likely covered this point in your initial meeting with the buyer, but if you have lingering concerns about the buyer's financial capability, and if the buyer is going to need a loan, find out more. Will the loan come in the form of a home equity loan or a loan secured by real property? If you offer seller financing, explain the kind of security you seek, and determine whether the buyer feels confident that he or she can meet your requirements.

- ✔ **Besides your spouse, is anyone else involved in your purchase decision-making process?** If the buyer relies on advisors or funding partners, you want those parties specified in the buyer's letter of intent and covered by confidentiality agreements. You may want to meet the other parties so you can explain your business and its attributes firsthand rather than through the buyer's translations of your presentations.

Listening for signs of uncertainty

When the buyer responds to your questions, don't interrupt. Let the buyer talk, and even ramble. If and when you start to hear the buyer's voice trail off with a statement like, "Oh, I don't know," follow up. People often trail off when they're not comfortable with the rest of what they have to say. Trailing off may mean the buyer is hesitant about your business but doesn't want to come out and say so. Or it may indicate hesitancy due to the nature (or truthfulness) of the answer the buyer's about to give. Follow up with a statement such as, "You seem hesitant about something. Do you have questions that perhaps I can answer or we can discuss?"

If your conversations lead to uncertainty about the buyer's intentions or abilities, simply reiterate your proposed price and timeline with a statement such as, "As we've discussed, I'm aiming to complete this sale by late June, at a purchase price of $400,000." Then ask the buyer if he or she is prepared to proceed with purchase discussions. Be frank, and admit if you sense hesitations that you'd like to discuss. Again, let the buyer talk without interruption. You need to learn as much as you can about whether an offer is likely to follow. Your findings about the buyer will likely fall into one of the following categories:

- ✓ **The buyer simply has unaddressed questions.** If that's the case, tell the buyer that your negotiations are your highest priority and that you want to be sure the buyer has all the information necessary to make the decision. To prompt a response, ask if the buyer has particular questions about how your business operates, its market, its financial condition, or your asking price and terms. By stating broad areas such as these, you can help restart the conversation and unlock the buyer's concerns.

- ✓ **The buyer has concerns about whether your business is a good fit,** either from an interest or a financial standpoint, or both. Ask if the buyer is hesitant due to concern over your business, your price and terms, or your general timeline. When you know the focus of concern, you can say something like, "Let's dissect your concerns and see if we can get them addressed." Then offer to review your business condition and its strengths and opportunities again, or to discuss ways the deal may be financed (which may lead to a discussion about the possibility of seller or SBA financing) and how you may be able to lengthen your timeline slightly if it addresses the buyer's need. You want to keep your discussion about the financial aspects of your sale general, more like a brainstorm than a negotiation, because you don't want to commit to sale price or structure details without input from your accountant, as described in Chapter 13.

- ✓ **The buyer is a serial shopper who can't or doesn't close deals,** which is a disappointing but important discovery that you're better off making sooner than later. When you ask about whether the buyer's prepared to proceed with purchase discussions, if your question is met with a lot of hemming and hawing, ask if you can help overcome hesitations with answers to any unaddressed questions. If the buyer doesn't have any issues to raise, ask if the buyer is considering other business purchase opportunities. Also ask if the buyer may be hesitant because past purchase efforts haven't panned out. If that's the case, ask what happened and listen carefully to the response. History often repeats itself, and if the buyer has walked away from the business sale altar before, put yourself on alert. If an offer isn't forthcoming, be ready to move on to other buyer prospects. If an offer does arrive, work to obtain a good-faith deposit to confirm the buyer's serious intention this time around.

Predicting the likelihood of an offer

At the same time that you're helping the buyer decide to make an offer, you need to decide whether an offer and subsequent purchase is likely. If a match-up isn't likely, face the facts and move on, sooner rather than later. The fastest way to forecast whether an offer is forthcoming is to assess whether you and the buyer are in the same pricing ballpark. Ask yourself the following questions:

- ✔ **What's the lowest price I'm willing to accept?** Probably, this price is somewhere between 70 and 85 percent of your asking price, if you started with a price that's somewhere between two and three times your annual seller's discretionary earnings and your business is reasonably strong. If your business isn't strong, and if you priced it anything above two times earnings, you may be looking at a final price that's even less than 70 percent of your initial asking price.

- ✔ **What's the highest price the buyer is willing to offer?** Usually, the buyer begins by figuring out how much the business needs to earn to provide a salary, plus enough earnings to repay loans that are required to make the deal possible and to give a reasonable investment return on the money the buyer puts down in cash. The buyer takes that total and multiplies by two to four to come up with an idea of a fair price (Chapter 6 explains how buyers and sellers arrive at the earnings multiple).

  As you try to peg how much the buyer will offer, the big variable is how much the buyer expects the business to generate for an owner's salary. The easiest clue is to find out how much the buyer has been making up until the time you began purchase discussions. If the buyer's been making $100,000 and your business will provide a salary of $50,000, read the writing on the wall — you probably don't have a very good match. People usually don't pay good money to get less than they could make without the stress of buying and owning a business.

Of course, every general rule has exceptions. If your buyer is retired and really wants a new challenge, money may not be the motivator. Or, if the buyer has big plans to take your business in a new, more lucrative direction, opportunity may outweigh income in the purchase decision. But if the buyer has to quit a high-paying job as part of the deal, don't count on the sale.

Nudging the Conversation toward Decision-Making Time

Before you can actually sell your business, you need to receive an offer, respond with a counteroffer if necessary, agree to a buyer's letter of intent, and go through the process of *due diligence*, where you and the buyer do all the research and homework necessary to confirm the condition of your business, its finances, and the buyer's ability to complete the deal. But first, you just want a serious, legitimate, well-priced offer, which may arrive verbally or in the form of a *letter of intent* — a document that outlines the buyer's purchase proposal and the terms being offered.

Although you won't release your selling memorandum until after you receive an offer and letter of intent, you've probably released the summary of your selling memorandum (see Form 8-2) so the buyer has a basic outline of your business and offer. Also, as the buyer indicates growing seriousness about making an offer, share your statement of seller's discretionary earnings so the buyer can understand how much the owner of the business can make. See Form 5-3 for help recasting your financial statements into a pro forma estimate of annual owner earnings.

Each time the buyer asks for information you can't divulge prior to an offer, or each time the buyer wants to discuss price or terms, use the opportunity to prompt an offer. For example, if the buyer asks for very confidential business information, you can say something like, "I've already begun to compile information like that to have ready for your review during due diligence. We can start that process immediately following the purchase offer. You may even want to note the request as part of the conditions and contingencies detailed in your letter of intent." At the risk of sounding like a broken record, repeat this response each time a request for private business information arises. Better that you get an offer with a long list of conditions and contingencies than never get an offer at all.

Calming a buyer's nerves

A business broker will tell you that a buyer gets very nervous when it comes time to put an offer in writing. The buyer will double-think everything from what your business is worth to what it'll take to own and run it to whether business ownership is really the right next step. It's your job, especially if you're working without a broker, to ease the buyer's tensions at the same time you encourage the buyer to make an offer. Some tips to help you along the way:

✔ **Explain that if the buyer's interested in taking the next step, he or she should present an offer so the two of you can sort out whether you're in the same ballpark on price.** The buyer knows your asking price, and you know that most likely the buyer will offer something less. You'll know how close you are, though, only after an offer is in your hands.

✔ **Remind the buyer (repeatedly, if necessary) that the offer presented before due diligence is non-binding.** Most offers come with what are called *contingencies*, which are conditions that must be met before the offer will become legally binding. Likely the buyer will make the offer contingent upon the results of due diligence. *Due diligence* — the next step in the sale process — is where the buyer examines your business and finances to confirm the condition is to the buyer's satisfaction. (Due diligence is the topic of Chapter 12.) The offer may also be contingent upon financing arrangements or other conditions (such as extension of your building lease, for example) that the buyer specifies as part of the offer.

Discussing possible offer details

Especially in smaller business sales and where brokers aren't involved, the buyer will likely deliver the first offer in person. Usually, this offer doesn't come out of the blue but as a result of buyer-seller discussions that lead to a firm decision by the buyer to begin to close the deal.

During your discussions, as soon as a buyer starts talking prices or terms, use the opportunity to ask the buyer to put the proposed terms in writing. Explain that after you have an outline of what the buyer wants to achieve, you can get your accountant involved. How the deal is proposed can be just as or more important than the price being offered, so don't hesitate to tell the buyer that you need to receive legal or accounting input before responding to a purchase proposal. At the same time that you're going back and forth to your accountant and attorney for advice, the buyer will be doing the same thing. The process is a little slow but entirely necessary, so don't try to rush it, and for your own good, don't leave your accountant out of the loop.

Getting an offer in writing

As soon as both you and the buyer — with input from your accountants and attorneys — are comfortable with the offer's general terms, it's the buyer's obligation to create and present a letter of intent to purchase your business. The *letter of intent* confirms the price, structure, terms, and conditions being proposed. Attorneys will tell you that the letter of intent "signifies the interests of the buyer and seller to complete the transaction." It's not usually a binding document, but it forms the basis for all future discussions that lead to your sale closing.

Even if the buyer personally presents an offer, unless your sale price is very low and your knowledge of and confidence in the buyer is very high, you still need to see a letter of intent that commits the buyer's offer to writing.

ON THE CD

Figure 11-1 (Form 11-1 on the CD-ROM) shows a sample statement of intent, provided by Sunbelt Business Brokers, to give you an idea of the kind of form that's presented with a small business offer. The Sunbelt form has two parts: the agreement to purchase and an addendum where the buyer lists conditions and contingencies (the addendum is shown in Figure 11-2 and on the CD-ROM as Form 11-2).

SUNBELT®

AGREEMENT TO PURCHASE

1. _____ (the "Buyer") agrees to purchase from _____ (the "Seller") the assets (the "Assets") of the business (excluding cash and accounts receivable) described as follows: the assets include any websites, all equipment, trade fixtures, inventory, supplies, trademarks, trade names, phone numbers and all other tangible and intangible assets used in the business known as:_____ (hereafter, "Business") located at: _____

2. The Purchase Price of _____ shall be paid as follows:
   a. _____ Deposit on the date of this Agreement, included in Down Payment to be deposited in the trust account of Broker within 3 business days of the offer acceptance by Seller.
   b. _____ Additional Deposit upon acceptance by Seller, included in Down Payment.
   c. _____ Balance of Down Payment due at the Closing in cash with certified check or bank wire.
      _____ Total Down-Payment
   d. _____ Balance to be paid to Seller pursuant to a Secured Promissory note in said amount payable as follows: _____ or more per month (including _____ interest) for _____ months.
   e. _____ Additional terms:
      _____ Total Purchase Price

3. The Closing shall take place on or before _____ A.M. / P.M. on _____, 20___ at the office of Sunbelt Business Advisors (hereafter, Broker). Closing costs shall be shared equally by Buyer and Seller.
4. The Purchase Price shall include inventory of $_____ at Seller's cost. If the actual inventory value is more or less, the Purchase Price shall be adjusted accordingly; however in no event shall the purchase of such inventory exceed $_____.
5. Seller warrants that at the time physical possession is delivered to Buyer, all equipment will be in working order and that the premises will pass all inspections necessary to conduct such business.
6. Sales tax, if applicable, will be paid for by the Buyer.
7. The Buyer and Seller agree to execute all documents necessary to consummate this transaction.
8. This Agreement contains the entire understanding of the parties and there are no oral agreements, understandings or representations relied upon by the parties. It may be modified only in writing and signed by both the Buyer and Seller.
9. The Seller represents and warrants that it has good and marketable title to the Assets being sold, and will satisfy all taxes, payroll, liabilities and obligations of the business at or prior to Closing. Seller will satisfy all requirements of the Bulk Sales Act or similar laws, if applicable.
10. The following adjustments and pro-rations shall be made at Closing: rent, utilities, _____, _____, _____.
11. In case any litigation is instituted to collect any sum due Broker, the Seller agrees to pay the expenses incurred by the Broker in connection with such suit, including attorney's fees.
12. Seller shall indemnify and hold harmless Buyer from all claims, liabilities, or obligations arising out of conduct of the Business prior to Closing.
13. Buyer shall indemnify and hold harmless Seller from all claims, liabilities, or obligations arising out of conduct of the Business after Closing.
14. If the Seller fails to accept this agreement by 5:00 P.M. _____, 20___, then the Buyer may revoke this Agreement and the Buyer's deposit will be refunded.
15. Both Buyer and Seller agree that any information provided by Broker has not been verified by Broker and both parties shall rely solely on their own due diligence and hold Broker harmless from all claims regarding this transaction.
16. Buyer agrees that if it should fail or refuse to complete this transaction within fourteen days after the Closing date (#3, above) unless amended in writing, then any funds on Deposit with the Broker will be forfeited without notice, and, at the Broker's option, shall be split 50% to the Seller, and 50% to the Broker.
17. Severability: The invalidity, illegality, or unenforceability of any obligation or provision under this agreement shall not affect or impair the enforceability or legality of any remaining provision or obligation under this agreement.

BUYER AND SELLER INDIVIDUALLY ACKNOWLEDGE RECEIPT OF A COPY OF THIS AGREEMENT
THIS IS A LEGALLY BINDING DOCUMENT. READ IT CAREFULLY. IF YOU DO NOT UNDERSTAND IT, CONSULT AN ATTORNEY. BROKER IS NOT AUTHORIZED TO GIVE LEGAL ADVICE.

BUYER hereby agrees to buy on the terms set forth above.   The SELLER agrees to sell on the terms set forth above. Brokers' commission as per separate Agreement.

Dated: _____   Dated: _____

BUYER SIGNATURE: _____   SELLER (Business Name): _____

Address: _____   SELLER SIGNATURE: _____

City: _____ State:_____ Zip: _____   Address: _____

BROKER By _____ It's Agent   City: _____ State:_____ Zip: _____

Agreement to Purchase_09_04

Figure 11-1: Sample letter of intent.

Letter courtesy of Sunbelt Business Brokers

SUNBELT®

Manager's Initials | Date

ADDENDUM TO AGREEMENT TO PURCHASE

The following Addendum and Contingencies are hereby made to the attached   Agreement to Purchase ,

Dated _____ on the Business known as   _____ :

Conditions of Closing:

Seller shall deliver to Buyer at, or prior to, closing the followi   ng: 1) Consents necessary to assign to Buyer, or assume by Bu   yer, any property leases the Business is party to.   2) All licenses, permits and franchise agreem   ents necessary to operate or acquire the Business shall be obtained by the Buyer or transferred to the Buyer by the Seller.

A Definitive Purchase Agreement, incorporating the terms of this   Agreement to Purchase, shall be agreed to by the Buyer and the Seller. Both parties shall work c   ooperatively and expeditiously to complete   such Definitive Purchase Agreement.

Contingencies:

The above contingencies shall expire and t   he Deposit shall become non-re   fundable without notice to the Buyer at _____ on _____(Contingency Expiration Date).   The Deposit shall be refunded to the Buyer upon Buyer's notification to the Seller   in writing, via Broker, prior to said   date, that the Buyer   is canceling this Agreement. The Business shall remain on the market unt   il the Deposit becomes non-re   fundable; however, Buyer may notify Seller, in writing, via Broker, t   hat the Deposit is non-refundable prior to   the Contingency Expiration Date. In such event, the Business shall be removed from   the market until the C ontingency Expiration Date, after which the business may again be marketed. In the event t   hat, prior to the Deposit becoming   non-refundable, the Seller receives and wishes to accept an Agreement to Purc   hase from another buyer,   Seller shall not   ify Buyer in writing, via Broker, of said other bona fide Agreements(s) To Purc   hase. From the date of sa   id notification, Buyer s hall have the earlier of 3 business days or the Contingency Expiration   Date above, to notify Seller in writing,   via Broker, that the Deposit is non-refundable or this Agreement to Purchas   e shall become null and void and Deposit   shall be fully refunded to Buyer. All other terms and conditions of the Agreement   to Purchase are to remain the same.

If the Seller fails to accept this Amendment by _____ P.M. _____ then the Addendum and the attached Agreement to Purchase may   be revoked by the Buyer and Deposit w   ill be returned to the Buyer. Receipt of copy of this Agreement is acknowledged.

Date: _____   Date: _____

_____   _____
Buyer   Seller

_____   _____
Buyer   Seller

Addendum to Agreement to Purchase_09_04

Figure 11-2:
Sample addendum to letter of intent.

Addendum courtesy of Sunbelt Business Brokers

Reviewing the Letter of Intent for Acceptance or Counter offer

Putting your signature on a letter of intent is sort of like watching the kickoff on a football field. It signals that the game has officially begun. So before you sign it, make sure you review it — carefully — and have professional advisors look it over, too.

As a motivated seller, it's tempting to fix your eyes on the buyer's proposed price as the make-it-or-break-it aspect of the offer, but that's a mistake — and it's part of the reason why involving advisors is so essential to the positive outcome of your sale transaction. How the buyer's offer is structured, the proposed timeline, and the payment strategy can combine to be even more important than the offered price. Your tax obligation varies depending upon whether you sell business assets or business stock; whether payments are specified for fixtures, furnishings, and equipment or for goodwill; and whether the proceeds will be taxable in a single year or spread over a longer period. Your accountant's advice is, literally, worth money in the bank.

When reviewing the buyer's letter of intent, here are some topics to cover with your legal and accounting advisors:

- **The proposed price and payment structure,** including how much is paid in cash, what kind of financing is necessary, and what sources of financing are being proposed.

  As you review the proposed payment structure with your advisors, you want to assess the buyer's ability to fulfill the proposed payment approach. You also need to weigh the tax implications of the proposed payment structure, working with your accountant to counter with a revised payment structure that better addresses your tax situation, if necessary. But realize that each time the deal is restructured to provide you a tax advantage, it probably eliminates a tax advantage the seller is counting on. Be reasonable, and ask for your accountant's input to arrive at a counterproposal that's fair and mutually beneficial to you and the buyer. Chapters 13 and 14 are full of information on how payment approaches are structured and what kind of tax implications apply to various payment approaches.

- **What the buyer is buying.** Nearly 95 percent of small-business buyers buy assets, but a few buy the entire business entity, and you need to be sure about what's being proposed and how the proposal will affect the taxes you pay on sale proceeds. (Chapter 6 includes a section that helps you get clear about the differences between asset and equity sales, and Chapter 14 dives into tax implications.)

- **How the buyer proposes to allocate the purchase price.** In addition to structuring the sale as an asset sale or an entity sale, *and* in addition to structuring the payment approach, the buyer's offer may also describe a price allocation approach. A buyer will want to allocate as much of the purchase price as possible toward the purchase of assets that can be deducted as business expenses (such as a seller's consulting contract) or toward assets with a short depreciation period, both of which provide tax advantages for the buyer. You, on the other hand, may want to allocate the purchase price differently, so that as much as possible of the price is allocated to assets you've held over time so the proceeds can be taxed at a lower capital-gains rate. See why you need your accountant's advice?

Chapter 14 includes details on how business sale proceeds are taxed, but in a single sentence here's what you need to remember: Payments for various assets are taxed at various rates, and the differences add up to real money in either your pocket or your buyer's pocket. If the letter of intent details a purchase price allocation that puts you at a serious tax disadvantage, work with your accountant to come up with a counteroffer that better balances the tax burden between you and the buyer.

If the letter of intent doesn't describe how the purchase price will be allocated, be ready, because this point will definitely arise during the negotiations that lead to the sale closing.

✔ **Variances from your sale offering.** Study the letter of intent carefully to determine whether the buyer is proposing a purchase that aligns exactly with your offering or proposing exclusions or additions that will affect your sale proceeds, taxes, or liability. Remember, most businesses sell for less than their asking prices — frequently as much as 30 percent less — so make sure you understand the concessions you're agreeing to.

✔ **The duration of the due diligence period.** The buyer will need time to investigate your business and financial condition. Typically, due diligence for a small business takes fewer than four weeks, unless real property or environmental assessments are involved, in which case a longer time period may be necessary.

If the buyer proposes an unduly long due diligence period, you can counter with a different deadline. Also, be sure that the letter of intent includes a clause that ensures that no information obtained during this investigation period will be disclosed to anyone other than the buyer's purchase advisors without your permission.

✔ **Requested warranties and representations**. Here's where your lawyer's knowledge will prove invaluable. Every purchase offer will include a request that you warrant or guarantee the facts presented about your company. However, not all warranty requests are the same, and language in this area matters greatly.

- The key phrase you want to include is that you have described your business condition *accurately to the best of your knowledge*. You're warranting *accuracy*, not *completeness*, because there may be facts of which you're honestly not aware. Also, you're warranting facts *to the best of your knowledge* or *to the best of your ability*, not *to seller's actual knowledge* or *upon due inquiry*. Should the buyer's investigation uncover negative surprises, this clause protects you by stating that you conveyed information to the best of your ability, not based on actual investigation of each fact.

- Finally, be sure you're clear about the definition of the term "seller" in the warranties and representations clause. Some buyers use the term "seller" to cover not only you but also everyone on your staff. If the buyer is asking you to warrant information from staff members, you may need to ask for a revision to the letter, or to limit access to your staff so you can ensure the buyer gets only accurate information.

✔ **Seller's future involvement.** The letter of intent may include a stipulation that you remain with the business for a period of time after the sale, and under what terms. It also may require you to sign a non-competition and non-solicitation agreement, also called a *covenant not to compete,* under which you agree not to approach customers of your business or pursue a similar profession or trade within a certain market area for a specified period of time. If the buyer requests that you remain involved with your business longer than you intended, or at a lower level of compensation than you want to agree to, counter with alternate terms. Also counter if the terms of the non-competition and non-solicitation agreements span an unduly large geographic area or time period, conditions that are unacceptable to most sellers and that rarely hold up when challenged in court.

✔ **Other stipulations.** Letters of intent may include the following clauses, which you should also review with your attorney:

- **Business as usual statement,** stating whether the owner is to continue running the business as usual during the closing period or whether the buyer requests that certain purchases or new agreements be put on hold or certain remedial actions be completed

- **Statement that the letter is nonbinding,** stipulating that neither party will be liable to the other if seller and buyer aren't able to agree on a satisfactory purchase agreement

- **Cancellation statement**, defining how each party can cancel the agreement and terms that prevent the buyer from using information to harm or compete against your company

- **Exclusivity agreement,** preventing the seller from considering competing offers during the due diligence period (be aware that this clause is only common in large deals where the buyer will be investing heavily in due diligence)

If you need to present a counteroffer, turn to Chapter 13 for advice on how to handle a buyer-seller negotiation, as you'll be wading into an important one.

Accepting the Buyer's Purchase Offer

When you're ready to sign the letter, here's what happens:

- ✔ If a broker is handling your sale, the buyer will provide a purchase deposit — usually 10 percent of the purchase price, to be held in an escrow account.

- ✔ If you're handling your own sale, your accountant and attorney can help you determine whether to request a deposit, called *earnest money*, and, if so, for what amount and how the deposit should be held. Most owners who sell on their own don't receive deposits, but if you do request a deposit, you need to present the buyer with a description of what events will trigger a return of the funds.

If a deposit is involved, open an escrow account with a company that deals with the sale of businesses and immediately place the deposit check into the account. Follow these steps:

1. **Open an escrow account, held by a neutral third party called an escrow agent, to hold the earnest money in trust until all the letter of intent's conditions are addressed.**

   Your broker (if you're using one) will help you set up an escrow account. Otherwise, you can contact an escrow company to open an account, or you can go through your bank's escrow department.

   Usually, escrow fees and other closing costs are split between the buyer and seller. When you open the escrow account, ask the agent to estimate the fee, which is incorporated by the escrow company into the final cost settlement sheet.

2. **The escrow agent provides a set of instructions to you and the buyer detailing the responsibilities the agent will fulfill and the conditions that need to be met by the buyer and seller before the earnest money deposit and closing documents can be released.**

3. **The escrow agent searches for business liens or judgments that need to be addressed or cleared before the sale can close.**

4. **While the escrow agent searches for liens or judgments, the buyer and seller conduct due diligence.**

   At this stage, the buyer determines whether anything about the business's condition needs to be addressed through owner actions or price adjustments.

5. **The escrow agent prepares the closing sheet and other documents while you work with an attorney to create a purchase and sale agreement.**

After a signed letter of intent is in your hands, your sale is officially underway. The next step is to launch the due diligence process. Turn to Chapter 12 for a rundown of what's involved next.

Forms on the CD-ROM

Form 11-1	**Sample Letter of Intent**	A copy of the agreement form a Sunbelt broker would present with a small business purchase offer
Form 11-2	**Sample Addendum to Letter of Intent**	A sample of the way buyers present sale offer conditions and contingencies

Part IV
So You've Got a Buyer! Now What?

The 5th Wave   By Rich Tennant

"The paperwork for your business sale seems to
be in order. Now, if we can tap a vein for your
signature we'll be all set."

In this part . . .

What you really want isn't a buyer but a check. You want this deal to be over and to end successfully, with smiles all around and a big celebration that accompanies the handover of the keys to your business.

First, take a deep breath. You still have some important work to do. The first chapter in this part guides you through the investigation period called *due diligence*, where your buyer examines the condition of your business and verifies the claims you make about its health and strength. The next chapter helps you work with the buyer and your advisors to negotiate the deal, including how the payment is structured, how the outstanding balance is financed, and what's involved if you're going to play the banker in the deal.

Chapter 14 picks through the details of financing and tax issues. Chapter 15 is your guide to closing the sale, and finally, Chapter 16 is all about transferring your business and moving on. Way to go!

Chapter 12

The Investigation Begins: Due Diligence

. . . .

In This Chapter

▶ Gathering the necessary paperwork for the buyer's due diligence

▶ Surviving the buyer's investigation into your finances and operations

▶ Conducting your own investigation of the buyer

. . . .

*1*f you like homework, you'll love due diligence. *Due diligence* is the process of research and investigation that takes place after you receive a buyer's offer to purchase your business and before the deal closes. When the buyer presents an offer and letter of intent, the proposal is usually non-binding and contingent on the buyer's ability to delve into details about your business. That means the buyer will close the deal if the business meets his or her expectations as discussed in your meetings together, or if, for those businesses that aren't up to par, you address specific conditions and contingencies to the buyer's satisfaction. During this stage the buyer's investigation revolves around your finances, your operations, and legal issues that affect your business.

Part of the assessment is on your end, too — usually, one of the specified conditions is that the offer is contingent upon the buyer's ability to come up with the financing necessary to make the deal happen, so you'll be using the period of due diligence to look into the buyer's financial capability. You also want to learn the buyer's plans for the business and to make sure that the buyer has the skills needed to run your business smoothly after the purchase goes through. This part of your investigation is important, especially if you agree to be the banker for part of the purchase price, or to accept deferred payments that are contingent on the business's future success.

From both the seller's and buyer's perspective, the investigation in front of you can make or break the deal. That's why you both have to proceed with, well, due diligence. Unless your sale is complicated by real estate issues or by environmental or other regulated factors that add complexity to the buyer's investigation, you and the buyer should be able to set and maintain a due diligence time frame of less than four weeks. This chapter outlines what's involved in this stage of the sale process, gives tips to help you protect yourself where confidentiality is concerned, and summarizes what responsibilities need to be addressed on both sides of the sale.

Preparing Paperwork That Bares All to the Buyer

Now that you're holding the buyer's letter of intent, it's time to open your files, financial records, and business operations for the buyer's inspection. By now, the buyer has probably provided you with not one but two confidentiality agreements. The first agreement is the one that your attorney drew up and that you signed in your accountant's office when you first met the buyer, right before you disclosed your business name. (Form 8-6 on the CD-ROM shows a sample confidentiality agreement provided by Sunbelt Business Brokers.) The second agreement is usually included in the buyer's letter of intent. If the letter stipulates that the buyer's offer is contingent upon due diligence investigation, this requirement is usually accompanied by a statement that prevents either party from disclosing confidential information obtained during the investigation to anyone other than the buyer's or seller's purchase advisors.

With confidentiality ensured, you're now safe to give the buyer a copy of your selling memorandum (on the slim chance that *selling memorandum* sounds foreign to you, Chapter 8 provides a guide to what's involved in this document).

 Before giving the copy to the buyer, number the cover and every page of the booklet — with the term "Copy #1," for example. That way, should pages get copied and circulated, you both can trace the photocopies back to this copy. The buyer has already signed a confidentiality agreement that prevents the sharing of information with anyone but specified advisors, but you still want to take additional steps to protect the information in your selling memorandum.

You also need to give the buyer access to the following list of backup information, which the buyer will review to verify the accuracy of the information in your selling memorandum and in personal discussions. After you assemble the material, move it to a place where you can invite the buyer to go for the due diligence review. Most sellers arrange for a meeting room in their accountant's office for this purpose. Unless the buyer specifically requests that copies of certain documents be sent to the buyer's accountant or attorney, and unless your accountant and attorney advise you to release the information, make this information available for perusal only in the setting you establish for due diligence review.

To keep the due diligence process moving, don't wait until the last minute to assemble this backup information. Gather it up and have it ready to present, even while you're awaiting a buyer offer. Not only will the advance planning save you a frenzied last-minute effort, it'll also keep the deal moving swiftly from the moment the buyer switches on the green light. Here's what to have ready to go:

- ✔ **Federal tax returns for the past three years.** The buyer wants to verify that you and your business made the amount of money shown on your financial statements. If your business files tax returns, have returns from the past three years ready for the buyer's review. If your business is a sole proprietorship, LLC, or S corporation that passes revenue through to you personally, be ready to show the Schedule C from your personal returns.

- ✔ **Business financial statements for the past three years.** Buyers need to see year-to-date and annual income statements (also called profit and loss statements) and balance sheets. When the request comes, don't pull out bits and pieces of paper. Work in advance with an accountant or bookkeeper to have standard, easy-to-understand reports prepared and ready for review. Turn to Chapter 5 for samples of the forms you need.

- ✔ **Current statement of seller's discretionary earnings,** which is the form that recasts your income statement into a pro forma estimate of how much money your business actually generates for your benefit. This form should be included in your selling memorandum. To see what it looks like, check out Figure 5-3 in Chapter 5.

- ✔ **Financial trends and ratios,** including sales growth, seasonality of sales, cost of goods sold in relation to sales revenue, inventory turnover, accounts aging, and liquidity. Chapter 5 helps you calculate these ratios and trends.

- ✔ **Accounts receivable, accounts payable, and inventory.** Have lists of current accounts receivable and accounts payable ready for buyer review, along with a report showing the aging of your accounts receivable. If your business is inventory-reliant, also have a copy of current inventory and value, along with a report showing your inventory turnover rate.

- ✔ **Current building lease.** Any buyer wants to see your building lease. If you're selling a retail business — especially a restaurant — the buyer needs to verify that the lease extends at least five years into the future and can be transferred to a new owner. Most bank loans also require that the building lease extend at least five years into the future. Short or non-transferable building leases can present a huge stumbling block in business sales, so take the time to get your lease in top form before due diligence begins. If you don't, plan on due diligence lasting until lease issues are resolved.

✔ **Franchise agreement.** If you're selling a franchise, turn to Chapter 1 and review the section on finding a buyer for your franchise. It details what's necessary to resell your franchise, including the importance of involving your franchise organization as early as possible.

✔ **A list of all fixtures, furnishings, and equipment** that will be included in the sale. Form 6-1 on the CD-ROM helps you prepare this list. Additionally, include the following:

- Photos of major equipment. Because your buyer completes part of the review outside your premises, photos help the buyer understand and verify your assets while also enhancing the attractiveness of your offering.

- Titles to show ownership for major equipment you own.

- Lease agreements for furnishings and equipment, if any.

- Equipment depreciation schedule from your most recent tax return.

✔ **Current contracts or agreements with employees, customers, vendors, and distributors,** including verification that the contracts can be cancelled by, or transferred to, a new owner.

✔ **Current business licenses, certifications, or registrations,** including verification of transferability.

✔ **Patent or trademark registration documents,** if any, showing whether the property is owned personally or by the business.

✔ **Copies of outstanding loan agreements,** if any.

✔ **Management records,** including a description of your business model (for help, see Chapter 7), billing rates or product price lists, sales reports, revenues by product line (see Form 8-3 on the CD-ROM), inventory lists, equipment or facility maintenance agreements and reports, and a copy of your business operations manual (to see what should be included in this manual, see Chapter 7).

✔ **Employee records,** including a list of employees, hire dates, and salaries (Form 8-3 includes a section you can use when creating this list), pension records, an organization chart, an employee benefit plan outline, and a copy of your employment policy manual, as described in Chapter 7.

✔ **Business formation documents,** including partnership agreements or articles of incorporation — or, if your business is a sole proprietorship, copies of your business license and assumed name registration.

✔ **Current client lists** or information on customer databases that will transfer to the new owner.

✔ **Current lists of major suppliers and distributors** with information on duration and nature of relationships and whether the relationships are under transferable contracts.

✔ **A summary of your business plan** (Form 7-1 on the CD-ROM shows what to include).

✔ **A summary of your marketing plan** (Form 7-2 on the CD-ROM shows what to include), along with copies of major marketing materials.

Use the checklist in Form 12-1 on the CD-ROM as you assemble information for the buyer's due diligence investigation.

Deals can fall apart during due diligence, and you don't want your sale to suffer that fate. Be ready to respond quickly to every information request the buyer makes, because delays don't just stall deals — they kill them.

Taking Precautionary Measures Before Due Diligence Begins

After signing a letter of intent to buy your business, most buyers want at least some exposure to employees and key business contacts such as major clients, distributors, or suppliers. It's your job to control those contacts so you can maintain the level of confidentiality you believe is necessary.

To maintain confidentiality about your sale intentions so employees, clients, suppliers, and competitors aren't tipped off about your sale plans until closing day, consider these steps:

✔ **Confide in one or a few (if your business has a large staff) trusted top managers,** telling them privately about the sale when the letter of intent has been signed and due diligence is ready to begin. Ask your lawyer's advice regarding whether you should obtain confidentiality agreements before sharing the news. This early confidential announcement to select managers is especially important if the buyer is counting on their continued employment. If that's the case, when confiding in the managers, assure them that their positions are secure under the new ownership.

The new owner may plan to offer incentives for the managers to aid in the transition — particularly if you're not staying on for a period of time — in which case you can explain that the buyer wants to meet with each one personally and to recognize and reward their loyalty. If not, you may want to offer an incentive of your own as a bonus not only for staying, but also for taking on the added responsibility of assisting the buyer's due diligence investigation and subsequent ownership transition.

This pre-announcement to top managers will work best if it includes the following information:

- A positive summary of the buyer's qualifications and expertise.

- A positive preview of what's in it for the manager, both in terms of a strong future for the business and immediate or near-term bonuses or other incentives or rewards for the manager's help in making the sale possible.

- An overview of the timeline you expect the sale to follow and the point at which you expect to announce the news to the rest of your employee team, as well as to customers, suppliers, associates, and media.

- Advice regarding how to keep the story under wraps, including how to deal with employee questions or suspicions that may arise before closing day. Managers can tell employees that you're interviewing a new top executive or that you're working on obtaining financing or growth capital, which allows you to be honest without disclosing the part of the story that may jeopardize the deal and the business.

- A request for assistance during the buyer's due diligence investigation. Before granting the buyer access to managers, ask managers to be prepared to answer buyer questions frankly and to decline to answer any question about which the manager doesn't have adequate knowledge.

Should managers give misleading information to the buyer, work with your attorney to protect yourself in the warranties and representations section of your purchase and sale agreement. This part of the document warrants that all facts presented by the seller to the buyer are accurate to the best of the seller's knowledge. Your lawyer may advise you to add wording that defines "seller" as you and not as everyone on your staff.

After making the announcement to top managers, requesting their confidentiality, and possibly offering them incentives for sale assistance, plan to introduce them to the buyer.

Use an outside-the-business location for key manager-buyer meetings so you don't set off alerts under your business roof. Your attorney's office is a good place for such meetings and for most other due diligence activities.

✔ **Limit the buyer's access to all other employees.** Realize that any access to employees is a risky move. If the sale doesn't close, you'll have thrown up a red flag and caused employees to doubt the security of the future of your ownership and, therefore, the stability of their jobs. Based on your knowledge of your employees' faith in you and your business, it may be worth the risk, especially if you feel your business can withstand the departure of employees if their insecurity about their jobs sends them to other employers. In most cases, however, you're better off not granting access to employees, or, if you do, making the introduction in terms that don't reveal your sale intentions.

When my husband and I sold our advertising agency, we introduced the buyer as someone who was considering joining our business as a top executive. We told the truth; we simply didn't admit that his presence would replace ours, as we really weren't yet sure that that would be the case. If you and the buyer agree to an approach like this, you can introduce the buyer to employees and a few business associates, such as clients or suppliers, if you feel such contacts are necessary.

✔ **Grant the buyer access to your accountant and attorney.** As much as possible, use your accountant and, to a lesser degree, your attorney to deliver information on your business. Move all the documents required during due diligence (see Form 12-1 on the CD-ROM) to the office of either of these professional advisors — preferably to your accountant's office, because so many of the buyer's questions will revolve around finances. Make this off-site professional setting the site of your buyer's research. This will cost you money, as professional advisors charge almost by the minute, and they'll almost certainly end up spending time on your behalf in addition to providing a meeting space and interacting with your buyer. But your buyer will get the necessary information, and you won't risk revealing your sale plans to others. As an alternative, if you're using a broker, you may be able to make the broker's office the site for due diligence information review.

✔ **Agree in advance how the buyer should contact your business**. For instance, you may agree that all buyer requests come to you directly, through use of your personal cellphone, home phone, or confidential e-mail address. Or you may require that all contacts go through your broker, accountant, or attorney. In any event, stipulate that no requests be left in messages, e-mails, or letters sent to your business, or you run the risk of others intercepting those requests.

The Buyer's Homework Assignment

During due diligence, buyers are working to find out two main things:

✔ That your business is in the financial condition and working order you represent it to be

✔ That there aren't any lurking problems — including financial, legal, or operational issues — that could threaten the future of your business and therefore the return on the buyer's investment

The buyer will conduct this research by poring over the hefty documentation you've compiled and handed over, by taking another stroll through your facility, and by asking still more questions of you. The buyer will probably conduct at least part of this review by working with his or her accountant and attorney, as covered by the confidentiality clause in the buyer's letter of intent. While the investigation is underway, your role is mostly to cooperate by compiling records to have available in a convenient location such as your accountant's office, by allowing access to your facilities and employees, by disclosing problems, and by highlighting opportunities so the buyer can complete the necessary fact-finding in the allotted time frame.

Get ready to make plenty of time available in your own calendar to devote to due diligence. The process is usually time-consuming and may eat into your evenings and weekends as well as your business days, because you'll be running and selling your business at the same time. To make your days bearable, and also to make your business a more transferable asset, if you can transfer some of your client contact and management responsibilities to key staff prior to launching the sale process, you'll be better able to juggle the tasks you need to handle. The upcoming sections describe what your buyer is trying to learn.

Verifying your business's financial health

When the due diligence process begins, the buyer will go right to work studying your financial statements and supporting documents. Don't be surprised if the buyer asks you to release copies of your financial statements and tax returns for a third-party review by the buyer's accountant. Check with your own professional advisors before handing anything over to an accountant you don't even know (they'll most likely tell you to share the requested information). If the buyer's letter of intent includes a clause ensuring confidentiality of information released to the buyer's advisors, the security of your information should be protected.

Here are some of the facts the buyer will be looking to confirm:

- **Business growth trends,** including how sales have increased over recent years, how sales by product line are growing, how cost-of-sales and operating expenses relate to overall sales, and how your revenue growth trends track against industry averages.

- **Business growth estimates,** including how the buyer's assumptions synch with your assumptions regarding the near-term future of your business.

- **Business financial management,** including how well your business has evened out or dealt with the effects of seasonality of sales, how your business handles billing and collections, how often clients challenge bills or receive billing adjustments, the condition of your accounts receivable, and whether you have any collection problems.

- **Business profitability,** including the strength of your current bottom line and whether the business is profitable enough to meet the buyer's earnings expectations. If it's not, the buyer will be studying how to trim expenses and/or raise prices to reach a level of profitability that justifies the purchase.

Investigation of your business finances consumes much of the due diligence effort. The good news is that most of the research is conducted outside of your business — in the office of your accountant or broker and far away from the curious eyes of employees or customers, unlike research of your operations, which has to happen under your roof.

Researching your operations

Your buyer gets a good look at your business during the initial tour, which — if your business is a retail establishment that attracts foot traffic — should take place during peak business hours, when your business is running at full tilt. (Chapter 11 helps you keep the reason for the buyer's visit under wraps even while you're introducing him or her around your business.) With a picture of your business already in the buyer's mind, you can probably handle much of the behind-the-scenes look at your company during off hours when employees aren't around, or even off-premises, where you can go over operational issues that don't require in-person inspection.

Your buyer wants to investigate the following operational issues, most of which can be accomplished in an off-premise location:

✔ **How your business runs** and whether it's likely to continue, fairly uninterrupted, upon your departure. Here's where your organization chart and operations manual are worth their weight in gold. Help the buyer understand that your business follows established processes to produce its products or provide its services, and that those processes will easily transfer to a new owner.

✔ **Strength and loyalty of your customer base.** Be ready to present the following information:

• How your business keeps, and will transfer, customer or client information. If you have customer databases, you can explain the system you use and show copies of the reports you generate.

• How your customer base has grown over recent years, if it has.

• How long your business has served key customers. Use this explanation to demonstrate customer loyalty, which is a key to customer retention. Also use it as an opportunity to explain that no single client accounts for the bulk of your business billings, if such is the case. (Buyers are rightfully concerned if one client, who may decide to leave the business following a sale, represents more than even 10 percent of annual sales revenue.)

• How your business relates to key customers. Unless yours is a one-person business, the buyer wants to see that customers are served by and have loyalty to a number of individuals beyond just you, the owner. Also, if your company serves customers face to face rather than by mail, phone, or online, the buyer wants to know that customers are familiar with and have a habit of coming to your location, which is a good indication of loyalty to your business.

✔ **What your business charges and how it handles billing.** In addition to providing service rates or product prices, describe how your business handles price increases and when the last increases took effect. This will be of particular interest if a buyer is trying to figure out how to increase your business profitability. Also describe how your company bills clients, extends credit, handles collections, and manages accounts receivable.

✔ **How your business produces its product or service,** including the caliber and condition of equipment, computers, and software. Be prepared to show asset lists, ownership information, equipment photos, equipment leases, maintenance records, and maintenance contracts. This portion of the due diligence review will probably require another walk through your business so the buyer can take a firsthand look at the condition of equipment.

✔ **How your business is staffed**, including how many full-time, part-time, temporary, contract, or freelance workers form your business team. When presenting your staff situation, if your business is large enough to have a number of managers and departments, show an organization chart. Describe how management and customer contact responsibilities are handled by others and not just by you, if that's the case. Also show your payroll obligation, which employees have employment contracts (if any), and how long each has been with, and who is most knowledgeable about, your company. If key employees have signed non-compete agreements, be sure to have copies of those agreements to present to the buyer. Finally, be ready to share an outline of your employee benefit plan, along with your employment policy manual, as described in Chapter 7.

✔ **Your business and marketing goals and growth plans.** If you're confident that the buyer will complete the purchase, you can provide a copy of your summary business and marketing plans (see Forms 7-1 and 7-2 on the CD-ROM). If you're having doubts that the buyer will close the purchase, present your plans but don't release written copies.

Additionally, be aware that the buyer will be investigating the size and health of your market, industry, and competitive arena, as well as the customer recognition and reputation your business name has in the marketplace. To help your buyer with this research, refer to the contents of your selling memorandum and provide additional information that supports positive conclusions (see Chapter 11 for tips on maintaining accuracy and integrity while presenting your business favorably).

Investigating legal issues that affect your business

In the appendix of your selling memorandum, you probably included a seller's disclosure statement. This statement, prepared with the help of your attorney and your broker (if you're using one), probably informed buyers of any legal issues your business faces, such as insurance claims, pending litigation, product liability concerns, or customer warranty obligations, to name a few.

Now that the buyer is getting a behind-the-scenes look at your business, he or she will want details on all potential legal obligations. Be ready to address the following list of questions:

- ✔ Does your business face any legal actions, pending litigations, or investigations?

- ✔ Does your business have any unfunded pension liabilities?

- ✔ Does your company owe or face employee unemployment claims, worker's compensation claims, or other liabilities?

- ✔ Does your business have any unpaid insurance premiums or unresolved insurance claims or disputes?

- ✔ Has your company provided product guarantees or warranties, and does it face product liability issues?

- ✔ Does your firm face — or is it undergoing — any tax audits?

- ✔ Does your business owe any outstanding taxes?

- ✔ Does your company face any local zoning ordinance issues?

- ✔ Do you have any disputes with your building owner or neighboring tenants?

- ✔ Does your business use any substances, materials, or products on or near the premises that may be considered an environmental hazard?

Meet with your attorney prior to the launch of due diligence to cover the list of legal issues detailed in your seller's disclosure statement, along with the kind of explanations you should be prepared to share if the buyer asks further questions. When the buyer does ask, be upfront with your responses. Also be proactive: If you're aware of an issue — even a small one — explain it and describe the actions you've taken or plan to take to deal with the problem.

Don't make the buyer dig to discover legal issues. Buyers know that running a business includes risks; they just want to know that the risks are being well-managed. If you're hiding facts, you're not managing them. Should your buyer pull skeletons out of the closet, your deal will likely be in jeopardy.

Your Homework Assignment

In addition to providing whatever information or resources your buyer needs for the due diligence process, your role includes one other major obligation. At the same time your buyer is investigating whether your business is in the condition you represent it to be, you need to conduct a similar investigation of the buyer's financial condition and business capability. In other words, you need to do some due diligence of your own. Your due diligence is especially important if your sale involves these two factors:

- ✔ **If you provide seller financing,** you want to confirm that the buyer is creditworthy and capable of running the business in such a way that it succeeds — so your loan will be repaid.

- ✔ **If you're staying on with the business** through a management or consulting agreement, you want to confirm that you can support and work with the buyer's management style, business plans, and personal reputation over whatever time period you agree to remain involved with the business.

The upcoming sections describe the due diligence investigation in front of you. Form 12-2 on the CD-ROM provides a checklist of information you need to gather.

Assessing the buyer's financial ability

During due diligence, your job is to collect enough information to determine whether your buyer is creditworthy, should you or a third-party lender need to provide financing. Certainly, you don't want to personally provide a loan if the buyer is a credit risk. You also don't want to hinge your deal on the buyer's assurance of third-party financing if you learn that the buyer's financial background will scare off most lending institutions. If you haven't already done so, collect the following information:

- ✔ **A copy of the buyer's financial statement.** If the buyer doesn't have a financial statement prepared and ready to submit, your bank likely has forms you can share with the buyer when you request this document. Or you can go online to www.sba.gov/sbaforms/sba413.pdf and download a PDF file of the Small Business Administration personal financial statement form.

- ✔ **The buyer's credit report.** The best way to check the buyer's credit is to obtain a credit report. The easiest way to obtain this report is to simply ask the buyer to provide a recent one from a reputable third-party credit agency. Alternatively, you can request a credit report, with the buyer's permission. Either use the credit bureau you use for verifying the creditworthiness of business customers or contact one of the many U.S. and international credit-reporting companies, like Equifax (www. equifax.com) or Experian (www.experian.com).

If you become the banker for your deal, make sure you protect yourself by heeding the advice in Chapter 14.

Researching the buyer's management experience and reputation

Especially if you provide financing or remain involved with your business during a lengthy transition period, how the buyer manages after the sale will matter greatly to you personally. You want to be sure that the buyer has the appropriate level of experience to make the deal work so that you get paid off and your ongoing involvement is enjoyable. Even if you don't carry a loan or remain involved after the sale, you want to be sure the buyer's ability and reputation are good. Should the business fail, a less-than-stellar business person may look for reasons to blame the past owner, perhaps citing misrepresentation of business conditions, which is an outcome you surely want to avoid.

To research the buyer's experience, take these steps:

- ✔ **Review the buyer's professional resume.** Look for unexplained time gaps or an unusually short stint in a key position. Ask what happened, and probe to find out as much as you can. Be wary if the answers you hear seem to place the blame for short-term positions on bad decisions by others rather than on understandable economic or market conditions. Also be wary if you find out that the buyer was released from or failed at positions that required similar experience to what it takes to run your business.

- ✔ **Conduct an online search** for both the buyer's name on its own and the buyer's name coupled with the name of each major firm on the buyer's resume. See what you discover, and look for any warning signals you should heed, such as negative publicity.

- ✔ **Ask the buyer to provide references** — personal, financial, and business — that you have permission to contact.

Before contacting references, agree with the buyer regarding how to introduce your request — that is, whether to reveal to the reference that the buyer is considering purchasing your business or to say that the buyer is interested in a top position in your company. The second option avoids the key fact but is still a true statement that allows you to maintain secrecy about the sale.

You'll ask the same questions either way, but you'll introduce your reason for the interview slightly differently. Following are some questions to ask:

- What size staff and budget has the person managed, and how would you describe the person's ability to manage both staff and budget?

- Has the person had to deal with business or personal financial challenges? If so, what was the outcome?

- How would you characterize the person's ability to develop new business?

- How would you describe the person's history of following through on business and financial commitments?

Whenever the reference expresses doubt, probe further. Ask whether the reference can recall a reason for what sounds like some hesitation in the answer. Remember, you're not trying to be assured that the buyer is a good person, so this is no time to play nice cop. You're looking out for Number One and trying to discover if the buyer presents any kind of management or loan risk.

Discovering the buyer's plans for your business

In your pre-offer meetings you discovered the buyer's general intentions, but now that the buyer is getting familiar with the inner workings of your business and where it faces particular challenges and opportunities, he or she may begin to form and share ideas about how to address the future. Find out about the following buyer plans:

- Will the buyer continue doing business in your same location and building?

- Will the buyer largely retain your current staff, or does the buyer foresee key staff changes?

- Will the buyer continue to offer the same primary products and services, or does the buyer envision major changes?

- Will the buyer retain your business name?

- Will the buyer immediately raise prices or change pricing or credit policies?

- Does the buyer plan immediate marketing plan changes?

- Does the buyer intend to keep you involved in the business for at least the near future, and do you agree?

If your feet get cold or you have second thoughts

As you help the buyer go through your business's details with a fine-tooth comb, you may find yourself catching the buyer's enthusiasm about your company's value and potential. Seeing your business through the buyer's eyes may make this same enterprise that's frustrated and exhausted you over the past months or years start to look like a darned good deal.

As the buyer starts talking about closing the deal, your feet — and heart — may start to feel heavy. You may find yourself wondering if you've priced too low, or if you should have negotiated a longer consulting or management contract. You may even start to think about ways to call the deal off.

Before doing anything rash, follow this prescription:

✔ **Recall why you started this process.** Flip to Chapter 1 and take another long and hard look at the reasons you wanted out of your business in the first place.

✔ **Remember that the past is a great predictor of the future.** If you were bored, burned out, short of energy or resources, in need of a lifestyle change, or just plain ready to retire when you decided to put your business up for sale, understand that those feelings are likely to crop back up in the near future.

✔ **Realize that if you bail out now, jumping back in won't be easy.** If you call this sale to a halt, changing your mind and trying to restart the sale process in the future may be a whole lot harder, as prospects may learn that you've changed your mind once before, and they may get cold feet as a result.

If you start to feel remorse, talk to your key sale advisors — your accountant, attorney, and broker, if you're using one. You worked with them to establish the asking price and to evaluate the offer on the table, and they'll probably help get you through your uncertainties.

If together you decide that your pricing concerns are warranted, you may work to schedule the deal so there's an earn-out that provides part of the payment based on future success, allowing you to capture some of the upside potential you're concerned about leaving behind.

Or perhaps you can structure a management or consulting contract that leaves you involved with your business for a period of time — if the buyer finds your ongoing involvement mutually beneficial. Use Chapter 13 as a guide to the options to consider as you structure your sale deal.

Mostly, your advisors will probably calm you down. They may also give you the same advice as I'm going to give you right now: Avoid advice from those who didn't help you put your deal together. If relatives, friends, or even associates tell you you're selling at too low a price or that you're going to go stir-crazy without your business, tune them out. They don't know what motivated you to sell; they probably don't know how businesses are valued and priced; and they almost certainly don't realize how hard you've worked to get your deal to this point.

Take a deep breath, know that the end is in sight, count your lucky stars, and turn the page to keep moving forward toward closing day.

In most cases, the answers to your questions about the buyer's plans will reveal positive actions intended to build upon the strengths and attributes of the business as you know it. Truth is, though, if you're getting paid in full *and* if you're not going to remain with the business during an extended transition period, then the buyer's next steps will be of interest but of no real bearing to you.

However, if the purchase offer is reliant on a seller-financed loan, deferred payments, or your continued presence in the business, then raise red flags if the buyer describes plans that you think can endanger the business's financial condition or the nature of business relationships with clients and employees. If the buyer doesn't pull away from such plans, you can revise the payment structure so that you're paid off at closing through buyer assets and third-party loans, or you can limit your ongoing involvement to a very short transition period. Just be sure not to tell clients or employees that business will continue as usual after closing day.

Forms on the CD-ROM

Form 12-1	**Buyer's Due Diligence: Preparation Worksheet**	A form to use as you assemble information to prepare for the buyer's due diligence investigation
Form 12-2	**Seller's Due Diligence: Checklist**	A form to use as you investigate the finances and plans of your buyer

Chapter 13

Structuring and Negotiating the Deal

....

....

*H*ow many times since you began the sale process have you heard stories about deals that fell through at the 11th hour? Or worse, how many times have you heard about deals that fell apart *after* closing, when businesses ended up back in sellers' hands, depleted of inventory, assets, and the value that existed on closing day?

The devil, as the saying goes, is in the details. Fortunately, the details can be carefully managed when you properly structure and negotiate your deal.

 The idea of dotting all your i's, crossing all your t's, and putting what feels like a million protective clauses in place may seem like a drag when all you really want to do is get the deal closed, but protections can save you from the threat of an after-sale disaster. That's why sale advisors — your attorney, your accountant, and your broker, if you're using one — are so essential. They force you to slow down long enough to structure your sale in a way that protects your interests in the very likely event that some of the purchase price is paid in deferred payments rather than at closing. Plus, they help you weigh the impact of each sale-structure option, because for almost every decision you face, taxes hang in the balance.

The goal of all your efforts is to negotiate a mutually agreeable sale structure that can be detailed in what's called a *purchase and sale agreement,* which is the centerpiece of all your closing-day documents. Chapter 15 describes the closing document and all that goes into it, along with how to handle closing-day activities. This chapter guides you through the menu of sale structure alternatives and helps you understand and negotiate the details that comprise the art of the deal.

Anatomy of a Sale Structure

As you, your buyer, and your sale advisors put your deal together, you juggle four variables:

- **What you're selling:** Business sales come in two forms: asset sales and stock sales. The vast majority of small businesses sell assets. When you price your business for sale, you determine what you *want* to sell — but like all things, that's up for negotiation when you and the buyer sit down to hash out the details and come to level ground. I explain the differences between the two sales types in Chapter 6. The upcoming section helps you understand the advantages (for you) and disadvantages (for the buyer) of entity sales so you know how to best negotiate in the event that you have that option.

- **The sale price:** When you accept the buyer's offer and sign the letter of intent, you agree to the buyer's proposed price — but that number is likely to shift before closing day. For one thing, due diligence may uncover issues that affect the price. For another, as you structure the sale with tax planning in mind, it may be to your advantage to make some concessions to allocate the purchase price in a way that minimizes your tax liability. Generally, don't expect the offered price to go up — that's not the direction that prices move between the day the letter of intent is signed and the day the sale closes.

- **Price allocation:** As if it's not enough to figure out how the price is paid, you also have to negotiate how the payment is allocated. Only rarely is the payment chalked up to a single line item, such as equipment. Instead, some or all the purchase price is usually spread across seven IRS-determined asset classes, which are detailed later in this chapter.

  Allocating the price across asset classes is tricky, because depending on how you allocate the price, either you or the buyer — but not both — will receive a tax advantage, and by IRS rules you both have to follow the same allocation. For that reason, price allocation is a major point of discussion and negotiation when you and the buyer — and your legal and financial advisors — are putting your deal together. The next section gives you a preview of the structuring strategy, and Chapter 14 goes into more detail about how sale proceeds are taxed.

- **Payment structure:** Very few sales end in a single, all-cash payout, so most sellers also have to consider a payment structure. Many businesses are paid for not at once but over time, with a closing-day down payment followed by various kinds of deferred payments, including seller-financed loan payments, balloon payments, or *earn-out payments*, where the seller gets paid a portion of future sales if the business grows as projected over the years following the sale closing. Under any payment plan, you want to see as much cash as possible at closing, if for no other reason than to reduce the collection risk that comes with deferred payments. On the flip side, your buyer will probably want to make as low a down payment as possible. That's why deal structure and negotiation go hand in hand.

Understanding the Fundamentals of a Seller's Sale-Structure Strategy

In most sale negotiations, price and price allocation are hot topics, because your decisions affect both how much money trades hands and how the money is taxed. Unfortunately, negotiation outcomes that benefit your tax situation rarely benefit your buyer's tax situation, and vice versa. Coming to a decision about the final price and how the price is allocated usually involves a fair amount of give and take during the buyer-seller negotiation process. The number and allocation you both agree to become part of your purchase and sale agreement. It's also what you report to the IRS when you both file identical versions of Form 8594, which reports how much money your business sold for and how the proceeds were allocated to various asset classes.

Before negotiating the final price, price allocation, and payment structure, get professional tax and financial planning advice. If the way the price is allocated or paid leads to serious tax burdens, you may be better off negotiating a lower price or a different deal structure. Your broker, if you're using one, will be helpful at this point, and your accountant will be invaluable.

As you already know, high taxable income leads to high taxes, and when it comes to sale proceeds, not all income is taxed equally. To the degree you can allocate sale proceeds toward asset categories taxed at lower rates, you'll come out of the sale with more money in your pocket. Also, if the price is paid over more than a single tax-year period, you can keep your annual income from soaring sky high during any one year, and you can probably keep your taxes a little lower as a result. If in a single year your taxable income goes way up, your *tax bracket* — the percentage rate at which your income is taxed — goes up too. If you accept full payment for your business sale at the time of closing or during the same calendar year as the closing, you may get pushed into the highest possible personal income bracket for that year.

To spare as much of your sale proceeds as possible from the bite of taxes, discuss the following issues with your accountant:

- ✔ **Allocating as much of your price as possible toward the purchase of fixtures, furnishings, and equipment.** The gain, or profit, you realize from tangible assets you've held for more than a year is treated as capital gain rather than ordinary income. Through 2010, capital gains taxes are set at 15 percent, which is considerably lower than most ordinary income tax rates. Your accountant will advise you regarding how much of your price you can legitimately allocate toward fixtures, furnishings, and equipment, because the items must be valued at fair market value.

- ✔ **Spreading income from sale proceeds over several years.** By offering a seller-financed loan, or by agreeing to an earn-out payment that provides you with a portion of increased business sales over the years following the sale, you can spread sale revenue over multiple years and defer taxes as a result. See Chapter 14 for more information on installment sales.

- ✔ **Avoiding the Alternative Minimum Tax (AMT), if possible.** See Chapter 14 for an overview of this tax and what triggers it.

To be sure you understand all the taxable income you'll realize from your sale, ask your accountant whether you need to plan for any unexpected income from what's called *depreciation recapture*. When you sell assets, if you've deducted depreciation for those assets over past years, you need to state the amount you deducted as ordinary income on your tax return for the year of the sale. For instance, if you purchased a piece of equipment for $10,000, and over the years you depreciated the asset $6,000, then your *adjusted basis* in the asset is $4,000. If you sell the equipment for $5,000, following the sale you have to recapture $1,000 of the amount you previously deducted for depreciation and claim it as ordinary income. Or, if you sell the equipment for $12,000, you have to recapture the full $5,000 you previously deducted for depreciation and claim it as ordinary income, plus you have to claim $2,000 (the difference between the purchase and sale prices) as a capital gain. You can see why this paragraph started with the advice to "ask your accountant."

By the time you and your buyer begin to negotiate the payment details, be sure you're well-armed with your accountant's advice about what you're trying to achieve in terms of the type of sale (asset or entity), price, down payment, and price allocation. With that information in mind, if the buyer proposes a deal that's dramatically off base, you can simply say that the proposed approach doesn't match up with your sale objectives. Don't rack up billable hours for your accountant to review a deal that you know is unacceptable. If you think the deal sounds like one you can live with, however, state that it looks good *subject to* — and those words are key — your accountant's review.

Agreeing with the Buyer on What Exactly You're Selling

The first factor in structuring your sale is to agree with the buyer on what you're selling — assets or stock. Chapter 6 goes into detail about the differences between asset sales and stock sales, which are also called entity sales. As you start negotiating your deal, it's worth reviewing that information again so you know what's what.

In a nutshell, be aware that nearly all small business sales fall into the category of asset sales for two big reasons. First, most small businesses are sole proprietorships, which can only sell assets because they have no stock to sell. (If your business is formed as a corporation or LLC, you have the choice of structuring your sale as an asset sale *or* an entity sale.) Second, even when a choice is available, most small business buyers prefer to buy assets, largely to distance themselves from hidden liabilities that can accompany an entity sale.

If you own a corporation or an LLC — especially if you own a C corporation — it's to your advantage to structure your sale as an entity sale rather than an asset sale. It's likely, however, that your buyer will negotiate for an asset sale instead. Obviously, you can't force the buyer to purchase your business entity — including its liabilities — if the buyer adamantly prefers an asset sale. You can, however, bridge the gap by working with your advisors and negotiating with your buyer to tilt the price or the price allocation to your favor, allowing you to make up for the tax concessions you make when accepting the asset sale approach. This section helps you see both perspectives so you know what's in the deal for you and what your buyer will try to avoid.

From the seller's point of view

To the owner of a corporation or LLC, an entity sale has some definite advantages:

- **Your proceeds are taxed at a lower rate.** In an entity sale, proceeds are taxed at the capital gains rate, which is currently lower than the ordinary tax rate that applies to at least a portion of the proceeds of an asset sale.

- **You avoid potential double taxation.** If your business is structured as a C corporation, when you sell assets you face *double taxation*. First, your corporation pays capital gains tax on the difference between the sale price and the price you paid (or the *adjusted basis*, which is the purchase price less depreciation) for the assets you're selling. Second, when you liquidate your corporation and distribute the proceeds to yourself and other shareholders, if any, they'll be taxed again, this time at the individual level and as ordinary income.

✔ **Business liabilities transfer to the buyer.** The buyer of a business entity assumes ownership of all but specifically excluded liabilities of the business, which eliminates the seller's risk of surprises if a totally unexpected liability claim arises in the future. If you sell assets, on the other hand, you retain responsibility for liabilities that you may not even learn about until after the sale. For example, if your business guaranteed a product, and following the sale a customer files a claim, the claim is your problem and not the buyer's problem, because the buyer purchased only assets, with the exception of itemized liabilities.

From the buyer's point of view

To a buyer, the biggest drawbacks to a stock or entity sale include:

✔ **Hidden liabilities transfer with the stock purchase.** An asset sale, on the other hand, carries no hidden liabilities. In an asset sale, the buyer purchases only assets and specifically listed liabilities. If product, employee, or other lawsuits arise after closing day, they're the problem of the seller, not the buyer.

✔ **The need to purchase all business assets,** including non-productive or non-essential assets that can be excluded from an asset sale.

✔ **The need to inherit the entity's depreciation history.** In an asset sale, a good portion of the sale price is usually allocated to the purchase of equipment, which can be depreciated over a short time period, allowing deductions that reduce the new owner's reported earnings and resulting taxes. Following an asset sale, the buyer can start depreciating the price of acquired fixtures, furnishings, and equipment at their *stepped-up basis*, which is the price the buyer paid for them. This tax write-off advantage doesn't apply to the buyer in a stock sale. Following a stock sale, assets transfer at their original price basis and with the existing depreciation schedule. That means if a major piece of equipment has been fully depreciated by the business, no depreciation opportunity remains for the new buyer to deduct.

In addition to the above-listed buyer drawbacks to an entity sale, buyers also realize several advantages:

✔ **Automatic transfer of advantageous leases and contracts.** In an asset sale, the buyer forms a new business entity. Because all existing contracts — leases, client contracts, even government contracts — are with your business entity, you have to transfer each one to the new owner. If you have a great long-term, low-rent lease, and if a transfer triggers a renegotiation, the transfer may lead to a real problem.

In a stock sale, the buyer purchases the entire business, so renegotiation isn't necessary because all contracts transfer with the sale.

✔ **Future tax advantages.** A nice tax advantage awaits the buyer (by that time the owner) of a business entity if the business is resold in another entity sale. At the time of resale, proceeds are taxed at capital gains rates, which apply only to the difference between what the owner paid you to acquire the business (the owner's *basis* in the business) and what the owner charges the new buyer.

The flip side: Asset sales do have pros for sellers

If your business is a corporation or an LLC and the buyer insists on an asset sale rather than an entity sale, you want to work to keep your selling price as close to your asking price as possible. You also want to structure the deal so tax benefits are in your favor to compensate for entity sale benefits you agree to forego. That all said, realize that asset sales also come with some seller advantages, especially in the following areas:

✔ **You can exclude non-essential assets from the sale:** Before negotiating your asset sale, you can exclude assets such as cash and investment accounts, equipment, vehicles, and other assets that your buyer may not want or be willing to pay extra for.

Your selling memorandum likely lists the major assets you plan to exclude from the sale, but if you plan to exclude additional items, be very clear about explaining them to the buyer at the beginning of negotiations to avoid surprises or snags at closing.

✔ **You can retain and lease back valuable assets:** By holding onto a valuable asset, such as your business building (if you own it), you spare yourself the taxes you'd incur if you sold the asset. Plus, if you negotiate

to lease the asset back to your buyer, or to structure a lease-purchase agreement, you gain an ongoing stream of income.

✔ **You can allocate some of the purchase price toward goodwill:** Your income from the sale of goodwill is taxed at the capital gains rate, which is currently far lower than the ordinary income tax rate you pay on proceeds from a consulting contract or the sale of equipment. Still, if income from the sale is high enough, you can be liable for the Alternative Minimum Tax (AMT). For more on the AMT and other tax issues you should discuss with your accountant, turn to Chapter 14.

✔ **Your due diligence is easier:** Due diligence goes faster in an asset sale than in a stock sale because the buyer doesn't need to search for hidden liabilities.

Income from the sale of an S corporation is taxed only once, at the individual rate. With advance planning, you can work with your accountant and attorney to explore the tax implications of changing your corporate status from C corporation to S corporation before selling your business in an asset sale transaction.

Setting the Final Sale Price

The buyer's letter of intent establishes the basic sale price for your business, but that number will almost certainly change as you go through due diligence, deal structuring, and the negotiation that leads to a closed deal.

The variables that affect the final sale price include

- **The condition in which your buyer finds your business and its assets.** If upon inspection the buyer finds your business or its equipment to be less valuable than presented, the buyer will want to negotiate a lower price.

- **How much you require as the down payment at closing.** Usually, the more you require in cash at closing, the more the buyer will work to negotiate a lower price. If you agree to receive a cash down payment, plus deferred payments that come in for months or even years after closing, you'll limit requests for price reductions.

- **Items you exclude from the sale.** Often, a seller can offset buyer-requested price concessions by excluding assets from the sale. The excluded assets can then be sold separately if they're not essential to the business, or leased back to the buyer in the case of a business building or a necessary piece of major equipment.

- **Your ongoing involvement with the business.** Many sellers agree to sign and accept compensation for a management contract as an alternative to a higher sale price. By paying you to remain with the business over a specified period of time, the buyer can deduct your management fees as a business expense, which provides the buyer with a far greater tax advantage than the depreciation deduction the buyer receives from a higher purchase price.

- **Tax implications.** Buyers will agree to pay higher prices if they're allocated to deliver the fastest possible tax write-offs. Sellers will agree to accept lower prices if they're allocated so that most sale proceeds are taxed at capital gains rates rather than at higher ordinary income rates. If your business is a corporation and you agree to an asset sale instead of a stock sale, which would result in far lower taxes, work with your broker and accountant to propose a deal structure that swings some of the tax advantages back in your favor.

When arriving at the final sale number, certain pricing aspects are pretty cut and dried. For instance, if your equipment is worth less than you estimated, the buyer is going to insist on paying a lower price than you initially asked for. Other aspects allow way more give and take. For example, if the buyer wants a lower down payment than you requested, and if you believe the buyer is creditworthy and an able manager, consider offsetting the request with a request for a higher earn-out payment or a higher price on your management contract. Realize that by structuring your deal differently, you can accept a different price than the one you initially asked for and still end up with nearly the same dollar amount in sale proceeds.

Keep in mind at all times that the art of the deal is tricky and requires the watchful eye of your accountant and your broker, if you're using one, at every turn and curve.

Don't even think about agreeing to a price or pricing structure without getting your accountant's advice early and often, and especially at these key points:

- ✔ **Before advertising your business for sale,** work with your accountant to decide whether you should aim for an asset sale or an entity sale, the minimum amount you want to request as a down payment, how you prefer to handle installment payments, and which major assets, if any, you want to exclude from the sale offering. By knowing what you want early on, you're more apt to steer your sale to an acceptable conclusion. Some sellers state their asking price and preliminary sale structure in the for sale ad so buyers can pre-qualify themselves and opt out if they can't meet the sale terms. Others state an asking price and wait to see what payment approach the buyer proposes. Either way, the final deal is the result not of what you ask but of what you agree to during negotiations. Buyers realize that the asking price and terms are negotiable.

- ✔ **Before signing your buyer's letter of intent,** go over the purchase offer with your accountant and come up with a counterproposal, if necessary, to see that your price and sale structure objectives are adequately addressed by the buyer's proposal. (See Chapter 11 for more information on accepting the buyer's offer.)

Allocating the Purchase Price

As part of your buyer-seller negotiations, and based on your accountant's advice, you and your buyer will allocate the purchase price for your business assets among what the IRS calls *asset classes*, including tangible and intangible assets, goodwill, accounts receivable, and other categories. How the price is allocated — how much is for tangible or physical assets; how much is for intangible assets such as customer lists, business processes, and even your agreement not to compete with the new owner; and how much is for the *goodwill* your business has generated (the value of your business name and the fact that your business is a going concern) — can be a big deal, because the way you allocate the price affects how your sale proceeds are taxed. This section provides a rundown of the asset classes and how allocation decisions occur. Before agreeing to a sale price allocation, always consult your accountant. With good advice, you may be able to avoid taxation at the highest rates.

Be aware that you and the buyer have to use the same price allocation, which you both report to the IRS using Form 8594, "Asset Acquisition Statement," following the sale. Don't wait until closing day to decide how to divvy up the price among the IRS-allowed asset classes, which are listed in this section. Make allocation part of your negotiations, and come to an agreement that can be included in your closing documents. Your accountant and your buyer's accountant will serve as valuable resources during this process. They both understand the importance of this step, because it fulfills an IRS requirement.

The IRS requires that your purchase price reflect the fair market value of tangible assets and that the price be allocated in the order presented in the following sections. For example, you have to add up the value of all cash and cash account assets included in your sale and subtract that amount from the purchase price before moving on to the next asset class on the IRS list, which covers certificates of deposits, government securities, and other marketable securities and currency. And down the list you go, working with your buyer (and your accountants) to allocate your price among classes until you get to the final class, which covers goodwill and which accounts for whatever portion of the sale price that hasn't already been allocated to the preceding six categories.

The other thing to remember is that the IRS can challenge how you allocate your price. It can question how you assess fair market value of tangible assets, for example, or whether the value you place on your intangible assets is reasonable. That's why third-party valuations (see Chapter 6 for more information on obtaining a professional valuation) are important in businesses with many complicated assets.

Cash

Cash and savings/checking accounts are the easiest assets to value. You simply total all cash that's transferring as part of the sale (not including certificates of deposit, because they're included in the next asset class) and subtract that amount from your purchase price before allocating the balance of your purchase price among the rest of the IRS asset classes.

CDs, marketable securities, and foreign currency

If you transfer any certificates of deposits or investments as part of your business sale, your second step in allocating your price — after the allocation for cash — is to allocate for the current market value of such investments.

Accounts receivable and debt instruments

The third asset class to which you allocate your purchase price covers accounts receivable, credit card receivables, and any loans due to your business (if those assets will be transferring as part of your sale).

Inventory

The IRS refers to the fourth asset category as *stock in trade*. If you're transferring inventory as part of your sale, you and the buyer need to agree on the inventory's fair market value. Because inventory qualifies as a deductible business expense, the buyer may want to allocate as much of the purchase price as possible to this asset class, but be aware that the value has to be defensible, which usually means that inventory should be valued at cost or fair market value, whichever is lower.

Tangible assets

The fifth asset class on the IRS list includes furniture and fixtures, buildings, land, vehicles, and equipment that's included in your sale. The IRS requires that you assess these assets at their fair market value, which allows some room for negotiation between you and your buyer.

The buyer wants to allocate as much of the purchase price as possible to tangible assets that qualify as business expenses or that qualify for rapid versus long-term depreciation. As the seller, you want almost the exact opposite. You want to set the fair market value of tangible assets as low as possible, because you have to pay tax on the sale proceeds, plus you want to allocate as much of the asset value as possible toward assets you've held long enough to qualify for taxation at long-term capital gain rates.

You have to pay ordinary income tax on the proceeds from assets you've held less than a year. For assets you've held longer than a year, you have to pay two kinds of tax — capital gains tax on the difference between the sale price and your *adjusted basis*, which is what you paid for the asset minus what you've deducted for asset depreciation; and ordinary income tax on what's called *depreciation recapture*, which is the amount you deducted for the asset's depreciation over previous years. See why you don't want to agree to anything without your accountant's advice?

Intangible assets, not including goodwill

The sixth IRS asset class covers all the intangible value of your business except what's referred to as goodwill and going concern value (those are covered by the final, seventh asset class).

Intangible assets include workforce in place, business books and records, operating systems and processes, marketing materials, correspondence, leases and contracts, customer base, supplier base, employee records, licenses, permits, trademarks and intellectual property or other rights granted by a government unit, telephone listings, Web address and site, a covenant not to compete, and other non-physical assets necessary for operation of the business.

The very most you can allocate to this class is the amount of the purchase price that remains after subtracting the fair market value of the preceding five asset classes. When you know the total that remains after all cash, investment, accounts receivable, inventory, and tangible asset values are allocated, you and the buyer will allocate this remaining amount between intangible assets and the final asset class, which covers goodwill.

As you negotiate this final allocation, your discussion will probably focus more on how the assets are paid for than on how the price is allocated between intangible assets and goodwill. In many deals, intangible assets are covered by payment for a covenant not to compete, or by a personal services contract between the buyer and the seller. The following sections list thoughts to consider as you determine how to accept payment for the intangible assets of your business.

Goodwill and going-concern value

Goodwill is the final asset class allocation. Its value is determined by what remains of the purchase price after allocations have been made to the preceding six classes.

Sellers love allocating as much purchase price as possible to goodwill, because the sale proceeds are taxed at capital gains rates, which through 2010 are set at far lower rates than the tax rates for ordinary income. Again, though, check with your attorney, because the revenue from goodwill can push your income high enough to trigger the Alternative Minimum Tax, or AMT.

Getting paid for intangible assets and goodwill

The buyer will almost certainly want your promise that you won't open a competing business right down the street, thereby threatening the value of the intangible assets and goodwill the buyer has just purchased. In return for this promise, which often comes in the form of a non-compete agreement, the buyer usually agrees to pay good money. The payment comes in one of two forms: a non-compete agreement or a personal services contract (or both).

Non-compete agreement

Money allocated toward the purchase of a covenant not to compete is amortized (or deducted) over fifteen years, even if the agreement lasts for, say, three or five years. For that reason, buyers try to limit how much money goes toward this item, because they'd rather allocate the price to items that deliver faster tax deductions and benefits. Sellers, however, want as much of the sale price as possible to be paid with a covenant not to compete, because the payment proceeds are taxed at the lower capital gains rate.

Personal services contract

If the buyer wants you to stick around, he or she will offer you a management, consulting, or employment contract, accompanied by payments that are usually offset by an overall business price reduction. The buyer will probably want to pay as much as possible toward an employment contract, because the fees can be deducted as a business expense, reducing taxable profits from day one. On your end, however, personal service contract payments are taxed as ordinary income, which means you pay more tax than you would on payments that qualify for taxation at capital gains rates.

If you accept a personal services contract as part of the deal, try to negotiate employment benefits and perks to offset the negative tax implications.

Also, be sure the scope of service you provide is clearly defined. For instance, if you agree to 160 days of service over a one-year period, you want to be sure you know what constitutes a "day" and what additional payment you'll receive for additional services you provide.

Finally, be very sure that the personal services contract is completely separate from the purchase and sale agreement. Should the buyer cancel the personal service contract for some reason, you want to be sure that its cancellation has absolutely no bearing on the sale agreement.

Studying the Payment Structure Menu

In a perfect world, you'd like your buyer to pay all cash at closing, with no tax implications. But no one ever suggested that business sales happen in a perfect world.

The first place buyers usually look for money is in the mirror, because the first place they turn to is their own resources. Buyers will tap their savings accounts, sell stock if they own some, or borrow against the equity in their home to come up with the money to purchase your business. They may even use retirement funds from 401(k) or IRA accounts, which are available with a long list of *ifs* that you can find out about by going to the site of BeneTrends at www.benetrends.com.

If the buyer's personal resources aren't enough to fund the deal, he or she will take loans — from banks, friends, family, and even you, the seller — to cover the purchase price.

If the buyer doesn't need a loan from you, you really don't care how the funds are assembled. But if you're loaning part of the money, you care — a whole lot — about where the rest of the money is coming from, and here's why: You need to know that the buyer's assets haven't been so thoroughly pledged toward other loans that there's nothing left for you to go after, should the buyer default on your seller-financed loan payments.

What follows is the menu of payment options, each with a brief explanation of what's involved and what red flags to watch for. Essentially, you have two major options: Do you want all your money right now, or you are you willing to receive your price over time? Your answer will affect how much your business sells for, because all-cash deals usually result in a lower price. It'll also affect how much tax you pay, because all-cash deals deliver sale proceeds in a single year, which may propel you into the highest of tax brackets. Read on.

Cash payoff

This approach takes little explanation. Cash is cash, and after you get it, you don't have to worry about whether the buyer is successful in your business or whether you'll be paid off at agreed-upon dates in the future. In an all-cash deal, you're paid off on closing day.

Before you decide this is the approach for you, note these two truths:

✏ **All-cash deals are rare.** In most deals, the seller agrees to accept at least some (often most) of the purchase price in deferred payments made under one of the other payment options in this section.

✏ **All-cash deals result in high taxes.** In the year you sell your business, your income will go up significantly, which will almost surely put you in a higher tax bracket than you're used to. If you get paid off all at once, your income will spike in that year instead of increasing gradually over a several-year period, probably leading to taxation at the highest possible rates.

Cash in hand, even with tax implications, is a pretty clean way to close a sale, but don't expect your buyer to offer a one-time payoff at closing. If your deal is the rare exception and your buyer offers to cash you out, thank your lucky stars and then go straight to your accountant to start tax planning.

Third-party financing

Third-party financing comes from a bank or other lender of the buyer's choice, and it rarely comes easily or without strings attached.

Banks are reluctant to lend funds to first-time business buyers, to buyers of very small businesses, to buyers without deep experience in the type of business they're buying, and to buyers whose loan applications aren't accompanied by very strong credit ratings and financial statements. They're also hesitant about loaning for businesses they don't view as very low risk based on other deals they've done, which is why buyers of certain well-known franchises may qualify for loans with greater ease than buyers of businesses with barely-known names. When they do loan funds, banks take one of two approaches:

✏ **Home equity loans,** which are really personal loans that provide funds for the buyer to make the purchase. If your buyer is using home equity to purchase your business, be leery of supplementing the deal with a seller-financed loan, simply because the buyer's primary source of collateral is already being tapped by the home equity loan.

✏ **Business loans,** in which the bank provides a loan that's usually limited to a portion of the amount of tangible assets being purchased, such as real estate, major equipment, and inventory. When offering business loans, banks usually work to write the loan under a government-guaranteed program such as those offered by the Small Business Administration.

SBA loans are funded by the bank but guaranteed in part by the Small Business Administration, making them somewhat easier to obtain. Be aware of these SBA loan considerations:

- The SBA is more willing to fund loans for business expansions than for acquisitions or start-ups.

- Getting an SBA loan can take months. Before delaying your sale in hopes of the buyer getting an SBA loan, do some advance planning. It's worth it to contact your banker or your SBA office to find out whether your business is likely to qualify for an SBA loan and what kind of sale structure is necessary to support the loan application. Many loans can be applied only toward the purchase of fixed assets, such as land and improvements or major machinery and equipment, so you need to allocate your deal accordingly. The most basic and frequently used form of SBA loan is the 7(a) loan. For information, go online to `http://www.sba.gov/services/financialassistance/sbaloantopics/7a/index.html/` or use the link included in the "Useful Links" portion of the CD-ROM. If you learn that your business and the terms of your deal don't match up with SBA financing requirements, you'll know to waive the buyer off from the hope of such financing.

If your buyer tells you that part of the payment will come from a third-party loan, get assurances by requesting a prequalification letter from the lender stating that the buyer is qualified for the loan and that the lender is prepared to provide the funding.

Stock exchange

A stock exchange is a payment option that applies only to a business being purchased by another corporation — typically one with publicly traded stock. This payment method is rare in the small business world, but it's worth it to know what's involved, just in case.

In a stock exchange, the purchaser pays with stock rather than with cash. Be aware of two drawbacks:

- You can't sell the stock you receive until it's either registered with the Securities and Exchange Commission (SEC) — a costly proposition — or held for at least two years.

- Unless the stock is widely and heavily traded, when you try to sell it you may have a hard time finding buyers or receiving a decent purchase price.

If a corporation offers to buy your business with stock, do some homework before accepting the offer. You can go to `www.finance.yahoo.com/`, enter the stock trading symbol, and see share price details and price performance charts that reach back five years. Unless you're very confident that the stock is a good mid- to long-term risk, accept stock for only a portion of your purchase price, if at all.

Cash down plus a seller-financed note

More typical than an all-cash deal is a deal where the buyer pays a portion (preferably a large portion) of the price at closing and signs a promissory note to pay the rest of the price, plus interest, over a specified time period. When you accept a promise of future payments, you're issuing what's called a *seller-financed loan*. When you hear business sellers say they have to *carry paper*, they mean they have to provide the buyer with a loan for a portion of the purchase price.

Buyers sometimes request that a portion of the purchase price be paid as a *balloon payment*, which is a lump-sum payment made at an agreed-upon future date, usually months — or even years — after the sale closing. The benefit to the buyer is that by replacing the need for ongoing monthly payments with the promise to make a future balloon payment, the buyer can keep early cash flow working to transition and build the business. The risk, which sits squarely with the seller, is that the buyer won't be able to make the payment when it's due. Chapter 14 has plenty of information on how to protect yourself when agreeing to deferred payments.

What's in it for buyers (and, indirectly, for you)

By offering to provide your buyer a loan, you boost your sale prospects in several ways:

- ✔ **You ease buyer concerns about the future success of your business.** By offering to accept deferred payments for part of the purchase price, you basically put your money where your mouth is in regard to your belief in a positive future for the business.

- ✔ **You discourage price reductions** by requiring that the buyer come up with only a portion of the price on closing day.

- ✔ **You speed up the sale closing,** because you don't have to wait for bank or SBA-guaranteed loans.

- ✔ **You provide your buyer with advantages,** including more flexible payment terms than a bank may allow and no loan origination or other fees, points that may give you negotiation leverage when other deal issues arise.

- ✔ **You can spread your business proceeds over more than one year,** so your year-of-sale taxable income doesn't spike so dramatically. By spreading the income over several years, you may spare yourself from paying income tax at the highest rate, or from paying the dreaded Alternative Minimum Tax (AMT).

How it directly affects you

You face both upsides and downsides if you become the banker for your deal:

- ✔ **Upside: tax advantages.** By allowing the buyer to pay the loan off over a number of years, you spread the tax impact from sale income over a longer period than would be the case with a one-time payoff.

- ✔ **Upside: interest income.** Say you offer a $250,000 loan at 7 percent interest. From interest alone you'll receive an additional $17,500 in annual proceeds from the deal. You'll pay taxes on the income, but the taxes will be spread over the term of the loan.

- ✔ **Downside: risk.** When you make a seller-financed loan, you sweeten your sale deal, but you also assume a big risk. The risk is that the buyer can default on payment obligations, which — sorry to say — happens way too often. If the buyer turns out to be a poor business or financial manager, and if the health of the business goes south, loan repayments are often one of the first casualties. That's why securing your loan with the ironclad protections described in Chapter 14 is so important.

- ✔ **Downside: value depletion.** Most seller-financed loans include clear conditions that allow you to foreclose and take your business back if the buyer defaults on loan obligations. But if your business has valuable inventory or physical assets, those assets could be gone by the time the business lands back in your hands, stripped of the value it had on closing day.

If you provide a seller-financed loan and if payments span more than a year after the sale, the portion of your sale that's taxable as capital gains can be deferred under what's called the *installment sale method*. Chapter 14 explains installment sales and other tax information. That chapter also has advice on financing, including the need for a personal guarantee to secure the loan with assets beyond those held by the business. That way, should the buyer wring the value out of the business, you'll have access to the buyer's personal assets in the event of loan default.

Don't offer seller financing simply to get the deal closed. Offer it only if you believe in the buyer's financial capability and the financial strength of the collateral the buyer's willing to put up to secure the loan.

Deferred payments: The earn-out deal

An *earn-out* is when you and the buyer agree that part of the buyer's payment will be based on how well the business does following the sale.

Especially if you feel that the business will continue to grow briskly, an earn-out is a great way to benefit from its future potential. Here's how earn-outs usually work:

✔ The earn-out takes the form of interim payments that are typically made quarterly, semi-annually, or annually over an agreed-upon period of time.

✔ The earn-out payment amount is calculated following a formula that's described in the purchase and sale agreement that you and the buyer sign at closing. (For more on the purchase and sale agreement, see Chapter 15.) Some earn-outs are based on increases in sales revenue; others are based on increases in gross profit. Over the period of the earn-out, the buyer pays the seller a portion of the increase as sort of a bonus for building and transitioning such a strong business.

✔ The earn-out may be set at a minimum amount. For example, the deal may be written so that the annual earn-out can't be less than a certain dollar figure.

✔ The earn-out may also be restricted by a maximum payment, so that the seller receives no benefit from the buyer's success beyond a certain point. The minimum and maximum earn-out amounts are usually called the earn-out *floor* and *ceiling*.

When a portion of the purchase price is paid as an earn-out, the deal's terms need to be detailed in the purchase and sale agreement. Here's wording from an actual closing document where the owner was paid for business goodwill through an earn-out:

"The purchase of goodwill shall be equal to 5 percent of Buyer's gross income for each of the first three years following the closing date, with a minimum payment of $50,000 per year and a maximum payment of $125,000."

The agreement also details how gross income is defined and how the calculation must be "made by an independent certified public accountant mutually agreeable to the parties." In other words, calculations made by the owner on the back of a business envelope don't count.

Navigating Negotiations

How your business sale concludes depends greatly upon how it's negotiated. This section lays out a road map to help you prepare for and navigate the negotiation, including what to expect, how to react, when to compromise, and how to keep the deal moving toward closing day.

Although you and the buyer will view the deal from very different vantage points, you should be able to agree on three things:

✔ You want the deal to conclude in a mutually acceptable purchase and sale agreement.

✔ You want the deal to conclude in a timely manner, maybe even by a certain date.

✔ You both want the deal to have an advantageous outcome. To you, that means receiving a reasonable purchase price that's paid with a good-sized down payment and well-secured deferred payments, allocated in a manner that saves you from extreme tax impacts. To the buyer, that means paying a reasonable price with a payment structure that allows for adequate business cash flow in the early months, allocated in a way that provides good expense and tax deductions and supported by your ongoing involvement, or at least your promise not to compete with the new owner.

If you and your buyer can customize and agree on the three points in this list, you can use these points as your negotiating objectives. Each time the going gets rough, you can remind yourselves that you both want the same outcomes and that you're only differing on how to achieve them.

Preparing to negotiate

Before you head into negotiations, be sure you've covered these four bases:

✔ **Have the buyer's signed letter of intent:** Don't even think about entering negotiations until you receive a firm proposal from the buyer, accompanied by a letter of intent that you've reviewed with your sale advisors, countered if necessary, and signed.

✔ **Understand your advisors' accounting and legal advice:** Before you even put your business up for sale, you should work with your accountant to determine the kind of price and sale structure you're aiming for. Then after you receive the buyer's proposal, meet with your advisors again, this time to determine how you can turn the proposal into a sale structure that delivers the most financial benefit and the fewest tax impacts.

✔ **Know your personal objectives:** Know what you need out of the sale in terms of amount of cash at closing and whether you're willing to offer financing — and, if so, for how much and how long. Also, know whether you want to remain involved with your business after the sale or whether you want to be free to move on as of a certain date, which you can set as a personal deadline.

✔ **Know what you consider to be deal-breakers:** Make a list of the issues that are absolutely essential to you. It may be that you want your business sold by a certain date, and that everything else is negotiable. Or, it may be that you want a certain price and no less, and that you're willing to walk away if the buyer can't meet your number. No one is suggesting that you set unreasonable deal-killers, but if you're absolutely positive that certain aspects have to be addressed, know those as you enter negotiations.

When you know your buyer is serious about purchasing your business and you're positive about what you want and need out of the deal, the negotiating dance begins.

Hashing out the details of the negotiation

If the letter of intent you both signed sets the basic sale price and sale description, as it should have, your negotiation will focus on the mechanics of the deal. Through negotiations, you need to clarify the following points:

- ✔ The structure of the sale — asset sale or entity sale
- ✔ The final price and price allocation
- ✔ The payment structure, including loan financing, if any
- ✔ How to deal with issues discovered during due diligence investigations
- ✔ How to structure your future involvement with the business
- ✔ How you'll handle the seller-to-buyer transition

Of those six factors, the first four are the major focus of the negotiation.

Minimally, follow these tips:

- ✔ **Don't start negotiating until you're ready.** Before you open negotiations, know your buyer's offer; obtain advice from your attorney, financial advisor, and broker; and set your personal objectives.

- ✔ **Do keep the negotiations moving.** If a buyer request requires legal or accounting advice, get the advice immediately, not tomorrow. Delays kill deals.

- ✔ **Do be sure you're negotiating with the right people in the room.** If the buyer's spouse or parent or whoever is going to call the shots, get that person in on the meetings. Otherwise, you slow things to a crawl, and — not to belabor the point — delays kill deals.

- ✔ **Do keep an open mind.** You may be stuck on a certain price or payment approach, but allow your buyer and your advisors to present ways you can meet your objectives and still vary slightly from your position. Remember, deal terms are often worth as much as money.

✔ **Don't forget your personal objectives.** If you enter negotiations wanting a certain amount of cash at closing, or a certain level of ongoing involvement, or whatever, use those objectives as your negotiation-navigating device. If you end up negotiating away from one of your objectives, balance your concession by negotiating an even better outcome for a different objective.

✔ **Don't try to up your price.** If you really think you deserve more for your business, offer to put an earn-out payment into the payment structure so you can realize some of the payment based on future performance — and at the same time let your buyer off the hook for closing day or short-term payments.

✔ **Do aim to achieve a win-win negotiation** by offsetting requests that are clearly to your advantage with offers that are clearly to the buyer's advantage.

✔ **Don't be afraid to protect your own interests.** It may feel awkward to press the buyer for a personal guarantee to secure a seller-financed loan or for access to business financials on a regular basis during the period you agree to accept deferred payments. But remember that such requirements are justified — they're normal business procedures, and they're necessary to a successful deal outcome.

✔ **Do remember your mutual objective,** which is a purchase and sale agreement, and do be flexible to get to that finish line.

For further guidance on handling negotiations, pick up a copy of *Negotiating For Dummies,* 2nd Edition, by Michael C. Donaldson (Wiley, 2007), which is full of negotiating advice, including what to do and what not to do.

Chapter 14

Handling the Fine Print: Financing and Tax Specifics

. . . .

In This Chapter

▶ Understanding what's involved with SBA loans

▶ Putting personal protections in place

▶ Minimizing and deferring taxes

. . . .

*U*nlike every other chapter in this book, this chapter is for reference only. Other chapters tell you what to do and ways to do it — how to decide you're ready to plan a business exit, how to prepare your business for a sale, how to place ads and screen respondents, and how to work with a buyer to structure and negotiate a sale deal.

When it comes to financing and taxes, this chapter doesn't try to tell you what to do. For that, you need to turn to your accountant for advice that's tailored to your unique situation. This chapter gives you background information to help you understand what your CPA is talking about when the topics of financing your sale and taxing the proceeds come up.

In the same way a traveler's language guide helps unlock key phrases but hardly makes you fluent in a language, this chapter gives you basic information but doesn't begin to stand in for the advice of your professional team when it comes to making financing and tax decisions and putting all the legal and tax paperwork in place. Instead, it serves as an orientation to the discussions, decisions, and processes that await you if your sale includes loans — either from the SBA or from you, personally — and in the definite eventuality that it includes tax impacts.

Deciphering the Rules of SBA Loans

When business buyers turn to banks for financing, they usually end up with either an equity loan against the value they've built up in their homes or other real property, or they luck out and get what's commonly called an SBA loan, which is a loan guaranteed through the Small Business Administration 7(a) loan program.

In spite of commonly used terminology, *SBA loans* aren't loans from the Small Business Administration. They're bank loans guaranteed in part (usually from 50 to 80 percent) by the SBA, which essentially plays the role of the loan co-signer, much like a rich uncle.

The advantage of an SBA loan guarantee through the 7(a) program is that a bank's position is somewhat protected, which makes loan approval somewhat easier than is usually the case when a bank issues a loan all on its own. Here are facts to know about SBA loans:

- ✔ An SBA-guaranteed loan is made by a participating American lending institution — usually a bank — with the assurance that the SBA stands behind the loan in the event of default.

- ✔ The SBA doesn't guarantee the loan's full amount — the bank has to assume risk for some 20 to 50 percent. For that reason, even if the SBA agrees to guarantee the loan, the bank may decline the loan application if it doesn't believe in the borrower's ability to repay the debt.

- ✔ When the SBA guarantees a loan, the guarantee assures the lender that in the event of loan default, the government will cover the bank's loss up to the percentage of the loan that was guaranteed. The borrower remains obligated for the full outstanding balance due. (To the borrower, an SBA-guaranteed loan may be easier than other types of loans to get, but it's no easier to get out of.)

Just because the SBA guarantees a loan doesn't mean loan approval is a cake-walk. The process takes longer than a regular loan application because the borrower has to be approved twice — once by the lending institution and once by the SBA. If your buyer plans on using an SBA loan, do everything you can to get the buyer started on the application process as soon as a purchase looks likely.

SBA-guaranteed loan requirements

Not all businesses qualify for SBA loans. Before hinging your hopes on your buyer's ability to get an SBA-guaranteed loan, realize that the nature of your business may be a big factor in whether a loan is even possible. Talk to your banker and your broker, if you're using one, to find out whether your business and your buyer are likely to meet the SBA requirements, which are summarized in the following list.

- ✔ The borrower must be able to repay the loan from business cash flow. If your business doesn't generate enough cash to meet its operating expenses, pay its owner's salary, and make loan payments, you can probably cross the wish for an SBA-guaranteed loan off the list of ways your buyer can fund the purchase.

- ✔ The borrower has to have good character and no current or pending criminal charges. If your buyer can't pass this test, the bank won't lend money, nor — if you're considering a seller-financed loan — should you.

- ✔ The borrower has to put up good loan collateral, and he or she — and every person who will own 20 percent or more of the business — has to personally guarantee the loan.

- ✔ The borrower has to invest personal assets in the business and take advantage of other available financing sources before requesting SBA loan guarantees.

- ✔ The business must do business for profit in the United States or in a U.S.-governed territory.

- ✔ The business can't be involved in real estate investments or lending, nor can it be a non-profit, religious, or charitable organization. The business also can't participate in speculative activities, gambling, or pyramid sales plans. And of course, businesses that are against the law or that sell products used in illegal activity are out of the running.

Additional SBA loan requirements apply to certain types of businesses, such as franchises, medical facilities, recreational facilities, and clubs, to name a few. The SBA also has restrictions on the size of businesses eligible for loans (in most cases, businesses with tangible net worth less than $7.5 million and net profit after tax less than $2.5 million), the size of projects considered for funding (generally between $150,000 and $10 million), and the maximum dollar amount the SBA can contribute to a single business (generally, $1.5 million, with certain exceptions).

The new SBA rules run hundreds of pages long. For general information, visit the SBA Web site and look into requirements for 7(a) loans (go to the "Useful Links" section of the CD-ROM and click on "SBA Basic 7(a) Information," or type this address into your Web browser: `www.sba.gov/services/financial assistance/sbaloantopics/7a/index.html/`). For more specific information, turn to a pro.

The SBA recently made changes to its business acquisition loan program. If you think your buyer will rely on an SBA-guaranteed loan, check with your banker or broker to be sure your sale will qualify. Following are a few of the key changes:

- ✔ The seller can't remain with the business as an employee who receives employee benefits. If you're staying on, your role will have to be that of a consultant.

- ✔ The buyer can't combine an SBA loan for the business purchase and a conventional loan for the real estate purchase, *unless* the conventional loan shares the first lien position on the real estate with the lender of the SBA-guaranteed loan.

- ✔ The borrower can't use home equity for the business purchase down payment unless he or she has sources of income outside the business with which to repay the home equity loan.

- ✔ If the loan is for more than $350,000, the borrower must get a third-party business valuation separate from the one used to set the purchase price.

- ✔ The seller must offer as much financing as possible. If you think your buyer will need an SBA-guaranteed loan, be prepared to offer some amount of seller financing as well.

Consider contacting an SBA loan broker for assistance so you can enter the sale process with your eyes wide open about whether your business is eligible and what's required of your buyer. You can find contacts by searching the Internet for "SBA loan brokers" or by asking your banker or accountant for names. Online, you can go to the site of BizBuyFinancing, a sister company to the online business-for-sale exchange site BizBuySell. BizBuyFinancing facilitates SBA financing for business purchases and is a consultant for specialty loans. It helps business buyers, sellers, and brokers obtain loans from $300,000 to $5 million. For information, go to www.bizbuyfinancing.com/.

Steps involved in obtaining an SBA-guaranteed loan

To obtain an SBA-guaranteed loan, your buyer begins by applying to an SBA partner bank or other lender for business financing, following all the bank's application procedures and requirements. The bank will determine if your buyer meets loan eligibility and creditworthiness criteria:

- ✔ **If the bank approves your buyer's loan application outright,** then no SBA loan guarantee is necessary.

- ✔ **If a bank senses loan application weaknesses,** it may require an SBA guarantee, which is granted only to applications that meet all SBA program requirements (see the previous section).

Be aware that the loan request doesn't go to the SBA until after the applicant has met the lender's requirements, so it basically gets reviewed not once but twice, which usually adds as much as three weeks to the overall approval process.

Becoming the Banker by Self-financing Your Sale

Even though seller financing is considered the norm in small business sales, provide a seller-financed loan only if you believe the buyer can and will pay off the debt. Even then, proceed with Murphy's Law in mind: If anything can go wrong, it's likely to go wrong in the worst possible way. This section helps you protect yourself with loan agreements, loan-recipient guarantees, and other actions that secure your interests and increase your chances of getting paid in full.

When you issue a seller-financed loan, the surest way to protect your financial interest is to get as large a down payment as possible on closing day. Most brokers and business advisors suggest getting a third to one-half of the money upfront. That way, if the worst happens and the business ends up back in your hands, at least you'll have the sizable down payment as well.

The next best way to secure your interests is to have your attorney draw up formal, legal documents that bind the buyer to loan repayment terms. One of those documents is a *promissory note*, which is a written, legally binding version of an IOU.

Don't even think of lending money on the strength of a handshake. Work with your attorney to get the loan's terms in writing. Normally, as part of the requirements of the written loan agreement, your buyer will put up business assets as loan collateral. Additionally, your legal and financial advisors may advise you to get the loan secured by other valuable buyer-owned assets. That way, should the buyer default on loan obligations to you, you have a greater opportunity for recovering the outstanding loan balance.

After your seller-financed loan agreement is set and the promissory note's signed, your attorney will file a Uniform Commercial Code (UCC) statement with your secretary of state's office. This filing creates a record of the debt agreement. Should Murphy's Law prevail, this filing makes it easier for you to start the legal collection process.

Obtaining a promissory note

A promissory note, sometimes called a *loan note* or a *note payable*, covers the following points:

✔ **The name of the promisor,** or the person promising to fulfill the obligations outlined in the note. The *promisor* is also called the *obligor* or the *maker* because he or she is making the repayment promise and is obligated to the loan terms.

- ✔ **The name of the promisee,** or the person accepting the promise outlined in the note (that's you). The *promisee* is also called the *obligee* or the *payee*.

- ✔ **The principal amount,** which is the sum of money being loaned under the terms of the note.

- ✔ **The interest rate,** which is usually close to what banks are currently charging for loans but often a little higher to account for the risk the seller is taking and the ease of financing the buyer is realizing. If you try to charge more than a slight increase over prevailing bank interest rates, however, your buyer could balk. Beyond that, *usury laws* cap how much you can charge, so check with your attorney or accountant to make sure you stay within the letter — or the percentage point — of the law.

- ✔ **Repayment terms,** including the interest rate and the payment due dates. Many notes include a *default clause,* which makes the entire outstanding amount of the loan due if the promisor fails to make a payment within a certain number of days of a payment due date.

The "Useful Links" section of the CD-ROM includes links to a couple of free legal advice sites where you can view sample copies of promissory notes. You can also go to this Web site: `http://www.expertlaw.com/library/business/promissory_note_form.html/`. Because laws vary from state to state, get legal advice before using a standard form and before presenting or signing any kind of a loan agreement.

If your loan covers real property such as your business building, a promissory note isn't enough. Instead, work with your attorney to write a mortgage and to file and record all the right deed forms.

Going a step further with a secured promissory note

It's not being negative to plan for an unanticipated loan default — it's being realistic. Protect yourself by asking the buyer to sign a *secured promissory note*.

In short, you should know that there are two kinds of promissory notes:

- ✔ With an *unsecured promissory note*, all you have is the buyer's promise that the payments will reach you on time following the terms of the loan. If the buyer doesn't come through with the payments, you have no path of recourse because your note is unsecured. If the buyer declares bankruptcy, you have to stand in line behind all secured creditors before getting paid. An unsecured loan is a formula for trouble.

✔ With a *secured promissory note*, the buyer gives you a legal right to *collateral* — valuable buyer-owned assets that you can seize and sell as recourse should the buyer not make payments as promised.

Collateral comes in a number of forms, including the assets of the business you're selling and personal assets owned by your buyer or other loan cosigners. Many lenders put a number of the following layers of protection in place.

Business assets as loan security

If your promissory note includes a security interest in business assets as collateral, then in the event of default, you have the right to take back the assets you sold, including accounts receivable, contract rights, business proceeds and products, equipment, assumed names and files, and so on.

When a borrower pledges business assets as collateral, watch out for two big dangers:

✔ **Beware of a subordinated position.** You take a *subordinated position* when another lender has first rights to the business assets, leaving you with access to what's left after the other lender's loan is repaid. For instance, if your buyer needs a bank loan in addition to your loan, or if your buyer needs a bank line of credit to operate the business, chances are good the bank will have first or senior rights to business assets. You'll be subordinated to a second position, and asset value may be already tapped out before you can get to it.

✔ **Beware of asset devaluation.** Before missing a payment, the buyer may run through existing inventory and may even sell equipment or assets to try to keep the business afloat during rough times. As a result, by the time of loan default, what's left may be a stripped-down operation you may not even want back, and if you get it back it may be without any real value.

To protect themselves, lenders who have to take a subordinated position — as well as lenders who are concerned about the possibility of business asset devaluation — require borrowers to offer additional collateral, usually by pledging a security interest in valuable buyer-owned assets outside the business, such as the buyer's home or other real estate.

A personal guarantee as loan security

Personal guarantees, which you'll hear referred to as PGs, are important because, in the event of a loan default, they allow you to go after personal assets if you can't go after business assets. They're also a little confusing, because they force you to deal with the fact that the person you've been calling your buyer may not end up being the *legal* buyer of your business. Read on for a little clarification.

Let's say you're selling your business to Jane Smith. If Jane decides to form a corporation or limited liability company (LLC) to hold the assets from your sale, that business entity — often referred to as NEWCO during the sale process — becomes your buyer, and Jane becomes the shareholder for NEWCO.

Likewise, if you're selling a corporation or LLC, you aren't really the seller; your business entity — often referred to as OLDCO during the sale process — is the seller, and you're the selling shareholder. (After the deal is done, you'll probably dissolve OLDCO and the buyer will rename NEWCO with the business name purchased from OLDCO. I wasn't exaggerating when I said this gets a little confusing.)

If you provide a seller-financed loan to Jane Smith's new corporation or LLC, the promissory note is between you and the business entity referred to as NEWCO, not between you and Jane Smith. She's not the buyer or the one taking the loan — NEWCO is.

If you want your loan to be backed by a personal repayment promise from Jane Smith — who you've probably grown to know and trust — you need the NEWCO promissory note to be backed by Jane Smith's *personal guarantee.* That way, if NEWCO defaults on the loan and there aren't enough business assets available to pay the loan off, you can go after Jane's personal assets. If Jane's married, you can (and your attorney will probably tell you that you should) obtain her spouse's guarantee, too, so you can go after the spouse's assets as well as jointly owned assets.

When you obtain Jane Smith's personal guarantee, she becomes the *guarantor* for the loan you provide to NEWCO. If you also get her spouse's guarantee, together they become the *guarantors.* Getting the spouse's guarantee along with your buyer's is especially important if you live in one of the ten U.S. states that at the time of this writing are designated as community property states (Alaska, Arizona, California, Idaho, Louisiana, Nevada, New Mexico, Texas, Washington, and Wisconsin). In these states, the property that's securing the loan is jointly owned, so you want to get guarantees from both owners.

To show you how a personal guarantee is worded, here's a clause from an actual purchase and sale agreement in which the buyer is a corporation and the person who formed the corporation and her spouse are the guarantors:

> *Subject to the provisions of this Section, Guarantors unconditionally and irrevocably guarantee the performance by Buyer of each and every Obligation. This guaranty shall be continuing and shall terminate only upon the satisfaction by Buyer of each and every one of the Obligations.*

In other words, thanks to their personal guarantee, Jane Smith and her spouse are promising to personally fulfill the loan obligations of NEWCO. If the value of NEWCO's assets should be tapped out or devalued at the time of loan default, everyone is clear about where they can turn next.

When providing a seller-financed loan, ask your attorney whether a *cognovit promissory note* is allowed in your state. A cognovit note is like any other promissory note except that it includes an extra provision that allows you, the lender, a very rapid path to judgment and collection should the borrower default on the loan. By signing a cognovit note, the borrower basically authorizes the lender to enter a judgment against the borrower — without notice — if loan payments aren't made following the terms of the agreement.

A third-party guarantee as loan security

If your buyer has no or very few personal assets with which to guarantee your loan, consider requiring your buyer to obtain a third-party guarantee from an asset-rich parent or other outsider.

If you go this route, don't be taken in by a lofty story about the third party's fame and fortune. Get a financial statement and credit report, just as you do when you assess your buyer's financial ability during your due diligence investigation, which is explained in Chapter 12.

Restricting stock share endorsements

If you're selling the stock of your business, another good protection that your attorney may recommend is to restrictively endorse your stock shares. This protection is important if your buyer is a private corporation (in other words, the person you sell to has set up a corporation to own your business) *and* if you make a seller-financed loan as part of the closing deal. In this case, you can protect yourself by attaching some strings or red tape to the transfer of your stock shares. If your attorney advises you to do so, you can *restrictively endorse* your stock shares so they don't become the outright property of your buyer until all debt is repaid.

Managing Your Sale Taxes

As I explain in depth in Chapter 13, the way you allocate the price affects how your sale proceeds are taxed — and how some sale structure decisions work *for* you and others work *against* you when it comes to taxation. At a glance, this list summarizes the major points to remember:

- ✔ If your business is structured as a corporation or LLC and you sell your entire business entity by selling your stock to a new buyer, you'll pay capital gains tax on the profit you realize from the sale, which at the time of this writing is set at 15 percent — a considerably lower rate than the rate at which ordinary income is taxed. With a stock sale, you usually end up paying less in taxes than you would with an asset sale.

- ✔ If you sell the assets of a C corporation instead of selling the stock, you pay taxes twice — once when your corporation pays tax on the profits from selling the assets and once when you pay tax on the money you distribute to yourself as the corporate shareholder when the corporation is liquidated.

- ✔ If you sell assets you've owned for less than a year, you'll pay taxes at your ordinary income tax rate for any gain, which is the difference between what you paid for the asset, called your *basis*, and what you sell it for.

- ✔ If you sell assets you've owned for more than a year, you'll pay taxes for any gain at the capital gains rate.

- ✔ If you accept a portion of the payment price in exchange for a non-compete agreement, the proceeds are taxed as ordinary income.

- ✔ If you agree to participate with your buyer in a consulting or management agreement, the income you receive from the arrangement is taxed as ordinary income.

After you receive your payment on the sale, sit down with your accountant and discuss any extra quarterly tax payments you may need to make to the IRS to cover your estimated tax liability in order to avoid penalties later.

Understanding a bit about the Alternative Minimum Tax (AMT)

The AMT is the taxpayer's Bermuda Triangle. It's that mystifying.

Basically, the AMT allows you only a minimum tax exemption instead of the long list of tax exemptions you may qualify for under the standard tax calculation. The AMT's purpose is to prevent wealthy individuals from claiming so many exemptions that they avoid most taxation altogether. But over the years the tax has begun to affect a growing number of middle-income earners as well.

You can't easily determine whether you're going to be affected by the AMT, but if you have a lot of deductions and long-term capital gains — such as those on your sale proceeds from goodwill and tangible assets — the AMT is apt to come into play.

Your accountant will calculate your taxes using standard and AMT methods, and — brace yourself — if the AMT is higher, you have to add the difference between the AMT and your regular tax to whatever your tax bill would have been under the regular tax calculation.

The only thing you can do about the AMT is to plan in advance, which requires your accountant's expertise. The tricky part is that planning to avoid the AMT puts you in a Catch-22. To keep as much of your sale proceeds as possible, you want to structure your sale by allocating the price to items that qualify for capital gains, because those come with a way lower tax rate than items that are taxed as ordinary income. The catch is that if you have enough capital gains, you may push yourself toward the AMT. Don't try to make the call without your accountant's advice.

Gaining tax advantages with an installment sale

In an installment sale, the buyer pays for your business in payments that span over more than a year's time. By giving your buyer a loan and allowing deferred payments, you can gain some tax advantages. The tax law for installment sales is complicated, but your accountant will advise you on how to use the structure to your advantage. At a glance, here are the highlights:

✔ As of 2000, owners selling assets that would be taxed at capital gains rates can defer paying some of the tax due until the payments are actually received.

✔ Installment sale tax deferrals don't apply to the sale of assets for which the proceeds are taxed as ordinary income, such as inventory or fixtures, furnishings, and equipment that was purchased within a year of the sale. They do, however, apply to the sale of assets you've held for more than a year. For those assets, the difference between what you paid (your *basis*) and the sale price is your capital gain. Under the installment sale method, you can defer paying taxes on these capital gains until the year you receive the buyer's payment.

✔ If part of your sale price is allocated to goodwill, and if your accountant tells you that your business is old enough to have the sale of goodwill qualify as a capital gain, then taxes on goodwill payments can also be deferred until they're received.

If you offer a loan to your buyer, take advantage of the installment sale tax method by allocating as much of your purchase price as possible to assets that will be taxed as capital gains rather than as ordinary income. Be sure to keep the risk of triggering the AMT in mind at all times.

Completing the IRS Asset Acquisition Statement

Your accountant will advise you to file various tax forms as part of or following the sale closing. One key form you and your buyer have to file if you're selling assets is IRS Form 8594, titled Asset Acquisition Statement Under Section 1060.

Don't wait until your tax return is due to complete Form 8594. During your sale negotiation, you and your buyer should agree on how you'll both allocate the purchase price so there's no dispute later.

The "Useful Links" section of the CD-ROM includes a link to this form, as well as a link to IRS instructions for completing it. Or you can go to www.irs.gov/pub/irs-pdf/f8594.pdf to download the form, and to www.irs.gov/instructions/i8594/index.html to reach the IRS instructions.

When submitting the form, be aware of several requirements:

- ✔ **Filing requirement.** You and your buyer both need to file a copy of the Asset Acquisition Statement (Form 8594) with your tax returns for the year of the sale.

- ✔ **Buyer and seller agreement.** When filing the statement, you and your buyer both need to make an identical statement of how assets are valued and the sale price is allocated. In other words, one of you can't say one thing while the other says something else.

- ✔ **IRS allocation review.** The IRS has the right to determine that the way you allocate the price is inappropriate. Unless the IRS determines otherwise, however, the way you and your buyer allocate the price on Form 8594 is binding, and you pay taxes on the proceeds accordingly.

See Chapter 15 for information on other tax and legal forms you're required to submit as part of your sale closing and business dissolution.

Chapter 15

Closing the Sale

In This Chapter

▶ Orchestrating the closing

▶ Understanding the forms you'll be signing

▶ Winding up your business activities

After the handshakes come the final laps of the business sale process, leading up to the day you and your buyer sign the final agreements and begin the long-awaited handoff of your business. Between now and when money changes hands, you have some serious work to do to prepare everything you need on closing day, make closing day arrangements, get your final sale documents in order, and, finally and happily, sign all the forms in all the right places.

Your business broker, if you're using one, will steer you through the twists and turns that come in the last throes of negotiations and closing your deal. If you're not using a broker, your attorney will guide you through the end process. If that's the case, spend the money to buy adequate time and advice from your lawyer. Remember the age-old advice that an ounce of prevention is worth a pound of cure. This isn't the time to cut corners or over-accelerate. Get the advice you need to avoid a future crash into problems that arise when sellers overlook legalities or technicalities along the way.

This chapter provides checklists of steps you need to take and topics you should go over with your lawyer or broker to be sure everything's in alignment as you head toward the finish line.

Clearing the Way for Closing Day

After you and the buyer, with your advisors, have structured your sale deal and agreed on final price and price allocation (flip back to Chapter 13 if any of these terms sound unfamiliar), it's time to close the deal on your sale. To prepare for the closing, you have to get the details in order, including the following tasks, decisions, and documents:

- **Set the closing date.** The date on which your sale closes can't be a moving target. You need to determine the exact date so you can prorate rent, utilities, payroll, taxes, and any other ongoing expenses that transfer with the sale. You may want to set the closing date on the last day of the month to make the process of prorating monthly charges as easy as possible, or at the end of a pay period so you don't have to prorate employee paychecks. Also, consider setting the closing for a weekday morning — when banks, government offices, and business offices are open — in case an issue arises that you need to address.

- **Establish final agreement on the purchase price.** If the buyer's due diligence investigation led to price negotiations, the results of those negotiations need to be incorporated into the final price that appears in your purchase and sale agreement.

- **Establish final agreement on price allocation.** You and your buyer have to agree on exactly how the final sale price is allocated among IRS-defined asset categories. Chapter 13 helps you weigh how price allocation affects your tax situation, and Chapter 14 includes a section on what's involved when filing the Asset Acquisition Statement. By closing day, you and your buyer should have a firm agreement so price allocation doesn't become a last-minute sticking point.

- **Satisfy the buyer's closing conditions.** Work with the buyer, with input from your accountant and attorney, to address any issues that arise from the buyer's due diligence investigation (see Chapter 12 for more information on what this investigation involves). Also be sure that you address any closing conditions listed in the buyer's letter of intent.

- **Assemble all documents required to transfer your business or its assets to a new owner.** If you're selling stock, you need to have your board pass a corporate resolution approving the sale. You also need to prepare and assemble all other forms your lawyer tells you are necessary to transfer or close your business in your state, including those required by your city or county offices and the office of your secretary of state or corporations commission.

- **Review any loan documents you'll be asking your buyer to sign.** If you offer a seller-financed loan, your attorney will prepare a promissory note (explained in Chapter 14) that details the loan agreement and repayment terms.

- **Review the security agreements your buyer will sign.** Chapter 14 includes information on securing seller-financed loans with business assets and personal guarantees. Prior to closing, work with your lawyer to prepare the agreements that your buyer, buyer's spouse, and third-party guarantors will sign to secure the loan in the event payments aren't made.

- **Confirm that the buyer has arranged for insurance.** Following the closing, you'll cancel your policies, so the buyer needs to have new policies lined up and ready to kick in on Day One. If you offer a seller-financed loan or agree to deferred payments for part of the purchase price, your lawyer will probably write an insurance clause into your purchase and sale agreement requiring the buyer to maintain insurance at levels comparable to the insurance you maintained. The agreement will probably also include other seller protections, like the requirement that you be notified in advance in the event of policy cancellation.

✔ **Review a preliminary closing or settlement sheet.** This is the document that lists all financial details involved in closing the sale, including the purchase price and all costs and price adjustments to be paid by or credited to you and the buyer. If you're using an escrow agent to close your deal, the escrow office will prepare this sheet. If your sale is being closed by an attorney, the attorney will prepare the settlement sheet. (The next section has information on the difference between escrow settlements and settlements in an attorney's office.) On the settlement sheet, costs include items like legal fees, escrow fees, and broker's fees, and adjustments include items like prorated expenses. If inventory or accounts receivable are being sold, the settlement sheet also shows adjustments to reflect the closing day value of those assets. As part of the negotiations leading up to the closing, you and your buyer will decide whether you'll both pay your own legal costs or you'll include legal costs in the closing fees, to be divided between the two of you. If you're using a broker, the broker will help handle this decision. If you're not using a broker, your attorney will likely address this point in preparation for the closing. If professional fees are being handled directly by you and the buyer, they won't appear on the selling sheet, but if they're being split, they will. You and your buyer should both review and agree to a preliminary copy of the settlement sheet to avoid surprises at closing.

✔ **Have all sale assets ready for transfer.** If you're transferring your lease, ownership of vehicles, a franchise agreement, patents, or trademarks, be sure that you take the steps necessary to obtain all necessary approvals and to have all titles or leases in hand to allow you to transition those assets on closing day.

✔ **Work with your buyer to prepare an employee announcement and a sale news release or fact sheet, which you can distribute immediately in the case of a news leak.** (Chapter 16 shows you how to craft both types of announcement.) Though you may hope to wait until the closing is firmly scheduled or behind you before you make your sale announcement, events may require you to jump the gun, and you and your buyer should be ready just in case. Even with every precaution, news of your sale may hit the grapevine before you want it to. You may get an anxious call from an employee, an inquiry from a reporter at the local daily paper, or a visit from a concerned client. If all goes as planned, you won't need to use these documents until after closing day, but by having them ready to go, if word of your sale gets out, you can corral the news by circulating a prepared set of facts.

If the leak involves the media, especially if it involves a local news outlet, you may be able to get the reporter to back off from releasing the story for a short period of time. If the story's release is likely to jeopardize client or staff relations, ask the reporter about delaying the interview and news coverage for one or several days while you take the necessary steps to finalize the deal and conduct essential internal communications. In return, pledge that the reporter's media outlet will be the first to get the news.

Form 15-1 on the CD-ROM includes a checklist of pre-closing steps. Use it for reference when you meet with your broker and attorney prior to the closing to be sure you take all necessary actions and prepare and review all necessary forms.

Knowing What to Expect: An Outline of the Closing Process

Your closing will probably take place in one of two ways: Either your attorney will prepare closing documents and guide you through all the closing steps, or you'll use an escrow agent in what's called an *escrow settlement*. In an escrow settlement, closing is handled by a neutral third party who holds the buyer's funds in trust until any buyer-requested conditions are cleared and any business obligations, such as liens or judgments, are removed.

If an attorney has been a key member of your sale team, you'll probably close your sale in the attorney's office. If you've used a broker for your sale and your attorney has been involved primarily to prepare or review necessary documents rather than to help steer the sale process, you'll likely close through an escrow office.

Closing in your attorney's office

If an attorney has been a key player throughout your sale process, he or she will handle many of the sale closing details. Your buyer may also use an attorney, in which case your two lawyers will work together on the closing documents and details, or you and your buyer may agree to have one lawyer act on behalf of both parties, which is usually the case because it avoids a duplication of time and fees.

Either way, here's what happens when an attorney guides the closing process:

1. **An attorney (or two attorneys working together on behalf of the buyer and seller) prepares the closing document, called the purchase and sale agreement, described later in this chapter.**

   If the buyer's attorney writes the agreement, your attorney will review it carefully before it's finalized.

2. **Your attorney advises you regarding any outstanding obligations that need to be cleared prior to closing.**

   Such obligations may include liens or judgments, as well as removal of conditions or contingencies (such as lease extensions or permit transfers) requested by the buyer in the letter of intent or raised during the due diligence investigation.

3. **You, your buyer, and your attorney meet to sign all final documents and transfer purchase funds.**

   This step is the official closing, described in this chapter.

Closing with an escrow settlement

If an attorney doesn't handle your closing, an escrow officer will. Back when you accepted the buyer's purchase offer and signed the buyer's letter of intent, if you required a good-faith deposit, you probably opened an escrow account at the same time. (The final section of Chapter 11 provides steps to follow when opening an escrow account.)

An escrow settlement involves these steps:

1. **You and your buyer follow all instructions provided by the escrow agent at the time you opened your escrow account.**

   These instructions detail the responsibilities the agent will fulfill and the conditions that you and the buyer need to address before the earnest money deposit and closing documents can be released. The conditions include addressing any contingencies stated in the buyer's letter of intent, such as obtaining financing, extending leases, and conducting due diligence.

2. **After all obligations are addressed — including any contingencies listed in the buyer's letter of intent — you and the buyer sign all closing documents, and the escrow agent transfers funds and records the sale.**

   Sometimes in an escrow closing, the buyer and seller sign forms individually, but a single session where all parties get together to sign the forms is more common, and way more efficient.

Drawing Up the Purchase and Sale Agreement

In the life of your business, probably nothing you sign rivals the importance of the purchase and sale agreement you sign on closing day. This single document states the price of the business you've spent years growing, describes everything you're selling, and spells out all the details about how you'll be paid and how your interests will be protected until the last payment dollar is in your bank account. If ever there was a perfect time to invest in the abilities of an attorney, this is the moment.

If your sale is uncomplicated and your purchase price is really low, like under five figures, the purchase and sale agreement may be fairly short. In that case, or if you have some legal savvy or know a lawyer who can give you some coaching, you can consider using a fill-in-the-blanks purchase and sale agreement form downloaded from an online legal resource such as www. lectlaw.com/. Conduct an online search for "business purchase and sale agreement forms" or "business purchase agreement" to find dozens of options. (The "Useful Links" section of the CD-ROM provides links to a number of such forms.)

Be aware that standard forms come with cautions, because legal requirements vary from state to state, making it necessary to modify most forms before using them. Starting with a standard form can save you money, but if you go that route, invest in some legal counsel to be sure the form you're using — and the way you've filled in the blanks — accurately describes your sale and protects your interests. Better safe than sorry!

For a sale covering a range of assets accompanied by a purchase price in the hundreds of thousands of dollars or more, the purchase and sale agreement may run dozens of pages, not including all the exhibits and attachments that support the agreement. In this case, covering all the necessary points makes for pretty heavy lifting and definitely requires the skills of a pro.

Who writes it

Your broker (if you're using one) may provide a purchase and sale agreement form that you can use as a framework, but whether you use the broker's template or one you obtain from a legal resource, you need to have the final document reviewed by an attorney, because it's full of legal details, obligations, and descriptions that are regulated by rules that vary from state to state. If you aren't using a template, go straight to an attorney to have your agreement written. When working with an attorney, here's what to expect:

✔ The buyer's or seller's attorney draws up the first draft (or reviews the draft if it was prepared with the help of a form document), and then the other lawyer reviews and amends the agreement. If the buyer's attorney writes the first draft, on review your attorney will pay special attention to sections that most affect you, such as representations and warranties, purchase price allocation issues, and payment terms and securities.

✔ In many sales, one attorney writes the agreement working on behalf of both the seller and the buyer, who split the legal fees.

What's in it

The following checklist details items an attorney addresses when writing the agreement:

✔ **Names** of the seller, buyer, and business, including locations.

✔ **Assets being sold,** including machinery and equipment, fixtures, inventories, accounts receivable, business name, customer lists, goodwill, and any other assets included in the sale. This section of the agreement will probably also list excluded assets such as cash, bank accounts, prepaid expenses, land and buildings, automobiles, or other assets being withheld from the sale.

✔ **Liabilities being assumed** by the buyer, including accounts payable, if any. In this section, the buyer will likely want to include a statement that no liabilities other than those listed are being assumed, including taxes or payables accrued through the closing date.

✔ **The closing date** of the sale.

✔ **Purchase price and allocation of the purchase price** to various asset classes such as accounts receivable, inventory, tangible assets, intangible assets, and goodwill. (See Chapter 13 for more information on allocation of the purchase price.)

✔ **Adjustments** to be made to the purchase price to allow for prorated business expenses such as rent, utilities, payroll and benefits, taxes, and other costs involved in operating the business. Also, adjustments may be included to account for closing day valuation of accounts receivable less accounts payable, and for final count and value of inventory, as described in the following section on finalizing the deal.

✔ **Personal seller agreements** such as a non-competition agreement or covenant not to compete, or an agreement to sign a management, consulting, or employment contract with the buyer's business.

✔ **The payment terms,** including the amount of cash paid on closing day, the amount payable following the terms of a promissory note that details a seller-financed loan, and the amount to be paid in agreed-upon future installments.

✔ **Security agreements,** including property listed as collateral, business operation requirements, and personal guarantee requirements if a portion of the purchase payment is covered by a seller's loan and buyer's promissory note. This section of the contract may include some of the following buyer restrictions and requirements:

- Maintain and operate the business following the sale agreement's terms and largely in the manner it was operated by the seller, including operating it on a regular and consistent basis and in accordance with all laws and regulations

- Maintain all purchased equipment

- Maintain insurance to cover all purchased equipment at levels comparable to those maintained by the seller

- Pay all taxes, fees, and assessments on time

- Keep all purchased assets free of liens and encumbrances beyond those in existence on the sale's closing date

Your agreement may also add a clause that gives you the right to inspect the purchased assets, books, and records.

✔ **Inventory** included in the sale.

✔ **Accounts receivable** included in the sale (or a statement explaining that accounts receivable are excluded from the sale), including a description of how payments received for accounts receivable will be applied to accounts after closing day and how uncollected receivables will be handled.

✔ **Seller's representations and warranties,** or "accuracy of representations and warranties," or some other title that basically means you're promising to tell the truth. These warranties include statements that you have the power and legal right to authorize the sale, that you have clear and marketable title to assets being sold, that financial records fairly present the business's financial conditions as of the date of the statements, and that you know of no obligations or liabilities beyond those disclosed as exhibits accompanying the agreement.

The legalese in this section of the agreement can be loosely translated like this: "Everything I've told you about this business, Mr. or Ms. Buyer, is accurate to the best of my ability, and I'm not aware of any facts that will affect the future of this business that I've glossed over or left out." Be absolutely sure you can make this promise to your buyer. If your buyer can later make the case that you've misrepresented facts — facts about business finances, taxes, assets, liens or liabilities, or future prospects — your buyer gains a giant loophole to walk through when defaulting on loan repayments. In all dealings with your buyer, tell the truth, tell the whole truth, and avoid making unrealistic projections about how well your business will do in the future.

✔ **Buyer's representations and warranties,** including warranties that the buyer has the power and legal right to authorize the purchase and that statements made by the buyer and the buyer's guarantors contain no untrue statements or omissions.

✔ **Seller's covenants,** including provisions for such actions as transferring employee benefit plans, paying employee wages through closing date, changing your business name to permit the buyer to legally begin using the name, and signing a non-compete agreement.

✔ **Employee termination clause** that basically says that as of closing day, you'll terminate all employees except those with employment agreements that are transferable to the buyer, and that you'll pay each employee all wages, commissions, and benefits earned up to the time of termination.

The buyer will probably agree to hire all terminated employees. This can't happen without some paperwork, however, because you have to close your federal employee identification number (FEIN) and the buyer has to open one. Then, employees need to reapply to have their employment transferred to the owner's business. For information on federal employer ID numbers, go to the "Useful Links" section of the CD-ROM or type this address into your Web browser: www.irs.gov/businesses/small/article/0,,id=98011,00.html.

✔ **Post-closing rights and obligations,** including such issues as rights for the buyer to offset the purchase price by the amount of liabilities or inventory valuation variances that become apparent after the sale settlement date. This section may also cover buyer obligations, especially if you offer a seller-financed loan as part of the deal. These obligations may require the buyer to carry insurance, allow you access to business books and records, and require maintenance of a minimum working capital level until the entire purchase price is paid in full.

✔ **Default provisions** that detail steps to follow should you or the buyer not follow through with the agreement's terms. For example, if the buyer stops paying, if unrevealed liabilities are discovered, or if you breach a non-competition agreement, this section defines litigation and dispute resolution agreements for dealing with the defaults.

✔ **Business transfer agreements,** including a bill of sale and assignments for the building lease, contracts, and intellectual property. If you're selling stock, this section covers the transfer of the business entity. If you're selling assets, this section describes your compliance with your state's bulk sales law (which requires you to notify all suppliers to whom money is owed within a certain time frame of the sale).

✔ **Statement of the absence or participation of brokers or finders.** Your contract needs to state whether brokers are involved and, if so, how they're compensated and how they'll be paid.

- *If no broker is used,* the sale agreement needs to state that fact. For example, here's wording from the seller's warranties section of an actual sale agreement: "Neither seller nor selling shareholders have employed any broker or finder in connection with the transactions contemplated by this agreement, or taken any action that would give rise to a valid claim against any party for a brokerage commission, finder's fee, or other like payment." The buyer's representations in the agreement include a similar statement.

- *If you use a broker,* the broker needs to be paid at closing, and your purchase and sale agreement needs to state how that payment will occur. For example, if your purchase price is $500,000 and the broker's fee is 10 percent, then the broker gets $50,000. When you listed your business, your brokerage agreement stipulated the commission rate and how the fee would be paid, and your lawyer can use that information when writing the broker section of your purchase and sale agreement. In most cases, you pay your listing broker the agreed-upon fee on closing day — either by a check or through the escrow settlement, just like in any other real estate closing — and the broker is then responsible for compensating cooperating brokers or agents, if any. This section will also include a statement that the broker makes no warranties as to the validity or authenticity of any information conveyed.

✔ **Obligation for fees,** including how you and the buyer will pay professional fees involved with the closing.

Finalizing the Deal: The Closing Ceremony

During the closing ceremony, you'll review, finalize, and sign all the documents necessary to transfer your business to your buyer. You need the following people in the room when you and the buyer sign the final closing papers, so as soon as you and the buyer agree on the closing date, start contacting all involved parties to set a time when everyone's available:

✔ Yourself and any other owners of your business.

✔ Your spouse (and spouses of other owners), especially if you live in a community property state (Arizona, California, Idaho, Louisiana, Nevada, New Mexico, Texas, Washington, Wisconsin, and Puerto Rico) where spouses have to sign business transfer documents.

✔ Your buyer or buyers.

✔ The buyer's spouse (or spouses, if there are multiple buyers), especially if you provide a seller-financed loan and require spouses to sign personal guarantees, which is essential in community property states and a good idea everywhere else.

✔ Third-party loan guarantors, if any, unless they sign personal guarantees in advance of the closing or provide powers of attorney to those in the room to sign on their behalf.

✔ Your attorney.

✔ Your buyer's attorney if the buyer requests.

✔ Your escrow agent, if you have one, and if you don't already have all the necessary escrow documents in advance.

✔ Your broker, if you have one. The ball is on the 1-yard line and your broker will want to make sure you score a touchdown.

✔ Anyone else whose signature is required on a closing form.

Here are the tasks you should expect to complete during closing:

✔ **Agree to make a final adjustment to the purchase price by a specified date,** usually within 15 days following the sale closing. This final adjustment will account for prorated rent, utilities, payroll, and other expenses that you'll cover up to the date of closing and that your buyer will assume from closing day on. Also, it will account for final adjustments to the value of inventory and accounts receivable as of closing day.

Your purchase and sale agreement will likely contain a clause like this sample from an actual agreement, explaining such price adjustments: "Expenses, including but not limited to utilities, personal property taxes, rents, real property taxes, wages, vacation pay, payroll taxes, and fringe benefits of employees of Seller, shall be prorated between Seller and Buyer as of the close of business on the closing date, the proration to be made and paid, insofar as reasonably possible, within 15 days of the closing date, with a settlement of any remaining items to be made within 30 days following the closing date."

If your sale includes inventory, to make the final price adjustment you probably need to take a physical count on closing day, after which you adjust your purchase price upward or downward accordingly. For example, your price may predict a closing day inventory amount of $50,000. However, if on closing day the inventory has an actual value of $40,000 or $60,000, the purchase price needs to be adjusted to reflect the difference. The final inventory count is usually done by a third party, such as RGIS (www.rgisinv.com/).

- ✔ **Review and sign the purchase and sale agreement,** which requires signatures by all owners of your business, as well as owners' spouses if you live in a community property state. If more than one buyer is purchasing your business, all buyers need to sign.

- ✔ **Review and sign loan documents,** including a promissory note, security agreements, and personal guarantees that need to be signed by the borrower, borrower's spouse, and third-party guarantors if you provide a seller-financed loan or accept deferred payments for part of the purchase price. Your buyer also needs to sign a UCC (Uniform Commercial Code) Financing Statement to record the financing agreement with the secretary of state.

- ✔ **Review and sign lease-transfer documents,** including your assignment of and the buyer's acceptance of assignment of the lease. If the buyer negotiates a new lease, these forms aren't necessary.

- ✔ **Review and sign vehicle ownership-transfer documents** if motor vehicles are included in the sale. Get signatures on all the necessary department of motor vehicles forms.

- ✔ **Review and sign seller's consulting or employment agreements,** if you agree to stay on with the business for a period of time following the sale.

- ✔ **Review and sign seller's non-competition agreement,** also called a covenant not to compete, if the buyer requests and agrees to one during sale negotiations.

- ✔ **Review and sign franchise documents** if the sale involves a franchise. Review the information in Chapter 1 on franchise resales for an overview of the unique steps required in franchise transactions.

- ✔ **Review and sign succession agreements** if the buyer will be assuming a profit-sharing plan or other employee benefit plans.

- ✔ **Review and sign the bill of sale,** which provides proof of the sale and transfers ownership of business assets detailed in the purchase and sale agreement.

- ✔ **Review and sign articles of amendment** to change your business name in order to free the business name for use by the buyer, who will amend the name from a working name to the business name being purchased as part of the sale.

- ✔ **Review and sign forms to transfer patents, trademarks, or copyrights** if intellectual property assets are being purchased.

- ✔ **Review and agree to the closing or settlement sheet** that lists all the sale's financial aspects, including how expenses and credits are allocated to you and the buyer.

- ✔ **Review and agree to the Asset Acquisition Statement,** IRS Form 8594, which shows how the purchase price is allocated to various asset categories. You and your buyer need to attach this form to your federal income tax return the year during which your sale takes place. (The "Useful Links" section of the CD-ROM includes links for downloading the form and instructions.)

- ✔ **Receive the buyer's check,** payable to you, for the purchase price or for the agreed-upon down payment. Oh happy day!

Form 15-2 on the CD-ROM includes a checklist of steps typically taken during the closing session. You may want to use it when you're meeting with your attorney or broker in preparation for the closing, ticking down the list to be sure you're ready for each closing day activity.

Post-Closing Housekeeping

Your lawyer will probably provide you with an outline of legal actions you and the buyer must take following the closing to formally transition the business. One thing you need to do immediately after closing is pass the following information on to the buyer to allow for an immediate operational transition:

- ✔ Alarm codes

- ✔ Computer and software access codes

- ✔ Safe combinations

- ✔ Customer lists, contact names, and background information

- ✔ Supplier lists, contact names, and background information

- ✔ Distributor lists and background information

- ✔ Keys to file cabinets, premises, vehicles

- ✔ Owner's manuals for equipment

- ✔ Your contact information, if necessary (that is, if you aren't sticking around to help with the business transition)

- ✔ Where to send material required by the purchase and sale agreement, such as financial statements, insurance policy verification, minimum working capital reports, and other information required to protect your interests if you provide a seller-financed loan or accept part of the purchase price in deferred payments

---

Don't pop the champagne before saying thanks

In the same way that it's nice after buying a house to find a welcome gift on the counter, after closing the deal to purchase your business, your buyer may appreciate a gesture of thanks and good wishes. Consider arranging in advance with your attorney or escrow agent to leave you and your buyer alone for a short post-closing ceremony. Minimally, share thanks and best wishes. If it feels appropriate to you, share a gift as well.

When my husband and I sold our advertising agency, many times during the negotiations, when legalities and business transfer issues felt overwhelming, the buyer of the agency would say, "Let's just put our hands around the candle and keep this thing going." Choosing a thank you gift was easy — we bought a crystal candleholder.

Dissolving Your Business Entity

If your sale is an asset sale rather than a stock sale, which is the case in 99 percent of small business sales, then after you transfer your business's assets to the new owner, your business will still exist, though likely without any value. If your business is structured as a sole proprietorship, you don't have to complete any paperwork — just be sure to pay off all outstanding taxes and bills due and your business automatically closes.

If you have a limited liability company or a corporation, upon closing you have to take care of a few legalities. Work with your attorney to complete the following steps:

- ✔ **Hold a meeting of the board, partners, or members and pass a resolution to formally dissolve the business.** Your attorney will advise you on how to file the resolution in your corporate minutes.

- ✔ **Notify the IRS that your business has been dissolved.** For a corporate or LLC dissolution, file IRS Form 966 within 30 days after the date of your dissolution resolution. To download the form, go to the "Useful Links" section of the CD-ROM, or type this address into your Web browser: www.irs.gov/pub/irs-pdf/f966.pdf.

- ✔ **File articles of dissolution with the secretary of state in the state your business was formed and in any other state where you've registered it as a business entity.** Contact the secretary of state's office or seek your attorney's counsel, as dissolution requirements vary from state to state.

> ✔ **File any other forms and take any other closing actions** that your accountant and attorney advise, including some or all of the actions listed in the upcoming section.

Ending Business Operations

Following the sale of your business, your business name goes on, but unless you sell your business entity, your business as it was structured ceases to exist. From paying bills for pre-closing obligations to canceling accounts to notifying tax agencies, plenty of paperwork accompanies the close of your business entity. Not all actions on the upcoming list apply to all businesses. For instance, if you sell your accounts receivable, you don't need to worry about collecting current, outstanding bills, as that becomes the responsibility of your buyer. Use the following list and get advice from your accountant or attorney to be sure you're touching all the bases required in your state and by your business as you end your business operation.

✔ Formally notify contacts for all business contracts that are being assigned or assumed by the buyer.

✔ Tell those to whom you owe money that your business has been dissolved and explain how their bills will be paid, either by you or by the new owner.

✔ Cancel state or county business permits or licenses, including any seller's permits and fictitious or assumed business names. Your attorney can help you with what's involved, or you can contact the office of your secretary of state for advice.

✔ Give notice and cancel your lease if you don't transfer it to your buyer.

✔ Cancel insurance policies, unless your buyer is assuming them.

✔ Pay off all bills and other liabilities that aren't being assumed by the buyer.

✔ Collect accounts receivable due, preferably before you announce the sale.

✔ Distribute all remaining assets to yourself if you're a sole proprietor, or to shareholders, partners, or members if your business is structured as a corporation, partnership, or LLC.

✔ Close your account with the IRS. Write to Internal Revenue Service, Cincinnati, Ohio, 45999 to close your employer ID number.

✔ Close all bank accounts and business credit cards. Be sure you don't just pay off your line of credit but that you close it down altogether.

✔ Close utilities accounts, or transfer them to the buyer's name.

✔ Pay final wages, payroll taxes, and fees due to the IRS and state and local tax authorities.

✔ File all necessary tax forms. Your accountant will advise you regarding the forms you need to complete. The IRS provides a "Closing a Business Checklist" that you can reach online by clicking on the link in the "Useful Links" section of the CD-ROM, or by typing this address into your Web browser: `http://www.irs.gov/businesses/small/article/0,,id=98703,00.html`.

Chapter 16 deals with the whole issue of announcing your sale — to employees, customers, suppliers, and associates — and successfully passing the baton to the new owner.

Forms on the CD-ROM

Form 15-1	**Closing Preparation: Checklist**	A list of issues to discuss with your broker and attorney prior to closing day
Form 15-2	**Closing Day: Checklist**	A list of closing day actions to discuss with your broker and attorney so you're prepared for the final deal

Chapter 16

Announcing the Sale and Passing the Baton

. . . .

In This Chapter

▶ Making the big announcement to employees and customers

▶ Telling the media about your business sale

▶ Staging a successful business transition

. . . .

*A*fter the papers are signed and the check is deposited, you can finally start talking about your sale. At this point, your challenge is no longer how to keep news of your sale under wraps; it's how to unfold the story in the right order and in the right way. Handling the business sale and purchase announcement well is a critical first step toward the new owner's success, which is especially important to you if you agree to accept deferred payments or compensation based partly on future business sales.

You and your buyer want to take care with how you make the sale announcement because there's a pecking order when it comes to sharing important business news. People who are most important to your business success — your biggest clients and most valued managers, for instance — need to hear the news first. You want to start with personal announcements to those whose ongoing support is most important to your business, and then move the announcement through your business world and into the larger community via media outlets. You also want to agree in advance with your buyer about how to handle the announcements and any costs involved.

This chapter provides a game plan for announcing the sale, including suggestions for employee, client, and supplier announcements; media announcements; and an outline for introducing the new owner to customers, suppliers, and business associates. It also describes post-sale actions that help pave the way for the new owner's success, ways to deal with the seller-to-buyer transition period, and ultimately, how to gracefully move yourself off center stage, whether that means moving out of the business altogether or into a supportive role.

Announcing the Sale to Your Employees

The first place to announce your sale is inside the walls of your business. Never let employees hear about the sale through the grapevine, or worse, through newspapers or other media channels. Tell them directly. Explain to them why you sold the business, tell them about the new owner, talk about the safety of their positions, and discuss how important it is that they help keep the story quiet until you and the buyer have the chance to announce the news to customers, associates, and media outlets. Before you started due diligence (see Chapter 12), you may have shared the news with key managers, whose support is important for a successful business transition. This is the time to tell the rest of your team.

When telling your staff, hold a meeting with all employees, if possible, to make the announcement. Plan what to say in advance so you're composed and you convey a complete story. Work with the buyer to be sure you're in agreement on all points.

Don't use e-mail to tell employees. First, it doesn't allow for discussion, which employees will want, and second, e-mails are too easy to forward to those outside your business.

Most sellers prefer to make the staff announcement with the buyer present. In some cases, the buyer prefers to make the announcement without the seller's presence, but more often the seller makes the introduction, announces the sale, and then turns the meeting over to the buyer. Often, the seller then leaves the meeting so the new owner can be alone with employees.

If the buyer can't attend this first post-sale meeting — because the buyer lives elsewhere, or maybe because the meeting has to be called on short notice due to an information leak (I talk more about the topic of leaks later in this chapter) — hold the meeting without the buyer's presence, but announce when he or she will be on-site to meet with staff, preferably within days.

Your turn: Explaining the situation

When announcing the sale to employees, tell the facts in this order:

1. **Explain that you want to make a confidential announcement that can't be shared outside the business for the next week, or however long you believe the news must remain confidential.**

2. **Announce that your business has a new owner.** Explain that conversations you've been having over the past months have resulted in the sale of your business, which you believe is a very positive step for everyone involved.

3. **Introduce the buyer and talk a bit about the buyer's experience and hopes for the business.**

4. **Assure employees that their positions will remain intact, if in fact the buyer plans for business operations to continue as usual.** Employees will wonder what's going to happen to them. If the buyer plans no staff changes, make sure you or your buyer say so right away.

5. **Tell why you're selling.** This was one of the first things the buyer wanted to know, and it's also one of the first things your employees want to know. Also tell whether you'll be remaining with the business for a period of time and, if so, for how long.

6. **Announce when the sale is scheduled to close (or when it closed).**

7. **State your announcement timeline.** Express the importance of releasing the news in a certain order — first to clients and then to business associates before it becomes public. Explain that the minute you're ready to make the news public, you'll let all employees know, but until then, ask for their support in keeping the news completely confidential.

8. **If the buyer isn't at the meeting, announce when the buyer will arrive to meet with staff.**

Neither you nor the buyer needs to reveal the purchase price or anything about the deal's terms. If employees ask, you can simply say that while you can't discuss sale specifics, you're happy to talk about your confidence in the buyer's ability to lead your business into a strong new chapter.

The buyer's turn: Establishing rapport and explaining future plans

When meeting for the first time with employees, the buyer will probably:

✔ Give a personal introduction, mentioning his or her business background and reasons for acquiring the business.

✔ Express enthusiasm over the business and its future.

✔ Announce plans to continue business as usual in terms of products and services, location, customers, and most important, staff. Even if the owner has plans to make changes down the road, unless they're very positive changes that aren't likely to ruffle any feathers, this probably isn't the time to say so.

- ✔ Explain that during the first staff meeting, he or she will discuss with employees how their employment will transfer to the new organization and give instructions for completing the necessary paperwork. To reassure employees, the buyer should make it clear that salaries, benefits, and commissions will remain unchanged, unless the buyer has specific plans to alter compensation programs.

- ✔ Share plans to keep refining and growing the business to make it even more competitive and well regarded.

- ✔ Show pride in the business and the chance to lead it into the future.

- ✔ Ask for ongoing support and effort from the employees, who as a team contributed to the buyer's confidence in the business.

- ✔ Convey openness to staff ideas and concerns if they arise.

Telling Customers and Business Associates

Most business owners wait until the deal is done before telling business associates and clients/customers about the sale. In businesses like restaurants and retail shops, where customers place a high value on consistent, unaltered service, the seller and buyer often never make the announcement. They just transition ownership and continue business as usual, until maybe six months down the road, when the new owner casually says, "Oh yeah, I bought the place six months ago."

If your business is one where your presence is visible and valued, however, you need to announce the sale quickly and strategically. Usually, that means going to your most significant customers, suppliers, distributors, and associates first, because your buyer will need their support most of all. You don't want them hearing about the sale from a competitor, a concerned employee, or a media article should the story leak out.

Sharing your news with key contacts

When telling key customers and associates, start by sharing the news one-on-one, preferably in person or during a phone conversation, and only as a last resort by e-mail. If you're staying around during a transition period, make that point clear, especially if the person you're talking to has relied heavily upon your personal input and expertise. Also make clear which key managers will be staying on as a way of indicating that you don't expect any immediate disruption in how business is done.

In addition to communicating that business services and quality will continue without interruption, be sure you explain the advantages you feel the buyer will bring to the business and to its business relationships. Describe the buyer's background and plans. Follow the same script used during your initial employee meeting, except instead of telling staff members what's in the deal for them, detail what positive outcomes you expect the customer or business associate to enjoy from the transition. Then schedule time as soon as possible during which you can personally introduce the buyer.

Spreading the word to everyone else in your business world

When it comes to announcing your sale to your full customer and business associate list, the size of your business will dictate how you proceed.

- ✔ **If your list of contacts is short,** pick up the phone and call each person. After all, one of the beauties of a small business is that it's small and personal. If you can make a personal announcement, pick up the phone and start going right down the list.

- ✔ **If your contact list is too long for you to call everyone your business deals with as a customer, supplier, distributor, or associate,** send out a mass fax, e-mail announcement, or letter, prepared in a manner that doesn't reveal the recipient list and that makes each message look as individualized as possible, using the following advice.

Wording the announcement

When you share your news, explain the sale in personal terms, and then attach the news release or a sale fact sheet (which I cover in the next section) to provide factual information. Follow these tips:

- ✔ Lead with the news. Don't make people wade through a paragraph, or even a few sentences, before telling them that your business has a new owner.

- ✔ Convey confidence in the buyer by sharing a brief bio and some encouraging facts about the buyer's intention to maintain and build on the quality currently expected from your business.

- ✔ Share your near-term plans, including the fact that you'll remain with the business for a while, if that's the case.

- ✔ Explain that you're sharing a news release that conveys all the facts.

Your announcement may read something like the one in Figure 16-1, adjusted — of course — to fit your own situation and personal tone. To deliver the announcement, you can send it by e-mail if your news is likely to be carried by media outlets and you don't want time to pass between when customers read about your sale and when they hear the news from you. If your announcement isn't likely to be covered by the media, or if it's likely to be publicized weeks after the closing, you can put your announcement on letterhead and mail it within a week or two of closing day.

After months of planning, it's time for me to make an exciting announcement on behalf of The Greatest Business. As of July 1, 2008, Jill Jones, a widely respected expert in our field, will become the business owner. After 22 years at the helm of the company, it was important to me that the business transfer to just the right person, and I'm so pleased to share my confidence in Jill's ownership. She plans to maintain the same staff, operation, and level of quality you're familiar with, and she also has wonderful plans to add services and systems that will make your experience with the business even more enjoyable and rewarding.

I will remain with the business for the better part of this year to assist in making the transition for Jill and for you seamless and enjoyable.

Attached is a news release detailing facts about the sale. Jill and I will be hosting a get-acquainted event later this month, so please watch for an invitation to arrive shortly.

For now, I share my most sincere thanks for all you've meant to me and to The Greatest Business, and my best wishes and highest hopes for a mutually beneficial future.

Figure 16-1:
A warm and friendly sale announcement.

E-mailing your message

If you e-mail your announcement, consider these recommendations:

- ✔ **Addressees:** If you send the same e-mail to all recipients, don't reveal the full list in the address portion of your e-mail — it makes the announcement look like a news blast instead of a personal note, and besides, no one wants his e-mail address to show up in a long list of others. To send your announcement to a number of people at once while keeping the recipient list hidden, enter your own address in the "To" line of the e-mail, and then enter all recipient e-mail addresses as *blind carbon copies* by using the BCC address option.

- ✔ **Subject line:** Keep the subject line to five to seven words, typed in upper and lower case (not in all capital letters). Include your company name so people recognize and open the note because it's from a familiar source. Don't announce your sale right in the subject line, as that's too abrupt, but do use the subject line to convey that the e-mail is worth opening. You can say something like, "Important news from The Greatest Company," or, "News I want to personally share with you," or, "An exciting announcement."

✔ **Body of e-mail:** Use easy-to-open and easy-to-read plain text for sending your e-mail. This isn't the time for a note that looks more like an ad or promotion. You want this to look like what it is — a personal announcement.

Making a phased announcement

Especially when the seller remains with the business during a transition period and when customers are loyal to the seller (as is the case with many personal service businesses), the buyer and seller may use a series of announcements to ease customers into the news that the business has been sold.

In such cases, the seller may introduce the buyer as someone who will be assuming a key position in the company, maybe even while the seller takes an extended time away from the business. Later, when customers have gotten to know the buyer and begun to transfer their loyalty, the buyer makes a second announcement, this one stating that the seller has retired.

Informing the Media

Whether or not you think newspapers, radio and TV stations, and blogs will carry the news of your sale, prepare a news release for distribution to all news outlets that carry stories about businesses in your community and business arena. As soon as the sale is finalized, distribute the release to all media outlets. By circulating a news release, you make the announcement formal and provide the facts in case media outlets do want to carry the story (and some will). Moreover, you put all the facts in one place, resulting in a news announcement you can share with customers, distributors, suppliers, and business associates.

If you don't issue a news release, prepare a sale fact sheet that covers buyer information, owner plans (stressing that staff, operations, services, quality, and location will continue unchanged, if that's the plan), the reason for the sale, the date of business transfer, and how the transition will occur, including whether you'll remain with the business, and if so, for how long.

To distribute your news, create a list of media outlets that serve your geographic area and industry arena, including the following:

✔ **Your local daily newspapers.** If you have news contacts at the papers, send your release to them. Otherwise, call the city desk or news desk and ask for the name and e-mail address of the person to whom you should send a business announcement.

- ✔ **Regional weekly and business publications.** If you don't have established news contacts, pick up issues of the publications or go online to learn the names and addresses of news editors.

- ✔ **Radio and television stations** that broadcast in your area. Send your release to the news director.

- ✔ **Industry and business publications,** including everything from the chamber of commerce newsletter to magazines that serve your industry or business arena.

- ✔ **Blogs** that carry news about businesses like yours in your community and industry.

To increase the chances your sale will make the news, submit your release in the most usable format for the intended recipient. Most news releases today are sent via e-mail, though many are still printed on paper to be faxed, mailed, or hand-delivered. When you contact each media outlet to confirm the editor's name and address, ask if the outlet prefers news releases sent by e-mail, and if so, whether it prefers the release to be sent as an attachment or in an e-mail message. Don't attach files or photos to an e-mail release unless the reporter or editor specifically instructs you to do so, as many news outlets don't open e-mail with unsolicited attachments. And don't use HTML or other markup languages, which aren't readable by all recipients.

For news releases that are mailed, faxed, or hand-delivered, print the release on 8½-x-11-inch white paper. Use wide margins and one-and-a-half or double-spacing. If your news runs more than one page, don't print both sides of the same sheet, as editors frequently tear off and forward only the first part of the release for production. Type the word "More" at the bottom of the page if the release continues, and start the next page by identifying the release in the top left-hand corner (for example, "The Greatest Business Sale, Page 2"). Following the final sentence of your release, type the pound symbol three times (# # #) to indicate that the release has ended.

Include the following information in your news release:

- ✔ **Who to contact for more information:** Give the name of the person who can be contacted for information or to schedule interviews — probably you — along with a telephone number for reaching that person directly. In printed news releases, contact information goes at the very top of the release. If you send the release in an e-mail, contact information goes at the conclusion of the message. Format the contact info like this:

    CONTACT INFORMATION:

    Contact person's name

    Business name

    Phone number with area code

    Contact person's e-mail address

    URL for your business Web site

- ✔ **When the news can be released:** Notify the media that the news is "For Immediate Release" by typing those words above your headline.

- ✔ **A headline:** The release headline should be active (in other words, it should include a verb), succinct (it should fit on no more than two lines), and typed in all caps, unless you're sending your release in an e-mail, where typing in all caps is taboo. Something as simple as THE GREATEST BUSINESS ANNOUNCES NEW OWNER would probably be just fine.

- ✔ **A dateline:** The meat of the news release begins with the name of the city and the abbreviation of the state from which the release originated, followed by a dash and the date the release is issued. For instance: Des Moines, IA — July 1, 2008.

- ✔ **Clear presentation of the facts:** Following the dateline, begin your news announcement. Tell who, what, where, when, why, and how in what is known as an *inverted pyramid* style. Here's what that means: Summarize your news announcement in the first sentence, followed in succession by the next most important facts in declining order, ending with the least important story elements. This allows an editor to cut your news release from the bottom, if necessary to save space, and still retain the most vital information.

- ✔ **Quotes:** Consider including a few short comments by you and the buyer.

- ✔ **Photos:** Consider including a photo of the buyer. When submitting news by mail or hand-delivery, enclose photos in the form of prints, slides, or on disk. Submit prints in a 5½-x-7-inch or 8-x-10-inch glossy format with captions attached.

If you e-mail your release, print a copy of it so that you have a reference handy when editors follow up to request additional information.

Seeing the Transition Period through to the End

If you're staying with the business for a period of time after the sale, get ready to adapt to some necessary changes. The first and biggest change is simply accepting the fact that the business isn't yours anymore. Your role, for as long as you've had the business, was that of the top decision-maker. You could make quick changes and alter how things were being done with the snap of your fingers. But from closing day on, someone else — the new owner — is in charge, and you need to change your role accordingly. Follow these tips to ensure a smooth transition:

- ✔ **Help the buyer become the boss.** It may not come naturally, but take a back seat or supporting role in business decisions. Also, be ready to redirect staff questions to the new owner rather than answer them on your own. Help everyone realize that someone new is at the helm.

✔ **Physically turn your workspace over to the new owner.** If your staff is used to coming to your office to have major decisions approved, then your office is where the business owner should sit, and you should sit somewhere else.

✔ **Make yourself scarce.** Especially right after the sale, find reasons to be away for periods of time so the owner can fill the leadership role without any feeling of competition. Be available to the owner and to fulfill all obligations as stated in your sale agreement, but be less available to staff, who may otherwise continue to rely on your input and decisions rather than transfer their allegiance to the new owner.

✔ **Take a vacation.** Celebrate the sale with a total change of pace and place. The time away will do you and the new owner a world of good.

✔ **Shy away from the word "I."** Especially in conversations with clients, you're probably used to saying things like, "I recommend . . ." or, "I think your best choice may be . . ." Help customers adapt to and embrace the new owner by saying things like, "Jill and I were discussing this and want to recommend . . ." or, "I think Jill has some good ideas I'd like you to hear . . ." In sports they call it passing or dishing the ball. It works equally well in the game of business sale transitions.

Even with all your best efforts to be a great player on the new owner's team, the time will come when the owner would rather steer the business without you in the co-pilot's seat. Sometime after the 90-day point, the buyer may want to cut your stay with the business short.

The truth is, about that same time, you also may be itching to move on. Just remember that you're obligated to fulfill the terms of the consulting or management agreement unless the buyer releases you from obligations, in which case you can insist that all conditions outlined in your purchase and sale agreement are strictly followed. When you do leave your business, remember that you're still obligated to the terms of your non-competition agreement.

After your sale is closed and your transition period has ended, you're free to embrace whatever's on your wish list. That may mean a long vacation, involvement with some great volunteer project, a position with another company, mentoring, coaching, serving on the board of a business start-up, or, as is often the case, ownership of another business. Your newfound free time also gives you time for money management. You do, after all, have sale proceeds to work with.

The sale of your business puts you in an exclusive category of entrepreneurial success stories. You built a business, contributed to the economy, served customers, upheld commitments to employees and suppliers, enjoyed the success of ownership, and, ultimately, harvested the value of your efforts on sale closing day. I know I won't be the first or last to say the word you've waited to hear all during the sale process: *Congratulations!*

Part V
The Part of Tens

The 5th Wave   By Rich Tennant

"If you ever decide to sell another business, don't say anything. You're lucky I convinced them that 'Ka-Ching, Ka-Ching!' was Swahili for thank you, thank you!"

In this part . . .

No one said that selling your business would be a cakewalk, but you can count on the information in this part to help simplify some of the trickier aspects.

The four chapters in this part present ten-part lists that you'll probably turn to again and again during the time between when you start to sell your business and when you hold the long-anticipated sale celebration party.

Chapter 17

Ten Deal-Killers to Avoid

Getting your business ready for sale, finding a buyer, completing negotiations, and making it through the closing process is an obstacle course with hurdles all along the way. Following are ten barriers you can overcome with good advance planning.

Setting Your Asking Price Too High

As they scan business-for-sale ads, buyers think about the price range they'd be willing to pay for businesses that catch their interest. If the asking price they see looks too high, most buyers simply move on, not even giving the ad a second look. Based on information conveyed by even the shortest sale ads, buyers conduct quick calculations to determine if an interesting business seems to be worth further consideration. John Davies, CEO of Sunbelt and observer of thousands of sale deals, says they're looking for businesses priced within a *box of reality*. If a business is priced close to what the buyer thinks is realistic, it gets a closer look. Otherwise, it suffers an immediate deal-killer: dismissal at first glance.

In determining whether your business is worth what you're asking, a buyer puts your price through a basic reality test by asking:

✔ Can your business fund the kind of salary the owner can earn in a full-time job running a similar business?

✔ In addition to a decent salary, can your business generate enough cash to provide a return on the investment the buyer will have to make in the form of a down payment?

✔ Can your business also pay the debt service on loans necessary to buy the business?

For example, if a buyer thinks running your business deserves a salary of $150,000, and if the buyer also thinks your business needs to make an additional $50,000 a year to provide a return on the buyer's personal investment and debt service, then your business needs to earn at least $200,000 a year. The buyer will multiply $200,000 by 3 (the midrange of the typical earnings multiple described in Chapter 6) to arrive at a price of $600,000. If your asking price is in the range of $600,000, the buyer is likely to give the offer more thought. If your price is way higher, the buyer is likely to simply move on to another ad.

Neglecting to Get Your Business in Salable Shape

A salable business is one with many attractive attributes and very few risks. A great location and a modern, appealing building are good attributes, as are a growing market area, high annual earnings, and a large and loyal clientele. On the other end of the spectrum, a lease that's about to expire is a risk, as is a business that relies on only a few large clients, with an operation that's run from the owner's memory rather than from formal, documented processes.

A buyer will overlook one or even several risks, especially if the risks are outweighed by attractive aspects, but if your business has too many risks or the risks are severe, you need to overcome the problems before offering your business for sale. If you don't, you'll either sell the business at a *much* lower price than you could earn otherwise, or you won't sell it at all.

Here are some factors that send buyers running in the opposite direction:

- Low earnings with declining sales and profits
- No key staff
- Weak operations
- Low name recognition
- A business building that's in poor physical condition
- A business facing high competition with low competitive advantage
- Dependency on a few clients
- A declining industry or market area
- An expiring or problematic lease

If any of the preceding traits apply to your business, turn to the advice in Chapter 3, which helps you get your business in salable shape before putting it on the market.

Lacking a Transition Plan

If a buyer doesn't see a clear plan for how clients, operations, staff, and location will transfer to a new owner, your sale is at risk. Likewise, if the bulk of your transition plan relies on your personal presence during the post-sale period, the buyer has reason for concern. A buyer needs to know that your business is ready to transfer hands smoothly because it offers products and services that have earned customer loyalty and because the way you run your business is documented and easy to move from the hands of one owner to another.

Be ready to present assurances that your business will transition easily, including these elements:

- ✔ Transferable contracts or agreements that firmly commit clients to your business
- ✔ Employment and non-compete agreements for key managers
- ✔ Operation and employment manuals
- ✔ A business plan and marketing plan (see Chapter 7 for help)
- ✔ Your personal commitment to remain involved for a period of time if business operations or client relations will benefit from a phased seller-to-buyer transition

Having a Short or Non-Transferable Lease

Especially if you're selling a restaurant or retail establishment that relies on customer visits and loyalty to the site, be sure you have a long-term and transferable lease. Most buyers won't even look at a site-reliant business unless the lease reaches at least five years into the future, and most financial institutions will consider business loans only if the lease runs at least five years, with options that extend for the length of the loan period.

If your lease has fewer than five years left on it, renegotiate the lease duration and ensure its transferability before offering it for sale. When the sale is certain, you'll have far less leverage with your building owner, who may view the change of ownership as a chance to lock in a higher rate. To conduct the lease renegotiation, meet with your building owner, explaining that you're in the midst of business planning and want to renegotiate your lease to secure your location for the foreseeable future. Work to include a lease transferability clause that allows you to assign the lease to a different owner should you sell your business, along with extension options that describe how the lease can be extended following its current term, and a rate escalation clause that limits and defines future rent increases.

Don't wait until the last minute to get your lease in order or you risk losing buyer interest, simply because the appealing place where your business experiences its success can't be secured for future use. If the worst happens and you find out the site can't be secured, and if your business is site-reliant, you need to consider establishing a presence in a new location before offering your business for sale, or reducing its price to accommodate for the short-term nature of your lease. When you do get the lease renegotiated, be sure to have your attorney review it before signing to ensure lease term, transferability, and rent rates are all adequately addressed.

Insisting on an All-Cash Sale

If you want all cash at closing, most business brokers will give you two words of advice: get real.

Except for the lowest-priced businesses, cash at closing is almost always out of the picture. If you insist on a single cash payment, your buyer may simply need to walk away. Or, as an alternative, the buyer may work to hammer the price downward to reduce the amount of cash that needs to be amassed.

What's more, if you insist on receiving all cash on closing day, you make yourself vulnerable to the highest possible tax rates. Purchase prices paid with a cash down payment followed by loan or deferred payments spread proceeds — and taxable income — over a multi-year period. In an all-cash deal, you have to claim all sale proceeds as income in a single year, pushing yourself into a higher tax bracket and thereby further reducing your net proceeds from the sale.

To avoid what are a long list of downsides to all-cash requirements, be ready either to provide seller financing or to accept deferred payments from a creditworthy buyer. Or, work to get your business pre-qualified for an SBA loan to make third-party financing easier for your buyer. Flip back to Chapter 14 for information on financing for your sale.

Covering Up Problems

Almost every buyer conducts a due diligence investigation (Chapter 12 tells you what to expect during this phase of the sale process). If your business has undisclosed problems, chances are they won't remain invisible to the buyer. And if the buyer discovers business problems you've failed to mention, the logical next thought is, what else is lurking in dark corners?

On the other hand, if looming risks do escape detection, they'll likely rear their ugly heads after the sale, at which time the buyer can rightly claim you misrepresented the condition of your business, which could very well provide grounds to sue for fraud. Remember, honesty isn't just the best policy. If representations and warranties are part of the purchase and sale agreement (and they almost certainly will be), honesty is a *requirement*.

So if your business faces risks, reveal them early on, along with your plans for dealing with or overcoming the situation.

Stretching the Truth

There's a fine line between promoting your business as a good purchase opportunity and exaggerating the opportunities that await a new owner. The line, however fine, is one you can't afford to cross over.

Playing fast and loose with facts and projections puts your sale in danger on two fronts:

- First, a smart buyer can see through hype that isn't backed by facts and supported by financial statements reflecting your claims. If a buyer thinks you're being less than frank or unreasonably grandiose about your business's condition, red flags will raise and the buyer will probably walk away.

- Second, most purchase and sale agreements include a section called "representations and warranties" in which the seller promises that information provided is honest and accurate. Exaggerating your business's health gives a buyer an excuse for defaulting on loan payments if the business falters and the buyer can prove that you misrepresented facts.

When it comes to forecasting the future, heed all cautions that your attorney advises you to take. These will likely include being frank about risks your business faces and how you're addressing them, and being upfront and honest about business liabilities and how you're working to clear them. Also be frank as to the reasons you're selling the business.

When describing your business's future, be careful to present projections not as promises but as *best-estimate forecasts* based on documented current business trends. Head to Chapter 5 for help on forecasting growth.

Taking Your Sweet Time When Communicating with Buyers

If a buyer expresses interest in your offer, reply immediately. The majority of sales start with Internet searches, and online shoppers expect the kind of rapid-fire response that e-mail has trained us all to expect. If you make prospects wait days or more for a reply, you'll probably lose them altogether. So check your e-mail daily, even if most days you don't get any bites; when you do get one, respond to potential buyers, pronto.

After you make contact, keep communications moving. If you promise to provide information or to check out a price or payment structure with your accountant, say when you'll be back in touch and don't miss your deadline. Especially if the request has to do with deal structure or with business financials or legalities, the longer you take to respond, the more the buyer's apt to think you're trying to solve or avoid a problem. That's why in the arena of business sales, the word is that delays kill deals.

If running your business eats up the hours in your day and you can't give adequate attention to your sale, hire a business broker. Chapter 4 helps you weigh the do-it-yourself versus use-a-broker decision, and Chapter 19 gives you ten things to consider when choosing and working with brokers.

Waiting Too Long to Qualify the Buyer

You may think you'll scare prospective buyers away if you start asking for things like confidentiality agreements and financial background information too soon. The opposite is more likely to be true. If you hand over information on your business without a confidentiality agreement, or if you respond in detail to buyers who haven't proven their financial ability to purchase your business, you're more than likely telegraphing the fact that you care more about unloading your business than about moving it into good, capable hands.

Chapter 10 provides a game plan for screening and communicating with ad respondents. It starts by helping you write and run ads that prompt buyers to pre-qualify themselves before responding. It also outlines the steps involved in requesting and obtaining confidentiality agreements and preliminary background and financial information.

Just about the only prospects who'll object to buyer-qualification requests are those who aren't qualified. Better you rule out such respondents early on, before they can divert your attention away from other, more capable prospects.

Refusing to Negotiate

Buyers view the asking price as a moving target and the starting point for negotiations. If your price is based on a formal appraisal or firm valuation formula, you may be less vulnerable to lower offers, but still expect some pricing give and take.

Most sale prices end up at around 80 percent of the asking price. For that reason, buyers often ask prices about 20 percent higher than what they expect to obtain. Sometimes, low-ball offers are as low as 50 percent of asking price, and on rare occasions, offers come in above the asking price. You won't find any specific rules for what buyers can offer or when you should walk away from a proposal. In general, though, if the buyer is qualified both financially and from a business standpoint, and if the offer comes close to what you think is the value of your business, keep talking. If it doesn't, don't hesitate to make a counterproposal.

Negotiating doesn't mean giving away the farm. It means listening and weighing every serious offer, both in terms of the price and the way the payment is structured. A low price structured with tax advantages that tilt in your favor may leave you in better financial shape than a higher-priced deal structured to the buyer's tax benefit.

Don't let numbers alone kill the deal. Work with your accountant to evaluate every offer. Turn to Chapter 13 for information on structuring the deal and Chapter 14 for background on tax and financing issues.

Chapter 18

Ten Business Marketplace Trends and Truths

In This Chapter

▶ Looking at some business sale facts and figures

▶ Checking out some business buyer and seller trends

*I*n the business sale arena, you won't find hard and fast rules. For instance, you won't always get 80 percent of your asking price; you won't always have to offer seller financing; and you won't always sell within six months or a year of listing day. However, the following marketplace trends and truths, documented by financial and brokerage industry surveys, will likely affect the outcome of your sale and apply often enough to make them worth noting.

The Number of Businesses for Sale Is Large and Growing

With a tsunami of business sales upon us, if you plan to sell your business in the foreseeable future, you'll be competing in a crowded marketplace. Consider these facts:

✔ According to U.S. Census Bureau statistics, more than 78 million Americans fall into the baby boom generation, born between 1946 and 1964. As they ready for retirement, those who own businesses are beginning to swell the number of businesses for sale. At the same time, the ratio of younger-generation workers to baby-boomer-aged retirees is dropping, resulting in a smaller pool of potential buyers for a growing number of available businesses.

✔ The Exit Planning Institute projects that over the next 10–15 years, eight million business owners will sell their privately owned businesses.

✔ Some 90 percent of businesses with employees are family-owned enterprises, but only a third will transition into the hands of a next-generation family member. Among the rest, many will be listed for sale.

✔ A PricewaterhouseCoopers survey finds that one out of every two business owners plans to sell within the coming ten years.

✔ Nearly 350,000 business sales are expected in 2009, up from 50,000 in 2001, according to the Federal Reserve's Survey of Consumer Finance.

Business Size Affects Sale Success

If your business has annual revenues of more than $750,000, it stands a good chance for a successful sale, but even with lower revenues, it'll still be attractive to buyers if earnings provide an owner salary of at least $100,000. Take a look at these pricing statistics:

✔ A widely cited figure among business brokers is that nearly 80 percent of business sales feature a business with annual revenues of $750,000 or less, fewer than ten employees, and an asking price under $500,000.

✔ Surveys by the business brokerage industry show that businesses with annual revenues of less than $750,000 sell at a rate of about 1 out of 5.5, or 18 percent. Businesses with revenues in the $750,000 to $2 million range sell at a rate of about 1 of 4, or 25 percent. Businesses with revenues from $2 million to $6 million sell at the best rate, with 1 of 3 selling, for a 33 percent success rate.

✔ The brokerage industry reports that as many as 20 percent of small businesses are for sale at any time. Those with the highest annual sales and earnings are the most likely to sell, for the simple reason that buyers want to earn an annual salary of at least $100,000 from the business they're purchasing. Most low-revenue businesses don't earn enough to deliver that kind of income, and for that reason, most buyers will pass them by.

If your business doesn't stand up to these numbers, take time to build sales, cut costs, and increase earnings before putting your business on the market.

Business Sales Take 5–12 Months on Average

Most business sale experts will tell you that it usually takes between 5 and 12 months to sell a business. But the time frame can vary greatly. When a buyer is waiting in the wings, the sale tends to go more quickly, and if a business is priced too high or has difficult sale terms, the sale tends to take much longer.

A survey of business brokers conducted by Businessesforsale.com found that 28 percent of brokers pegged the time it takes to sell a business at 6 months, 31 percent said 9 months, 21 percent said 12 months, and 10.5 percent gave a time span of longer than 12 months.

Nearly all sale advisors agree that unreasonable price and terms have the greatest negative effect on the sale timeline, followed closely by a lack of documentation — such as asset and inventory lists and valuations, financial statements and trend reports, and supporting tax returns and other data — to justify the asking price.

Most Businesses Aren't Ready for a Sale

Business brokers report that the vast majority of businesses aren't prepared for a sale because they have profitability, production, staffing, and/or inventory problems that need to be addressed and overcome before the business is put on the market.

A 2006 survey by GW Equity and the University of Dallas found that 80 percent of U.S. business owners with $1 million to $150 million in annual sales were considering selling their businesses, and more than 75 percent were thinking of doing so by 2009. What's more, the survey found that most owners wait until they're ready to retire before starting the sale process. Some advice: Don't wait. Getting your business ready for sale takes time, as does the selling process. If you want to sell, start early, and begin by building business strengths and eliminating high risks (see Chapter 3 for help).

Most people who buy businesses are middle-aged, used to middle management, and not eager to assume large risks. They want a business that looks like a sure success and that's offered at a fair price, with terms that make the purchase attainable.

Healthy, growing, low-risk, easy-to-transfer, well-presented businesses sell fastest and at the best prices. They have a strong management team, strong and growing financial performance, efficient operations, distinctive and highly desired products and services, and a broad and loyal customer base.

Business Brokers Have the Highest Sale Success Rates

Businesses sold through brokers have a much higher listing-to-closing rate than those sold through realtors or offered directly by business owners. Brokers account for about 10 percent of all business sales, and they successfully close between one out of four and one out of seven listings, depending on who's counting. Real estate agents close about one out of twenty business listings. For-sale-by-owner (FSBO) businesses close at a lower rate.

A major reason that many businesses never sell is because business buyers never learn about the sale offering. Brokers overcome this problem, which they attribute to insufficient market exposure, by placing many ads in many places, both in print and on a number of business-for-sale Web sites. Brokers also have access to a deep database of qualified buyers whom they can contact. If you're selling on your own, plan to emulate the pros by getting the word out in not one place but many, following the advice in Chapter 9.

$250,000 Is the Median Asking Price

BizBuySell, the largest online business-for-sale marketplace, evaluated 40,000 business sale listings and determined that the median asking price for a business in the United States in 2007 was $250,000. This equaled an asking price of .92 of annual revenue and 3.47 times annual earnings. When determining your asking price, keep the following facts in mind:

- Most businesses end up selling for 20 to 80 percent of annual sales, with an average price of 45 percent of sales. To end up with this kind of proceeds, most business sales begin with an asking price set at 2 to 4 times earnings, as described in Chapter 6.

- Buyers typically negotiate downward from the seller's asking price. In the BizBuySell analysis, completed sale prices averaged .73 times revenue and 2.79 times earnings.

- Many sellers overprice by 20 to 30 percent, thereby reducing buyer interest and inquiries.

The best asking price is within 10 to 15 percent of the sale price you're willing to settle for. This kind of price leaves you room for negotiation without risking loss of the buyer's initial interest.

Most Sellers Are 55+

More than half of today's small businesses are owned by people age 55 or older. Most consider their business their primary source of retirement income. To free cash for their golden years, they plan to sell — soon. In fact, a report from the Alliance of Merger & Acquisition Advisors indicates that by 2009, one out of six baby-boomer-owned businesses will be on the market.

Despite the fact that baby boomers are ready to sell, retirement isn't the number one reason for business sales. The top reason is owner burnout. Other prominent reasons include health issues and a personal desire to diversify the owner's time and financial holdings.

Most Shoppers Shop Online but Buy Locally

More than 95 percent of businesses are purchased by someone currently living in the same area as the seller's business. However, 90 percent of initial buyer inquiries for small businesses come from Internet business-for-sale listings. On the www.bizbuysell.com site alone, some 700,000 buyers conduct over a million searches monthly, viewing 2.3 million business-for-sale ads. Add to that the shopping traffic on dozens of other major online business-for-sale sites, and the number of opportunities to introduce your business to online shoppers is simply huge.

Just because your buyer lives around the corner, don't assume the buyer's search will start in the local newspaper. Do what the brokers do and list your business online. Furthermore, announce your sale in trade journals or on industry association Web sites, if they're prominent in your field. Chapter 9 provides advice for writing online ads that work and for getting your ad posted on major business-for-sale sites.

Most Shoppers Never Buy

Here's a stunningly disappointing fact: Within the business brokerage industry, research shows that nine out of ten people who search for businesses for sale never close a deal. And of those who do close, they almost always buy a business other than the one they initially inquire about. The fallout between interest and action is due to two main factors. First, most business shoppers have never purchased a business before, and they don't realize until they start responding to ads just how much is involved and how unprepared they are to complete the purchase process. Second, when they start looking, buyers realize how many options they have, and their attention gets diverted from the business that first caught their eye to one that seems a whole lot more interesting, successful, and affordable.

To convert shoppers to buyers, you have to write and place ads that

✔ Emphasize the attractiveness of your business

✔ Stress your business's proven track record and financial success

✔ State a reasonable price

✔ Present workable sale terms

✔ Invite inquiries, to which you respond quickly, clearly, and in a manner that builds upon the buyer's initial interest

All-Cash Deals Cost Time and Money

Sellers who require 40 percent or less of the purchase price at closing usually close their sales more quickly, both because a lower down payment makes it easier for the buyer to get the funds together and because the seller's offer to accept deferred payments conveys confidence in the business. Also consider these other facts:

✔ Up to three-quarters of all sellers end up financing 60 percent or more of the purchase price

✔ Sellers who require all cash at closing get about 70 percent of their asking price on average, whereas sellers who offer payment terms receive 85 percent

If possible, plan to offer seller financing and to make that offer clear in your business-for-sale ads. When inquiries come in, quickly qualify each prospective buyer's financial capability. If the buyer doesn't have personal funds sufficient to cover the required down payment, along with reserves to provide operating capital, find out where the buyer plans to get the funds, and request a commitment letter that confirms when the funds required will be delivered. Or move onto the next prospect.

Chapter 19

Ten Things to Consider When Hiring a Broker

Most business sellers know two things about brokers: They handle a lot of the heavy lifting that's part and parcel of a business sale, and they charge a commission. In order, most sellers would tell you the second fact first.

Beyond the fee that brokers earn — which, keep in mind, they earn only if they succeed in selling your business — is a lineup of other facts to consider. Following are ten things to know about brokers, including what to look for when considering a broker, questions to ask before signing a listing agreement, how to work with a broker, how to understand broker fees, and other useful facts and advice.

What Are the Broker's Qualifications?

Some brokers work full time selling businesses, and others do it as a sideline to some other job. Some specialize in selling businesses in certain industries, or of certain sizes. Some have undergone professional training and certification — and those are the ones you most want to work with. When interviewing brokers, discover their qualifications by asking these important questions:

> ✔ **Are you certified?** Find out if the broker is a Certified Business Intermediary (CBI), which is the gold standard in the business brokerage world. As part of the CBI certification, a broker has to have adequate experience, complete association courses, pass a final exam, and pledge to uphold a code of ethics.

✔ **Are you a member of the International Business Brokers Association?** The IBBA is the largest international non-profit association for people and firms engaged in the various aspects of business brokerage and mergers and acquisitions. To verify your broker's membership, you can go to the IBBA business broker search site (`http://bbms.ibba.org/Broker-Search.asp`) and conduct a quick search for the broker's name. The "Useful Links" section of the CD-ROM also links you to the site.

✔ **How long have you served as a business broker?** Ideally, you want to work with a broker with a track history that goes back at least several years, because you'll be counting on the broker's experience to guide you through the twists and turns that you're sure to encounter as you market your business, screen and negotiate with prospects, and close your sale deal. Plus, a broker with long-standing experience is likely to have expertise, contacts, and a wealth of buyer prospects that will make selling your business easier.

✔ **Do you work full time or part time as a business broker?** This question is important because you want to know whether the broker is likely to be on the job when a question or need arises.

✔ **Do you have a real estate license?** Most business brokers are licensed realtors, which is a requirement in many states and important to you if your deal includes the sale of a building or other real property.

If you have a choice, and you probably will, opt for a broker who's certified, experienced, and working full time in the field.

Does the Broker Have Good Web Presence?

First things first: Find out if the broker has a Web site. If not, keep looking around. Nearly all business-for-sale searches start online. If you list with a broker whose offerings are invisible to Web users, you're almost out of sight.

Visit the broker's site to see how fast it loads, how easy it is to use, and the kinds of businesses it offers for sale. If you like what you see, ask for information about how the site is used:

✔ **How much traffic does your brokerage site generate?** How many people actually visit the site each month? Given the fact that nine out of ten people who shop online for a business never buy, you want to know that the broker's site generates hundreds — or preferably thousands — of hits each month, so that in addition to the "just looking" traffic, you stand a chance of getting your ad in front of some valid buyer prospects.

✔ **How many offices in your network use this site?** Obviously, if the brokerage has offices in many cities, states, and countries, your listing will have broader exposure than if you work with an independent firm with a single office.

✔ **How many brokers are in your office?** A brokerage with a number of brokers benefits from staff synergy, as does its Web site, which becomes the hub for all brokerage listings and a magnet for those seeking business opportunities in your market area. A broker working independently can only attract so much business, but a multi-broker firm is likely to attract more listings, more site traffic, more buyer inquiries, and more successful closings.

✔ **How many businesses are currently listed on your site?** You can get the answer to this question by a quick site visit, but it's worth it to ask the broker directly so you can ask follow-up questions, including whether the number of businesses listed for sale has gone up or down over the past months, how long the typical listing remains on the site, what kinds of listings pull the most traffic, and other facts that may help you as you make your broker decision and prepare your sale announcements.

✔ **How many qualified buyers are already in your database?** Part of the reason you hire a broker is to gain access to a greater number of potential business buyers than you could on your own. In addition to posting your sale online and announcing it through other forms of advertising, find out whether the broker has a list of prospective buyers that the broker will contact directly.

What's the Broker's Recent Track Record?

You want to select a broker who's been successful selling businesses like yours. You can find out a lot about the broker's experience and success levels, and also about the business-for-sale marketplace you're entering, by asking the following questions.

✔ **How many businesses like mine did you sell last year?** You probably wouldn't list an urban condominium for sale with a broker who specializes in ranch properties. Likewise, you probably don't want to list a small professional services business with a broker who specializes in selling heavy industrial firms. To find out whether the broker is experienced selling businesses like yours, ask:

- **How many businesses in my size range did you sell last year?**
  You probably won't know your sale price when you interview brokers, but you can provide your annual sales or earnings figures as the basis for your research. For instance, you can say, "My business does $1.75 million in annual sales. What's your experience selling businesses of approximately that size?"

- **How many businesses of my type did you sell last year?**
  Businesses are usually categorized by the way they make money — manufacturing, service, retail, agriculture and mining, financial services, real estate, transportation, and so forth. Find out whether the broker has experience selling businesses in your specific business arena, because such experience will prove valuable as you discuss pricing your business and structuring your sale.

When asking these questions, find out statistics about the entire brokerage office. What you're looking for is a broker, and a brokerage, that excels in sales of businesses like yours. You also want to know that the individual you're working with is among the top performers in the brokerage and not the new kid on the block.

✔ **How many businesses did you list last year?** In addition to learning about closed sales, find out how many businesses the broker — and the broker's firm — listed for sale last year, along with the listing-to-sale success rate. Ask:

- **How many of the businesses you and the brokerage listed ended in closed sales?** Especially if you're interviewing several brokers, the closing rate helps you compare firms by putting their listing-to-sale rates side by side. A brokerage with a high sale-closing rate likely attracts the most salable business listings *and* manages the sale process most effectively, which is probably the exact combination you're seeking.

- **On average, how long were last year's listings on the market before they ended in closed sales?** More than anything, the answer to this question will give you a feel for what's in front of you in terms of time span.

✔ **How many of the site's listings did you represent?** This gives you a good idea of whether the broker is a major player in the brokerage and what kind of volume the broker handles. If the broker's numbers are very high, ask how the broker manages to devote time to each client. Ideally, you want to work with a broker who's well-regarded and in high demand and who has a proven program for managing volume without sacrificing customer service.

How Does the Broker Market Listings?

A major reason owners list their businesses for sale with brokers is to gain the leverage of a professionally managed marketing program. Beyond posting your ad on the brokerage site, find out how else your business will be advertised by asking these questions:

- ✔ **In addition to your own brokerage site, what other online business-for-sale listing sites do you use?** The three largest sites are currently `BizBuySell.com`, `BizQuest.com`, and `BusinessesforSale.com`. Find out if your listing will be posted on any of those. Ask to see ads posted for recently closed listings, and ask if the ads for your business offer will be similarly sized and how long they'll be posted. With nearly all buyer searches beginning online, be very hesitant about choosing a broker who isn't familiar with and committed to online advertising.

- ✔ **Do you place classified print ads for your listings?** Sometimes, brokers place *blind classified ads* that promote your offering (without revealing your business name) in select newspapers or targeted industry publications. Ask if the broker uses this approach and whether it's a likely tool for advertising your business. No one answer is correct. Mostly, you want to hear the broker's rationale and to be assured that the broker is willing to use all advertising approaches that make sense when marketing your business.

Also ask the broker to show you a sample of the selling memorandum (or selling book) he or she prepares for clients so you can get a sense of the caliber of document the broker prepares and presents to buyer prospects. (See Chapter 8 for information about what usually goes into a selling memorandum.)

What Do Recent Clients Have to Say about the Broker's Performance?

The broker's Web site or marketing materials may include testimonials from clients who've listed with the broker. Additionally, ask the broker to provide names of owners who've sold over the past six months and who you can contact for references. When you reach the owners, ask them the following questions:

✔ Would you use the same broker or brokerage again?

✔ Do you have advice on ways I might handle the relationship most effectively?

✔ Did you like or dislike the broker's availability and communication style, and why?

✔ Were you satisfied with the level of confidentiality maintained for the sale while working with the broker?

✔ If you could change one thing about working with the broker, what would it be?

What Does the Broker Charge?

Most brokers charge what's called a *success fee,* which is a commission based on a portion of the price paid at closing for your business. Usually, the commission is 10 percent.

Some brokers charge part of their fee as an upfront retainer to cover expenses they incur to market the business. Others charge hourly fees for services they provide even if you don't list your business with them. (The final section of this chapter covers such services.)

The most common fees you should be aware of when listing with a broker include

✔ **Broker's fee:** The broker's fee is usually 10 percent of the business purchase price, or a pre-established dollar amount such as $10,000, whichever is greater. The broker's contract probably defines the purchase price as "including, but not limited to, cash equivalents, notes, liabilities assumed, earn-outs, licensing fees, and no-compete and consulting agreements." The fee typically is due in full to the broker no later than at sale closing.

✔ **Cancellation fee:** Most broker contracts state that if you cancel or withdraw your listing, or if you enter into a purchase and sale agreement without the broker's approval, the broker's fee is due immediately.

✔ **Trailing fee:** This fee is due to the broker if you sell your business to a source referred to you by the broker after your listing with the broker has expired. The broker calls these *protected prospects.* If you sell your business to a person on the protected list within a defined period (for example, two years) of your listing's termination, the listing agreement likely obligates you to pay the broker the full commission. Most broker agreements also state that if you relist with another broker who sells your business to a person on the protected list during the defined time period, you may be liable for full commission to both brokers.

How Does the Broker Price a Business?

Pricing your business is a big job and a step where brokers are usually worth their weight in gold. Ask the broker for information on the following points:

- What method does the broker use to establish the asking price for a business like yours?
- What percentage of variance does the broker advise you to expect between the asking price and the closing price?
- Over the past year, what's the average percentage of asking price received by the broker's closed listings?

If you're prepared to share your most recent annual sales and earnings figures (see Chapter 5 for information on calculating your seller's discretionary earnings), you may ask the broker for a very preliminary asking price recommendation.

Has the Broker Been Sued?

When it comes to the broker's professional reputation and reliability, you want to know two things:

- Has the broker ever been sued by a listing client or a business buyer, and if so, when and why? Business sales are complex and require an attention to detail that, if overlooked, can lead to errors and omissions that result in client complaints, if not lawsuits. In addition to asking the broker directly, you can check on the broker's reliability by conducting a Better Business Bureau search (http://search.bbb.org/).
- Does the broker carry professional liability insurance? This type of insurance protects service businesses in the event that a provider is somehow negligent and a client suffers financial harm. There's only one answer you want to hear when you ask if your broker carries professional liability insurance, and that answer is "Yes."

Will the Broker Agree to Carve Outs?

Most broker agreements are called exclusive listing agreements because when you sign the agreement, you grant the broker the exclusive right to sell your business or its assets. In other words, you agree not to work with a number of brokers at the same time. The exclusive broker has sole rights to your sale for as long as the listing agreement lasts, which is typically not less than six months.

The one exception, if your broker agrees to it, is that you may negotiate a *carve out* or *limited exception* for a certain buyer prospect. For instance, if you've already been talking to a partner or associate as a buyer prospect, you may exclude that person from the listing agreement, and therefore from the sale commission. Unless you have a prospective buyer waiting in the wings, this clause doesn't really matter, but if you know of someone who may become your buyer, be sure to get a carve out written into your listing agreement or you'll pay the commission on the sale in spite of the fact that you brought the buyer to the deal.

Usually, before signing a listing agreement, you can get the broker to approve one or a very few exceptions, but expect the agreement to come with a few strings attached. In most cases, you have to agree that if you're going to sell to one of the parties listed as an exception, you'll do so within 30 days of the listing. The broker may also require that you agree to a minimal fee of somewhere between $1,000 and $2,000 to cover the broker's time, effort, and counsel in putting your selling memorandum together.

Will the Broker Assist You Even without a Listing?

Many brokers offer services, even without a listing agreement, for an agreed-upon fee.

If you feel you're the best one to market, represent, and negotiate your sale but you want some help pricing your business or creating your selling memorandum, find a reputable broker and discuss contracting for help.

For somewhere in the range of $1,500 or $2,000, a broker may be willing to help you get your business-for-sale documents ready for presentation. The broker may even offer to credit the fee against the sale commission if you decide later on to list your business with the broker.

Chapter 20

Ten Answers to Have
Ready for Buyers

In This Chapter
▶ Planning your answers to frequently asked questions
▶ Using facts and figures to bolster your business offering

*W*hen a buyer comes calling, be ready. Too many deals never close because the seller takes too long to deliver the information the buyer needs to make the decision and negotiate the deal. This chapter helps you prepare answers to ten issues on almost every buyer's mind. Whether or not the buyer actually asks, make sure you communicate your answers. Also, have all the information you may need at your fingertips and ready to present, using the list contained on the Cheat Sheet in the front of this book. Your sale will be on surer footing as a result.

Why You're Selling

If you don't answer the question about why you're selling, the buyer's imagination will take over, likely leading to the wrong conclusion that your business is faltering and you want out.

A common myth among business buyers is that owners don't part with truly good businesses; they only sell duds. In fact, the opposite is true. Among businesses that sell, most are close to picture-perfect, on an upswing, and in terrific health. Otherwise, the deals wouldn't make it to closing day, or they'd close at sacrifice prices.

The number one reason sellers sell is that they're burned out and ready to do something else. If that's your case, you can be honest without being so blunt. Instead of saying "burned out," say that after 8 or 18 or 28 years, the time's right to turn your success story over to a new owner with fresh energy and ideas, one who's fired up and ready to grow the business to an all-new level of success.

Chapter 1 helps you focus on your reasons, and after you're clear about why you're selling — whether for health, lifestyle, or retirement reasons — be frank with buyers.

When you're explaining your motivation for moving on, you have to account for one of two scenarios:

- **If your business is strong and growing,** explain why you're selling at this time, and make sure you explain that your business is in great shape for an ownership transfer and facing great prospects for the future. See the section "What Your Business Prospects Look Like," later in this chapter, for more info.

- **If your business isn't in great health,** discuss its prospects, and explain why you want to sell it to someone with the ability and energy to invest in the turnaround detailed in the business and marketing plans that you turn over to the new owner. (See the section "What Your Business Risks Look Like," later in this chapter, for guidance.)

What You Plan to Do after the Sale

The seller wants to know two things about your post-sale plans:

- **Are you willing to stick around to help with the ownership transition?** Put the buyer's mind at ease by offering to sign a management or consulting contract and to remain with the business for a short period after the sale. Even if the buyer doesn't take you up on the offer, your willingness indicates your faith that the buyer won't discover disappointing facts after the deal is done. Likewise, if you agree to accept some amount of the purchase price in deferred payments, you convey your belief that the future of the business is promising.

- **Do you intend to remain actively employed in the same business arena, and if so, will you be a competitive threat?** If you're going to retire, the buyer will probably be pleased, because you won't be taking on a potentially competitive role, and you'll likely be around and available should future questions arise. Likewise, if you're relocating to a distant market area, you won't be a competitive threat. Still, the buyer will probably request a *non-compete agreement,* also called a *covenant not to compete,* to ensure that you won't end up vying for the same customer list you're selling. Chapter 15 explains how this agreement is covered in the closing documents for most sales.

How Much You Earn from the Business

The vast majority of business buyers purchase for financial reasons. They look for a business that makes enough money to provide a great job and income for its owner, plus a good return on the investment required to make the deal possible. Most business ads tell how much the company does in annual sales, but the real question on the buyer's mind is, "What's in it for me?"

The quickest way to assure a buyer that your business can deliver a good living for its owner is to share how much it makes for you each year. This figure, called *seller's discretionary earnings,* is key to whether the buyer will continue negotiations, so don't hem and haw. Be ready with the following information (turn to Chapter 5 for help in preparing these documents):

- **Your seller's discretionary earnings (SDE) statement.** This document combines information from your income statement with adjustments that back out all expenses that represent owner benefits, one-time non-recurring expenses, and discretionary expenses that another owner may choose not to make. The result is a report of how much your business earns for you annually. It's one thing for you to say your business makes you $100,000 a year plus good perks; it's another to pull out a single sheet of paper (or turn to a single page in your selling memorandum) and point to a formal statement of annual owner earnings.

- **Trends for how earnings have increased over recent years.** Your buyer wants to know that the earnings figure you present isn't a one-year fluke. Don't even wait to be asked before showing earnings for the past three to five years, including the average rate of growth and how that trend leads to positive future projections.

Why Your Asking Price Is Reasonable

A great many deals fall apart because the price is unreasonable, either in fact or at least in the buyer's mind. Save your business from that fate by providing the buyer with the rationale you used to establish your asking price, including the following information, which I walk you through in Chapter 6:

- **The appraisal value of your business:** If you've had your business professionally appraised or valued, you can share or summarize the report that formally justifies your price.

- **Your multiple of earnings:** Explain how you arrived at your multiplier and why it's reasonable, based not only on your business's attractiveness but also on sale prices for similar businesses in your market area and industry. (Keep in mind that most businesses sell for two to four times earnings. Chapter 6 has a form for arriving at a reasonable multiplier.)

- **The value of your tangible assets:** Include your fixtures, furnishings, and equipment so the buyer can see what portion of the price is backed by physical assets.

- **The value of your intangible assets:** Include the values you place on such intangible assets as workforce, clientele, operations, intellectual property, and brand name or business goodwill.

Presenting or defending your pricing rationale is a great way to underscore your business's strength. It allows the buyer to see the value of all the assets you're selling, which likely add up to even more than the price you're asking.

How Your Business Has Grown over Recent Years

Although buyers decide to purchase based on their belief in your business's future, they base their offer on an assessment of how the business has performed over recent years.

Show your growth trends by presenting business financial statements and other indicators of your success. Include any of the following points that apply to your business situation:

- **The growth rate of your sales and earnings** for the past three years. (Chapter 5 includes a chart that helps with this presentation.)

- **The number of new customers you've added** over recent years, including a description of how your clientele is also increasing in profitability and loyalty, if that's the case.

- **The number of staff you've added** over recent years, including how you've increased sales or earnings per employee over the same period.

- **New products or services you've added** and how the new offerings have resulted in customer and sales increases.

- **Physical plant improvements** that make your place of business more efficient, effective, competitive, attractive, and capable of increased production and profitability.

✔ **Price increases that have been favorably accepted** over recent years.

✔ **Other indications of your business strength and momentum,** such as increased square footage to accommodate growing clientele or operations, improved rankings by community or industry evaluators, increased publicity and marketplace visibility, and improved performance against competing businesses.

How the Business Will Transfer and Run without You

For understandable reasons, a buyer may come to the negotiation table with nagging questions about whether your success story can be handed off like a baton in a well-run relay. In dealing with the buyer's concern, it's not enough for you to feel comfortable that the pass-off is possible. What's important is that the buyer feels certain the transfer will be successful. To assure the buyer, be ready to provide facts that prove that the transition will be as close to seamless as possible.

Present a clear transition plan for each of the following areas:

✔ **Business location:** If your location is important to your business success, as is the case with most restaurants and retail establishments, let the buyer know that the space is secure for at least the next five years. If necessary, negotiate with your landlord in advance to extend your lease, and make sure that the lease is transferable to a new business owner. If you own your building and it's not part of the sale, be ready to lease the space to the buyer, and have supporting documents ready for the buyer's review. If your place of business is online, describe how your Web space is owned by the company and ready for transfer to the new owner.

✔ **Operations:** Assure the buyer that you've created a business plan, marketing plan, operations manual, and employment policy manual documenting how your business works. (If you don't have such documents, turn to Chapter 7 for help.) You don't have to present these documents — the keys to your success — until you accept a buyer offer and begin due diligence. And you won't release them to the buyer until after all the papers are signed on closing day. In early conversations, though, let the buyer know that your systems and approaches are detailed in writing and ready for handoff.

✔ **Workforce:** The buyer will relax, probably a lot, when you explain that you have one or several top employees or managers who know the business well, whom customers know and trust, and who will almost surely stay on after the sale. If you have employment contracts with key staff, have them ready to present during due diligence. Also, if you have signed non-compete agreements with these key employees, that fact will come as more good news to the buyer.

Why Customers Will Remain Loyal

Customers are the lifeblood of business, and your buyer will want to know whether your customer list is fortified or anemic and whether it's likely to transition easily after a sale. Be ready with this information:

✔ **Number of accounts or customers** your business serves. Buyers want to see a long list that can survive the smattering of defections that typically occur after a sale.

✔ **Duration of major customer relationships.** Buyers view long-standing relationships as a sign of customer loyalty and relationship durability. When those relationships are backed by contracts or written agreements, buyers view them as even more valuable.

✔ **Percentage of sales that come from your top three customers.** Buyers want to know if all your eggs are in one or only a few baskets. If they are, work on building a bigger stable of major clients before putting your business up for sale.

✔ **Length of time it takes to win a customer.** If your customer base is large and customers come and go with frequency, turnover isn't as threatening as it is in a business where acquiring a customer may take months or longer. Be ready to explain what it takes to attract new clients, and if the process is slow or complicated, tell the buyer the number of prospects already in the pipeline.

✔ **Customer purchase patterns.** If your business sales are seasonal, time your sale (if possible) so the buyer rides the wave of the upcoming season's sales, revenues, and customer communications.

If your customer relationships are tied to you personally, offer to stay on for a period after the sale to help with the owner transition. Better yet, if you have time before the sale, begin to transition customer relationships to key managers so your business is less dependent on your personal presence at the time of the sale.

What Your Business Prospects Look Like

Avoid offering such a rosy projection that the buyer can later say you misrepresented business conditions, but by all means provide an accurate assessment of how you see a positive future for the business. Rely on facts by presenting the following information:

- **Growth projection:** Chapter 5 includes a section that helps you forecast growth based on recent, actual sales and earnings increases.

- **Market and industry growth projections:** Chapter 2 includes a section on how to analyze the growth trends of your industry and market area. Use the findings to present your market outlook to the buyer. If your business is facing a less-than-favorable industry or market situation, present steps you've taken or planned for overcoming the situation.

- **Future plans:** Refer the buyer to your selling memorandum (described in Chapter 8) for a list of actions you believe could propel future growth (or reverse declines, or surmount problems).

Remember that buyers usually want to do more than just take over a success story. They want ideas on how they can direct a new, even more exciting chapter for the business. By presenting such ideas for the future, including ways to overcome challenges, you can inspire the buyer to see the upside potential for your business.

What Your Business Risks Look Like

In the same way that you'd want to know your risks before investing in real estate or stock, your buyer wants to know what kind of risks come with your business. Sellers typically don't want to introduce the topic of risks, preferring to focus on positive attributes instead. But risks are on the buyer's mind, and if you don't address the issue, the buyer may be scared off by what amounts to paper tigers.

Most risks that concern buyers fall into one of the following categories, all detailed in Chapter 2:

- Low or declining sales and earnings

- No key staff to provide continuity after the sale

- Unprofessional operations, including poor financial records

✔ High competition and low competitive advantage

✔ Dependency on only a few customers

✔ Declining industry or market area

✔ A problematic or non-transferable business lease

If your business is plagued by any of these risks, overcome them if you can before offering your business for sale. Renegotiate your lease, turn around earnings, improve operations, hire key staff, and expand your customer base, if possible.

Where you can't turn things around before the sale, present the risk frankly, along with ideas for how the buyer may reverse the situation.

Remember, buyers know businesses are rarely risk-free. They just want to be assured that your business is a low-risk investment.

What Payment Terms You're Open To

The quickest way to convey your belief that your business carries few risks — while also enhancing attractiveness to a buyer — is to offer to carry a loan or accept deferred payments for part of the purchase price.

By saying "You can pay me later," you're basically assuring the buyer that you believe the business will survive the sale transition just fine. You're also making it easier for the buyer to complete the deal, because financing is necessary in nearly all small business purchases, and the most common source of financing is usually the seller. In fact, sellers who insist on an all-cash-at-closing deal usually end up with lower sale prices, simply because it can be difficult for the buyer to come up with that much cash out of pocket or from third-party lenders.

Most sellers settle for a sizeable down payment on closing day and an ironclad promissory note to cover the balance of the price. Chapter 14 provides information on financing the sale of your business. Take the time to decide — before putting your business on the market — whether you're willing to sweeten the deal by making seller financing part of your offer.

Appendix

About the CD

System Requirements

Make sure that your computer meets the minimum system requirements shown in the following list. If your computer doesn't match up to most of these requirements, you may have problems using the software and files on the CD. For the latest and greatest information, please refer to the ReadMe file located at the root of the CD-ROM.

- A PC with a Pentium or faster processor; or a Mac OS computer with a 68040 or faster processor

- Microsoft Windows 98 or later; or Mac OS system software 7.6.1 or later

- At least 32MB of total RAM installed on your computer; for best performance, we recommend at least 64MB

- A CD-ROM drive

- A sound card for PCs; Mac OS computers have built-in sound support

- A monitor capable of displaying at least 256 colors or grayscale

- A modem with a speed of at least 14,400 bps

If you need more information on the basics, check out these books published by Wiley Publishing, Inc.: *PCs For Dummies,* by Dan Gookin; *Macs For Dummies* and *iMacs For Dummies,* by David Pogue; *Windows 95 For Dummies, Windows 98 For Dummies, Windows 2000 Professional For Dummies,* and *Microsoft Windows ME Millennium Edition For Dummies,* all by Andy Rathbone.

Using the CD

To install the items from the CD to your hard drive, follow these steps:

1. **Insert the CD into your computer's CD-ROM drive. The license agreement appears.**

   Note to Windows users: The interface won't launch if you have autorun disabled. In that case, click Start⇨Run. In the dialog box that appears, type **D:\start.exe**. (Replace D with the proper letter if your CD-ROM drive uses a different letter. If you don't know the letter, see how your CD-ROM drive is listed under My Computer.) Click OK.

   Note for Mac users: The CD icon will appear on your desktop; double-click the icon to open the CD and double-click the "Start" icon.

2. **Read through the license agreement, and then click the Accept button if you want to use the CD.**

   The CD interface appears. The interface allows you to install the programs and run the demos with just a click of a button (or two).

What You'll Find on the CD

The following sections are arranged by category and provide a summary of the software and other goodies you'll find on the CD. If you need help with installing the items provided on the CD, refer to the installation instructions in the preceding section.

Software

You'll find the following software on your CD:

- ✔ **Word Viewer:** A freeware program that allows you to view but not edit Microsoft Word documents. Certain features of Microsoft Word documents may not work as expected from within Word Viewer.

- ✔ **Adobe Reader:** A freeware program that allows you to view but not edit Adobe Portable Document Files (PDFs).

Shareware programs are fully functional, free, trial versions of copyrighted programs. If you like particular programs, register with their authors for a nominal fee and receive licenses, enhanced versions, and technical support.

Freeware programs are free, copyrighted games, applications, and utilities. You can copy them to as many PCs as you like — for free — but they offer no technical support. *GNU software* is governed by its own license, which is included inside the folder of the GNU software. There are no restrictions on distribution of GNU software. See the GNU license at the root of the CD for more details. *Trial, demo,* or *evaluation* versions of software are usually limited either by time or functionality (such as not letting you save a project after you create it).

Chapter files

The chapter files on the CD all fall into one of the following categories:

- ✔ **Adobe Acrobat (PDF) files:** Most of the files on the CD are in PDF format, so you can't change them, but you can print them out and record the answers to the questions as you go through the process of selling your business, and I highly recommend that you do so. Many of the documents work well for bringing along to your various meetings so you can make sure you've covered all your bases, so to speak.

- ✔ **Word documents:** All the PDF files are also in Word format, created so you can save them to your computer and fill them out electronically. I've also included a Word document of helpful links to various Web sites that you may find useful as you embark on the sale process and see it through to the closing and beyond. Feel free to add to the list as you discover other sites you find useful.

- ✔ **Excel spreadsheets:** Some of the forms are Excel spreadsheets, which you can use to help you do calculations at the touch of a key. Simply plug in the numbers and follow the guidance I provide in the corresponding chapters.

The following list summarizes all the chapter files on the CD:

Form 1-1   Setting Your Business Sale Goal and Objectives

Form 2-1   Sales and Profit Growth Trends

Form 2-2   Business Attributes: Rating Your Strengths

Form 2-3   Business Capabilities: Prioritizing Importance and Rating Strengths

Form 2-4   Business Transferability: Assessing Your Sale-Readiness

Form 8-3   Selling Memorandum Template

Form 8-4   Customer Profile

Form 8-5   Business Client Profile

Form 8-6   Sample Confidentiality Agreement

Form 9-1   Profiling Your Likely Buyer: Checklist

Form 10-1 Prospect Qualification Form

Form 11-1 Sample Letter of Intent

Form 11-2 Sample Addendum to Letter of Intent

Form 12-1 Buyer's Due Diligence Preparation Worksheet

Form 12-2 Seller's Due Diligence Checklist

Form 15-1 Closing Preparation Checklist

Form 15-2 Closing Day Checklist

Links

Web site addresses throughout the book lead to helpful information on everything from appraising your business to helping your buyer obtain financing to close the deal. To save yourself the need to type in what's sometimes an overly long URL, you can also use the Links section of the CD-ROM to go directly to the following sites:

`http://www.sec.gov/info/smallbus/qasbsec.htm`: This link leads to the U.S. Securities and Exchange Commission site that helps business owners wrestling with the issue of whether to take their company public.

`www.gvalue.com`: This link leads to the home page of GCF Valuation, where you'll get a good idea of the services valuation specialists provide and how they work.

`www.census.gov`: This link provides population and resident characteristics for U.S. communities, which you may find helpful when you describe your market area to prospective buyers.

`www.bizbuysell.com`: This link connects you to the site that promotes itself as "The Internet's largest and most heavily trafficked business-for-sale marketplace."

`www.bizquest.com`: This link leads to the site self-described as "The Internet's oldest and most-established business-for-sale marketplace."

`www.businessesforsale.com`: This link leads to a U.K.-based business-for-sale site that lists international and U.S. businesses.

`http://www.sunbeltnetwork.com/component/sbsearch/?view=results`: This link takes you to a page of business-for-sale ads presented by Sunbelt, which you can review as good examples to follow.

`http://www.sba.gov/services/financialassistance/sbaloantopics/7a/index.html`: This link takes you to the page of the U.S. Small Business Administration site that explains the Basic 7(a) Loan Program.

`www.sba.gov/sbaforms/sba413.pdf`: Use this link to access a PDF file of the Personal Financial Statement provided by the U.S. Small Business Administration.

`www.equifax.com`: A link to one of the major credit reporting companies.

`www.experian.com`: A link to one of the major credit reporting companies.

`http://finance.yahoo.com/`: This link takes you to the Yahoo! Finance page, where you can research the share pricing trends should a buyer want to use company stock to buy your business.

`http://www.benetrends.com/home/index.php`: This link takes you to the site of BeneTrends, which offers information on how retirement funds can be used for business investments.

`www.bizbuyfinancing.com`: This site links to the site of a firm that assists with specialty loan consulting and SBA loan financing.

`http://www.expertlaw.com/library/business/promissory_note_form.html`: This link leads to a free promissory note form that's intended for general information purposes and for review by an attorney prior to use.

`http://www.lawdepot.com/contracts/promissory-note-form/index.php?ad=mainpage&a=t`: This link leads to a promissory note form that you can complete online and purchase.

`http://www.businessnation.com/library/forms/promissory.html`: A site full of fee-based legal forms, including promissory note forms.

`www.irs.gov/pub/irs-pdf/f8594.pdf`: A link to a PDF file of IRS Form 8594, Asset Acquisition Statement Under Section 1060.

`http://www.irs.gov/instructions/i8594/index.html`: A link to instructions for IRS Form 8594, Asset Acquisition Statement.

`http://www.lawdepot.com/contracts/business-purchase-sale-agreement/`: This link leads to the LawDepot Purchase and Sale of Business form, which you can fill out and purchase online for subsequent review by an attorney.

`http://www.lectlaw.com/forms/f048.htm`: This link leads to the Lectric Law Library Contract for Sale and Purchase of Business form, a free form that provides general information for your use and for review by your attorney.

`http://www.freelegalforms.net/index.cfm?index=forms&file name=form16372.htm`: This link leads to a free form you can complete to create an Agreement for Purchase and Sale of Business, to be reviewed by an attorney prior to use.

`http://www.rgisinv.com/`: This link leads to the site of RGIS Inventory Services, the largest inventory company in the world.

`www.irs.gov/pub/irs-pdf/f966.pdf`: A link to a PDF file of IRS Form 966, Corporate Dissolution or Liquidation, which must be filed within 30 days of corporate dissolution.

`http://www.irs.gov/businesses/small/article/0,,id=98703,00.html`: Use this link to reach the IRS "Closing a Business Checklist."

`http://www.irs.gov/businesses/small/article/0,,id=98011,00.html`: This links to IRS information on Federal Employer Identification Numbers, including what steps to take to close your number following the sale of your business.

`http://bbms.ibba.org/Broker-Search.asp`: This link leads to the Broker Search page of the International Business Brokers Association, where you can look for member brokers in your home area or check to see if a broker you're considering is a registered member.

Troubleshooting

This CD-ROM includes programs that work on most computers with the minimum system requirements. Alas, your computer may differ, and some programs may not work properly for some reason.

The two likeliest problems are that you don't have enough memory (RAM) for the programs you want to use, or you have other programs running that are affecting installation or running of a program. If you get an error message such as Not enough memory or Setup cannot continue, try one or more of the following suggestions, and then try using the software again:

- **Turn off any antivirus software running on your computer.** Installation programs sometimes mimic virus activity and may make your computer incorrectly believe that it's being infected by a virus.

- **Close all running programs.** The more programs you have running, the less memory is available to other programs. Installation programs typically update files and programs, so if you keep other programs running, installation may not work properly.

- **Have your local computer store add more RAM to your computer.** This is, admittedly, a drastic and somewhat expensive step. However, adding more memory can really help the speed of your computer and allow more programs to run at the same time.

If you have trouble with the CD-ROM, please call the Wiley Product Technical Support phone number at 800-762-2974. Outside the United States, call 317-572-3994. You can also contact Wiley Product Technical Support at http://www.wiley.com/techsupport. John Wiley & Sons will provide technical support only for installation and other general quality-control items. For technical support on the applications themselves, consult the program's vendor or author.

To place additional orders, or to request information about other Wiley products, please call 877-762-2974.

Index

• K •

• L •

Wiley Publishing, Inc.
End-User License Agreement

READ THIS. You should carefully read these terms and conditions before opening the software packet(s) included with this book "Book". This is a license agreement "Agreement" between you and Wiley Publishing, Inc. "WPI". By opening the accompanying software packet(s), you acknowledge that you have read and accept the following terms and conditions. If you do not agree and do not want to be bound by such terms and conditions, promptly return the Book and the unopened software packet(s) to the place you obtained them for a full refund.

1. **License Grant.** WPI grants to you (either an individual or entity) a nonexclusive license to use one copy of the enclosed software program(s) (collectively, the "Software") solely for your own personal or business purposes on a single computer (whether a standard computer or a workstation component of a multi-user network). The Software is in use on a computer when it is loaded into temporary memory (RAM) or installed into permanent memory (hard disk, CD-ROM, or other storage device). WPI reserves all rights not expressly granted herein.

2. **Ownership.** WPI is the owner of all right, title, and interest, including copyright, in and to the compilation of the Software recorded on the physical packet included with this Book "Software Media". Copyright to the individual programs recorded on the Software Media is owned by the author or other authorized copyright owner of each program. Ownership of the Software and all proprietary rights relating thereto remain with WPI and its licensers.

3. **Restrictions on Use and Transfer.**

   (a) You may only (i) make one copy of the Software for backup or archival purposes, or (ii) transfer the Software to a single hard disk, provided that you keep the original for backup or archival purposes. You may not (i) rent or lease the Software, (ii) copy or reproduce the Software through a LAN or other network system or through any computer subscriber system or bulletin-board system, or (iii) modify, adapt, or create derivative works based on the Software.

   (b) You may not reverse engineer, decompile, or disassemble the Software. You may transfer the Software and user documentation on a permanent basis, provided that the transferee agrees to accept the terms and conditions of this Agreement and you retain no copies. If the Software is an update or has been updated, any transfer must include the most recent update and all prior versions.

4. **Restrictions on Use of Individual Programs.** You must follow the individual requirements and restrictions detailed for each individual program in the "About the CD" appendix of this Book or on the Software Media. These limitations are also contained in the individual license agreements recorded on the Software Media. These limitations may include a requirement that after using the program for a specified period of time, the user must pay a registration fee or discontinue use. By opening the Software packet(s), you agree to abide by the licenses and restrictions for these individual programs that are detailed in the "About the CD" appendix and/or on the Software Media. None of the material on this Software Media or listed in this Book may ever be redistributed, in original or modified form, for commercial purposes.

5. **Limited Warranty.**

   (a) WPI warrants that the Software and Software Media are free from defects in materials and workmanship under normal use for a period of sixty (60) days from the date of purchase of this Book. If WPI receives notification within the warranty period of defects in materials or workmanship, WPI will replace the defective Software Media.

   (b) WPI AND THE AUTHOR(S) OF THE BOOK DISCLAIM ALL OTHER WARRANTIES, EXPRESS OR IMPLIED, INCLUDING WITHOUT LIMITATION IMPLIED WARRANTIES OF MERCHANTABILITY AND FITNESS FOR A PARTICULAR PURPOSE, WITH RESPECT TO THE SOFTWARE, THE PROGRAMS, THE SOURCE CODE CONTAINED THEREIN, AND/OR THE TECHNIQUES DESCRIBED IN THIS BOOK. WPI DOES NOT WARRANT THAT THE FUNCTIONS CONTAINED IN THE SOFTWARE WILL MEET YOUR REQUIREMENTS OR THAT THE OPERATION OF THE SOFTWARE WILL BE ERROR FREE.

   (c) This limited warranty gives you specific legal rights, and you may have other rights that vary from jurisdiction to jurisdiction.

6. **Remedies.**

   (a) WPI's entire liability and your exclusive remedy for defects in materials and workmanship shall be limited to replacement of the Software Media, which may be returned to WPI with a copy of your receipt at the following address: Software Media Fulfillment Department, Attn.: *Selling Your Business For Dummies*, Wiley Publishing, Inc., 10475 Crosspoint Blvd., Indianapolis, IN 46256, or call 1-800-762-2974. Please allow four to six weeks for delivery. This Limited Warranty is void if failure of the Software Media has resulted from accident, abuse, or misapplication. Any replacement Software Media will be warranted for the remainder of the original warranty period or thirty (30) days, whichever is longer.

   (b) In no event shall WPI or the author be liable for any damages whatsoever (including without limitation damages for loss of business profits, business interruption, loss of business information, or any other pecuniary loss) arising from the use of or inability to use the Book or the Software, even if WPI has been advised of the possibility of such damages.

   (c) Because some jurisdictions do not allow the exclusion or limitation of liability for consequential or incidental damages, the above limitation or exclusion may not apply to you.

7. **U.S. Government Restricted Rights.** Use, duplication, or disclosure of the Software for or on behalf of the United States of America, its agencies and/or instrumentalities "U.S. Government" is subject to restrictions as stated in paragraph (c)(1)(ii) of the Rights in Technical Data and Computer Software clause of DFARS 252.227-7013, or subparagraphs (c)(1) and (2) of the Commercial Computer Software - Restricted Rights clause at FAR 52.227-19, and in similar clauses in the NASA FAR supplement, as applicable.

8. **General.** This Agreement constitutes the entire understanding of the parties and revokes and supersedes all prior agreements, oral or written, between them and may not be modified or amended except in a writing signed by both parties hereto that specifically refers to this Agreement. This Agreement shall take precedence over any other documents that may be in conflict herewith. If any one or more provisions contained in this Agreement are held by any court or tribunal to be invalid, illegal, or otherwise unenforceable, each and every other provision shall remain in full force and effect.